S0-BER-757

THE RIVER'S IN MY BLOOD

University of Nebraska Press: Lincoln & London

Riverboat Pilots Tell Their Stories

JANE CURRY

The River's in My Blood

Publication of this
book was aided by a
grant from The Andrew
W. Mellon Foundation.

Copyright 1983 by the
University of Nebraska Press
All rights reserved

Manufactured in the
United States of America

The paper in this book
meets the guidelines for
permanence and durability
of the Committee on
Production Guidelines for
Book Longevity of the Council
on Library Resources.

Library of Congress Cataloging
in Publication Data

Curry, Jane, 1945-
The river's in my blood.

Bibliography: p.
Includes index.
1. Inland navigation – United
States.   2. River boats – United
States.   3. Pilots and pilotage –
United States.   I. Title.
HE629.C87 1983   386'.35044'0977
82-11068   ISBN 0-8032-1416-2

386.35044
C97

83-5117

FOR CAP'N T. DAVE

Illustrations by David Routon

CONTENTS

MAPS

THE OHIO AND MISSISSIPPI RIVERS
This map of the Ohio River from Pittsburgh to Cairo and the Mississippi River from St. Paul to the Gulf of Mexico shows towns and cities along the waterways, locks mentioned in the text (all locks are indicated by arrows), other tributaries, and the states through which they flow. Mileage numbers are indicated in parentheses after location names. It is 979.3 miles from Pittsburgh to Cairo on the Ohio River, for example, and the numbering begins with Mile 0 in Pittsburgh. Cincinnati is at Mile 470.3, which is the distance in river miles from Pittsburgh. Mileage numbers on the upper Mississippi begin near Cairo with Mile 0; numbers on the lower Mississippi begin with Mile 0 in the Gulf and end with Mile 955.8 at Cairo Point. Courtesy of the Delta Queen Steamboat Company.

*I remembered that it was the custom
of steamboatmen in the old times to
load up the confiding stranger with
the most picturesque and admirable
lies, and put the sophisticated friend
off with dull and ineffectual facts.*

Mark Twain

PREFACE

This project all started in 1973 because of a fantasy nurtured on the fifth
floor of a graduate library in Michigan. If I could be doing anything I wanted
(besides, that is, writing first drafts of dissertation chapters, sneaking Milky
Way bars past keen-eyed librarians, and initiating study breaks with fellow
sufferers in the stairwells), what would it be? Well, I could try being Charles
Kuralt's assistant and comb the country finding worm groaners in Florida or
eccentric gardeners in Tennessee. Not a bad idea, but the job, I was sure,
wasn't open. Besides, my number one fantasy, lying droopy if not dormant
after a delightful trip from St. Louis to Cincinnati on the paddlewheel steamer
Delta Queen in 1972, was to ride into the Mississippi River sunsets on a
steamboat. With nothing to lose but my ten-cent postage stamp and the time
to write a letter, I barged ahead, creating for myself a job I thought I would like
and the Delta Queen Steamboat Company should initiate. This ideal job would
resemble a cross between informal lecturer on history, Twain tradition, and
river folklore and gregarious hostess in antebellum hoops—sort of a Gail Storm
of the inland waterways plus mortarboard.

Betty Blake, then president of the company, replied promptly, saying she
liked my view of the steamboat and my "understanding of the position."
Imagine my surprise, since to my mind I had invented this particular post. But
it was no time to quibble. So for the summer of 1974 I gave talks, flew kites off
the paddle wheel, led sing-alongs, emceed nightly shows, called out bingo
numbers, conducted calliope tryouts, circled the sundeck followed by jog-
walkers, and occasionally sought relief from my duties by hiding out in the
pilothouse. Of course, I had read and reread Mark Twain's *Life on the Mississippi*,
so I was eager to meet genuine steamboat pilots. The guitar player fueled that
interest when he reported to me a conversation he had overheard between one of

the old southern pilots and two older lady passengers ("who looked," he said, "like a damned freight train had run over 'em.") To the utter delight of the ladies, the pilot had smiled broadly and said, "There musta been a recess in heaven what with all these angels walking about!" Of course, the guitar player was no slouch with the expressions himself. Not long after my arrival, he had put his arm around my shoulder in fatherly counsel and announced with crossed eyes, crooked smile, and a southern drawl that I was "the sweetest little thing that ever wee-wee'd between two slipper heels." No doubt about it—I had definitely escaped the rarefied air of my cluttered cubicle.

In those many hours spent on the lazy bench listening to pilothouse palaver, I heard typical conversations about children, wives, pensions, today's youth, and America's shortcomings. According to Captain Harry Louden, for example, America has "gone aground." A character in Richard Bissell's novel, *A Stretch on the River*, decides he will go for a mate's license so he can get into the pilothouse and hear the pilots talk—he supposes they discuss the channel and tell stories like Samuel Clemens.[1] But when he goes up to scrub floors, he is treated to a conversation about laundry detergents and vacuum cleaners used by the wives at home. Unlike that mate, I was not disappointed by what I heard. The pilots did talk about the equivalent of the vacuum cleaners, but they also waxed nostalgic about former channels, new cutoffs, old wrecks, cub piloting, salty masters, ghosts on the bridge, and other captivating echoes of Mark Twain's recollections. And, like the stranger Mark Twain refers to, I may have been hoodwinked by those occasional "stretchers."

I returned to the *Delta Queen* for a month in the summer of 1976 as relief cruise director and became convinced that the stories of these pilots should be preserved. Those working as trip pilots on the *Delta Queen* had "retired" from towboat work with private companies or careers with the Army Corps of Engineers; they had piloted for the old Federal Barge Line, taken LSTs (landing

---

[1] Samuel Clemens took the pen name "Mark Twain," by which he is universally known. There are two predominant stories regarding Clemens's choice. One claims he took the name because it is a river term; "mark twain" is sung out when sounding the water's depth with a lead line to indicate a depth of twelve feet. Clemens claimed he took the name because it had been the pen name of Isaiah Sellers, a riverman and newspaper columnist whom Clemens had caricatured. This story may have been fabricated; Ernest E. Leisy argues in his essay, "Mark Twain and Isaiah Sellers" (*American Literature* 12, January 1942), that there was no "original Mark Twain" other than Sam Clemens himself. Then again, Richard Bissell notes in *My Life on the Mississippi, or Why I am Not Mark Twain* that "getting at The Truth on Mark Twain is at least twice as difficult as Was Hamlet Really Wacky?"

crafts) down river during World War II, and witnessed a technological explosion in their traditional profession. Three pilots gathered on the bow for general jawing would in all likelihood represent 150 years of river experience among them. They had begun their careers on steamboats (some even on wooden-hulled steamboats), had piloted the diesel descendants, and had returned to steam in the twilight of their river lives. They, and others like them, could personally document the impact of technology on their profession and illustrate what features of their craft had defied change.

I resolved to begin as soon as possible recording the oral narratives of these and other riverboat pilots and captains.[2] In the summer and fall of 1977, I spent three months riding aboard the *Delta Queen* and *Mississippi Queen* steamers, interviewing the pilots and others at outposts along the way. Since then I have interviewed retired pilots and captains in their homes in Chattanooga, Tennessee; Huntington, West Virginia; Sewickley, Pennsylvania; Paducah, Kentucky; Akron, Ohio; Davenport, Iowa; and elsewhere, and have ridden a diesel towboat, the *Ann King*, pushing fifteen barges of grain from St. Paul to St. Louis. My own limited river travel has taken me the length of the Mississippi and Ohio rivers several times, up the Illinois River as far as Kampsville, a stretch on the Cumberland River to Kentucky Lake, and a snippet of the St. Croix up to Stillwater, Minnesota. I taped the first interview in Winona, Minnesota, in December of 1976, windchill -50°. My last major collecting trip ended in Paducah, Kentucky, in September of 1979, windchill +95°.

Of course, I started out talking to pilots and captains I had worked with; they told me about others, and these men, in turn, told me about others. Eventually, my collection included interviews with approximately fifty river folks, some of which were taped in the pilothouse (aboard the *Delta Queen*, *Mississippi Queen*, *Ann King*) where the stories often unfolded naturally in the

---

[2] The distinction here between *pilot* and *captain* bears explanation. A pilot is called "Captain," as in Captain Clemens. The master of the boat is in charge of the overall operation of the vessel, may or may not be a pilot, and is also called "Captain." Some pilots have master's license and can perform both functions. It used to be customary to carry two pilots and a roof captain on boats (and this is still the way it is done on Delta Queen Company boats). The roof captain, or master, was not involved in the actual navigation of the boat except as overseer, unless extraordinary circumstances prevailed. On modern towboats there are no more roof captains; instead, one of the pilots serves both functions and the boat therefore carries one pilot and one master-pilot. Nearly all of the men I interviewed were pilots, and many had served at one time or another as captains (masters) of their assigned boats. Exceptions included five of the last roof captains on the river—Captains Ernest Wagner, Gabriel Chengery, Jim Blum, Verne Strekfus, and "Doc" Hawley—all of whom have spent their entire careers on excursion steamboats.

course of a watch.[3] Represented among the fifty are pilots and captains from all stretches of the Ohio and Mississippi rivers, who had a variety of experience that spans the spectrum from steam packets, towboats, and excursion boats to diesel towboats.[4] They had worked for private industry and for the government. They were as old as 102 and as young as 22. The had piloted as long as sixty-four years and as little as one trip. Because I was interested in the changes in piloting during the twentieth century, I made a special effort to talk with old-timers in their seventies and eighties who could describe firsthand a river with few locks and dams and infrequent buoys. If anything, my sample of pilots and captains is skewed toward those with thirty-five years of experience or more. The piloting profession is predominantly male and, to my knowledge, almost exclusively white.[5] Because I was a woman in this male world, some stories were no doubt inaccessible to me, especially off-color ones. However, I am not convinced that very many male interviewers would have been allowed to tape those stories either; I was told a few of the tales but only sans tape recorder. Almost without exception, the pilots were gracious, hospitable, and eager to share their memories with a fellow river rat who knew that there is very little romance to twelve-hour work days and cramped crew's quarters.

To avoid the caricature that often results from the effort, I have not attempted to transcribe dialect, though I have preserved regional flavors by

---

[3] A list of the pilots and captains interviewed is given in the Appendix, along with the place and dates of interviews and any other pertinent information. In the text I will either refer to the captain's name in introducing his remarks or I will indicate the name in brackets afterwards. Since the other information is available in the Appendix, I will not repeat it in the text. Duplicate copies of my tapes and transcripts have been deposited with the Inland Rivers Library in Cincinnati and the Minnesota Historical Society in St. Paul.

[4] These pilots and captains had also worked other rivers, such as the Tennessee, the Cumberland, the Illinois, the Missouri, the Muskinghum, and the White.

[5] That is, I know of no black or oriental pilots. I do know of at least one native-American pilot-captain. One woman, Captain Lexie Palmore, currently has a first-class pilot's license for a considerable stretch on the lower Mississippi and lower Ohio rivers and pilots for the Delta Queen Steamboat Company. Another newcomer (though from an old river family), Martha Ritchie Dennison, is likewise a licensed pilot. Also from an old-time river family, Captain Linda Williams, thirty-two, drowned in 1979 while working as master on the *Tom Reynolds* near Davenport, Iowa. A letter in the *Waterways Journal* signed by Captain Mary L. Hammond of Fort Thomas, Kentucky, suggests that there are more women additions to the pilot ranks. Since I talked with only two women out of the entire group, I will use the pronoun "he" when referring to pilots and captains in general.

faithfully adhering to intonation patterns, phrasings, figures, and rhythms. I have not laundered the language to excise terms, particularly racial ones, that will offend many sensibilities, because that would not be true to the language and ideas of the pilots. I have, however, removed mumblings such as the "uh's," "you know's," "well, I tell ya's," and other false starts common to oral interviews.

In Chapter 1 the rambling and sometimes repetitious quality of the narratives has been preserved to illustrate the common form as well as the content of a story. In subsequent chapters I have edited passages more stringently to remove the repetitious and irrelevant remarks that often detract from the point or punch of a recollection. Generally, I have used ellipses only to indicate a significant gap in the original transcription. For linguists, folklorists, or anthropologists interested in the complete form of the oral narratives, original tapes and transcripts are available for study (see footnote 3). A glossary is provided for readers unfamiliar with river terms.

Because I was first drawn to this project by stories that seemed impossibly Twain-like given the vast changes in both rivers and equipment since the 1850s, and because I wanted to underscore both change and continuity, I have used several sources in preparing this book that give more range than my collection alone could offer. I have relied on Mark Twain's own account of piloting, *Life on the Mississippi*, the considerable nonfiction river literature available in published form, the published and unpublished memoirs of pilots and captains from the 1850s to the present, novels written by rivermen and river enthusiasts, a collection of taped interviews done in 1957–58 and deposited in the Inland Rivers Library at Cincinnati (see Introduction, footnote 18), and a collection of taped interviews of U.S. Army Corps of Engineers veterans.[6]

This book is not so much about the river itself, nor even about the boats, past and present, that ran the river; this book is about the pilots and captains who have worked the river, many for fifty to sixty years of their lives, pilots still living, and pilots long dead. On the one hand, their stories recapture the spirit of Twain-era pilots, and on the other, they reveal a realistic reconciliation with the figure of the businessman-pilot who, unlike Mark Twain's kings, might be mistaken for a banker on the streets of Hannibal.

---

[6] These twelve interviews were recorded in September 1980 for a history-of-dredging project recently undertaken by the Corps and are deposited with their historical division in Washington, D.C. I served as interviewer for these tapes.

ACKNOWLEDGMENTS

I couldn't have done this alone. A project of this sort runs up numerous debts of gratitude, the acknowledgment of which is but feeble repayment to those persons and groups who gave so generously of their particular gifts. Almost without exception, the pilots themselves were enthusiastic, hospitable, gracious participants. They told me of other pilots, made phone calls or wrote letters to pave my way with an old friend or former partner, and willingly shared—in lively discourse or rambling pilothouse reveries—the experiences of their lives on the river. In my notebook are the names of many other pilots I would like to have talked with, names that would be familiar to many in the river community; but though the temptation is great to just keep talking, one finally has to be content with a representative group. I thank all those pilots who gave me so much of their time for letting me write their book.

The considerable expenses for travel, equipment, tape, transcription, and time were covered by grants from several sources. I am grateful to the National Endowment for the Humanities for a 1977 summer stipend; to the American Council of Learned Societies for a 1978 grant-in-aid; and to the Alice O'Brien Foundation of St. Paul, Minnesota, for funds to underwrite tape transcription. I was awarded a junior faculty leave by Lafayette College (Easton, Pennsylvania), which freed me from teaching duties for one term and allowed me to ride boats and talk to pilots. Lafayette's Committee on Advanced Study and Research helped pay for tapes and typing. I appreciate both the financial assistance from Lafayette College and the considerable encouragement of colleagues.

The Delta Queen Steamboat Company gave me access to their pilots, who served as the catalysts for the entire project. Particularly I want to remember the late Betty Blake, who first hired me in 1974, and to thank Bob Waring, who arranged for me to be relief cruise director, giver of talks, and pilothouse lounger for over three months in 1977. The entire crew of the *Delta Queen* helped me out in many ways that summer. I want to thank Captain Gabriel Chengery, then master of the *Delta Queen*, and Henry Mitchell, chief purser and friend, both of whom offered complete cooperation in everything from providing liberal access to the pilothouse to finding an empty crew room for me to sleep in.

All of the following people contributed to this project. Jim Swift of the *Waterways Journal* provided me with numerous names and addresses of pilots and sent along other tidbits of information from time to time. Ralph DuPae, who works with the Murphy Library of the University of Wisconsin at LaCrosse, also supplied names, addresses, and photos. He helped me choose photos from the library's extensive river collection for inclusion in the finished book. Yeatman Anderson III, curator of the Inland Rivers Library at the Public Library of Cincinnati and Hamilton County, and his staff cheerfully accommodated me and my rental recorders for several days while I taped the Knoephle Collection. Eleanor McKay, curator of the Mississippi Valley Collection at Memphis State University, sent me copies of 1972 William Tippitt interviews that were clearer than those I had obtained through patch-recording from his tapes. Russell Fridley, director, and Elizabeth Knight extended the institutional backing and services of the Minnesota Historical Society. Sandra Rae Miller shared her research on women pilots. Captain Loren "Shorty" Williams made a call on my behalf, and Jerry Tinkey arranged for me to ride as a guest aboard the Mid-America Transportation Company's towboat, *Ann King*. Captain Gordon Nelson, who called me "Steamboat," and his crew answered endless questions and made me feel welcome on the ride from St. Paul to St. Louis. Diagrams in the text that illustrate river terms are based on sketches provided by Captain Lexie Palmore.

Willard "Bill" Moore read sections of the manuscript and provided the critical perspective of a folklorist. Lee Chambers-Schiller also read portions of the manuscript and offered suggestions; but even more important, she's seen the entire fantasy unfold—from the stairwells of the Michigan library to the completion of the book. When I first timidly suggested my idea for this project, David Johnson immediately responded with the kind of enthusiasm and endorsement that strengthened the resolve of the Mississippi Screamer. I want to thank all of these people, and any I have inadvertently overlooked, for their valuable help and their reassuring confidence.

More than anyone else, my husband, David Lund, is a part of this book. He believed in the value of what I was doing and in my ability to do it. He shared my fantasy and nurtured my dreams. He made it possible for me to devote full time to it for three years; he gave technical advice when asked; he listened to stories and read early drafts; he recharged my spirits when energies flagged or my confidence sputtered. For these and other love offerings, I affectionately and publicly thank him.

Mark Twain, 1895

INTRODUCTION

Echoes: The River Changes, the River Stays the Same

The trade weekly of the river industry, the *Waterways Journal*, routinely announces the arrival of new, high-horsepower diesel towboats, advertises for the most sophisticated boating equipment available, and editorializes on behalf of progressive river management and effective congressional lobbies to further the economic self-interest of the industry. It also features an "old-boat" column, "Twenty Years Ago" and "Forty Years Ago" jottings, and space for the river fraternity to learn of one another's doings. The very format of this publication reflects an acknowledgment of the long, rich tradition they carry on and an accommodation of that legacy to the technological triumphs of a new age. Despite progress in the form of controlled rivers, radar, sonar sounding devices, long- and short-range radios, intercoms, search lights, and hydraulic steering levers, it is, as a recent editorial proposed, "an industry that still rings with echoes of the Mark Twain era."

In both cultural and individual terms, the river—specifically the Mississippi—has been particularized in the American imagination by Mark Twain. For countless foreigners as well, to say "steamboat" or "the Mississippi" is to speak with one breath of America's best-known river and her best-loved spokesman. To be sure, other major American writers of the nineteenth century used the river—Henry David Thoreau took us on the Merrimac and Concord; Herman Melville outfitted his Mississippi steamer with a motley assortment of humanity in *The Confidence Man*. But Thoreau is remembered as interpreter of the mainland woods and Melville as glorifier of the open sea. It is not DeSoto's Mississippi we imagine, though he "discovered" it. It is not LaSalle's or Jolliet's, though they explored it. It is Mark Twain who has charted the Father of Waters for Americans, and Mark Twain's Mississippi symbolizes rebirth, freedom of conscience, eternal flux, endless continuity—a kind of divinity. In *The Adventures of Huckleberry Finn*, the river is a sanctuary for Huck and the escaped slave, Jim. An avenue of escape from civilization and its codes, the river carries danger and death as well as potential freedom. In Part I of *Life on the Mississippi*, Mark Twain describes a natural force basically indifferent to man and his civilizations—neither merciful nor hostile, good nor evil—that creates and destroys at will. The river can be loved; it must be respected.

Those who choose to match their ingenuity against the Big River—the steamboat pilots—speak of it, as Samuel Clemens and Horace Bixby did, with affection, awe, and reverence. Part II of *Life* revealed a man torn between a belief in the inevitable progress of change and a desire to retrieve a simpler past. As a businessman (though not always a successful one), Mark Twain agreed with the need to improve the river to facilitate commerce, but as an old riverman, long removed from the scene of his boyhood ambitions, he regretted the change and resented West Point engineers who "knocked the romance out of piloting." Though he knew what "miracles" Captain Eads had worked on the jetties in the Passes, he scoffed at efforts to control the majestic Mississippi through the science of engineering: "the Commission might as well bully the comets in their courses and undertake to make them behave, as try to bully the Mississippi River into right and reasonable conduct" (*Life*, chap. 28).

The men who worked the river, in the person of the steamboat pilot, had been for Mark Twain exemplars of the traits traditionally linked to our image of the American character. His pilot used wit, ingenuity, nerve, and judgment in daily confrontations with the vagaries of one of nature's cagiest adversaries and was justly rewarded as "monarch" of the river. In sum, Mark Twain saw the old-time pilot as the personification of the free, unfettered, independent, rugged, mobile, ingenious American.

While Mark Twain's river could carry the weight of symbol and his pilots the mantle of monarchs, that same river, of course, was and is significant in practical economic, social, and political terms. [1] The steam packets of yesterday and the diesel towboats of today were and are commercial vehicles, the river an inexpensive conveyor of commodities. When Mark Twain returned to his river in 1882, he declared that "Mississippi steamboating was born about 1812; at the end of thirty years, it had grown to mighty proportions; and in less than

---

[1] For details of the part played by the inland rivers in the economic development of the country, see Louis C. Hunter, *Steamboats on the Western Rivers*, particularly Chapter 1.

thirty more, it was dead! A strangely short life for so majestic a creature" (*Life*, chap. 22). His own piloting career lasted from 1857 to 1861; when the Civil War came, commerce was suspended and his occupation was given over for those that followed: silver miner, newspaper reporter, gold miner, special correspondent, lecturer, "scribbler of books."

Some say the Golden Age of Mississippi steamboating was the 1840s and 1850s, when the river enjoyed a near monopoly as the main transportation route used by eastern markets.[2] In the 1840s steamboat tonnage on the Mississippi, even exclusive of New Orleans, was greater than that of all Atlantic ports combined, with some boats already operating with loaded tows. Though steamboats were almost as numerous and certainly more splendid in the two decades after the '50s, the seeds of decay already existed: canals, stage and express lines, plank roads, and especially railroads were growing steadily in importance.[3] In 1860, the total tally carried on the western waters was ten million tons; by 1880, it had doubled to twenty million tons and would continue to increase until 1895, "when a precipitate decline set in, which reached its nadir by the time World War I broke out."[4] So Mark Twain was a hasty gravedigger.

The government's failure to continue improving the river and, most devastating, competition from the railroads made packet boats a vision of nostalgia by the second decade of the twentieth century. In 1923, however, the Inland Waterways Corporation (known as Federal Barge Lines) was formed and is considered, along with the implementation of lock-and-dam systems that guaranteed a nine-foot channel in both the Ohio and Mississippi rivers, responsible for the revival of commercial river traffic. In 1976, the Mississippi system (main channels and all tributaries of the Mississippi, Missouri, Illinois, and Ohio rivers) carried more freight tonnage than the Great Lakes, the Intra-Coastal Canal, and the Panama Canal combined.[5] Major industries are dependent on inland waterways to carry such principal commodities as grain, soybeans, coal, iron and steel products, crude petroleum, distillate and residual fuel oils, gasoline, fertilizers, prepared animal feeds, and countless other

[2] This varies, of course. A report by the Inland Waterways Commission fixed the Golden Age in the 1860s to early 80s.

[3] Mildred L. Hartsough, *From Canoe to Steel Barge*, pp. 101, 109.

[4] William J. Petersen, *Towboating on the Mississippi*, p. 9.

[5] Ibid., p. 17. The Mississippi System carried 510,502,000 tons; the Great Lakes 91,486,000 tons; Intra-Coastal Canal 96,950,849 tons; the Panama Canal 121,010,654 tons.

products. According to the annual river study prepared by the Waterborne Commerce Statistics Center of the U.S. Engineers for 1978, river commerce on the Mississippi system had reached an all-time high of 552.9 million tons.[6] Mark Twain would be pleased to know that the river wasn't "dead past resurrection" in 1882.

Particularly in the middle decades of the nineteenth century, the Mississippi system served as a passageway to settlement as immigrants from abroad and from the older states peopled the frontier. The first settlers traveled primarily by overland routes, but when steamboats displaced keelboats and made river passage a two-way route (and a cheaper proposition—steamboat cabin fares averaged three cents a mile for distances of fifty miles or more, which included berth and meals; stagecoach fares were about six cents a mile, excluding meals and lodging at hotels), most people settling in the Ohio Valley emigrated by river.[7] By the beginning of the American Revolution, only a few hundred settlers had crossed the Alleghenies, but by 1789, approximately 250,000 had immigrated to the Mississippi Valley, mainly via the chief highway to the West, the beautiful Ohio.[8]

The great immigration period for the upper Mississippi regions was 1848 to 1860; even after the railroad reached the Mississippi, settlers continued to take passage on steamboats for the remainder of their journey to the Minnesota and Dakota territories. Many Irish and German immigrants worked at their first jobs as deckhands on steamboats. But often immigrants, who generally took deck passage to save money, were the first victims of explosions, collision, and disease. George Washington Cable's novel, *Gideon's Band* (his father was a steamboat owner and captain), based on his own experience on the river, takes as its subject the intrigue of rival steamboat owners and an unfortunate effect of the river passageway to settlement—the spread of cholera during the epidemic of the late 1840s, which took a disproportionate toll among the immigrant deck passengers who had anticipated a new start in a new land. Later, in the early twentieth century, steamboats helped disseminate a happier "infection," what has come to be recognized as indigenous American music—jazz. Several musicians, including Louis Armstrong, Baby Dodds, Joe Howard, and Davey Jones, played with the "Fate" Marable orchestra aboard Streckfus steamers

---

[6] *Waterways Journal*, June 14, 1980.

[7] Edward Quick and Herbert Quick, *Mississippi Steamboatin'*, p. 117.

[8] Hartsough, *From Canoe to Steel Barge*.

plying the Mississippi. And jazz, long a resident of New Orleans, steamed upriver to new audiences.[9]

The river has tickled the American fancy as Mark Twain's symbol of romance, power, and divinity; it has carried commodities to new markets, a people to new countries, disease to new victims, music to new listeners. The modern 10,500-horsepower diesel towboat—continually moving, pushing fifteen to forty loaded barges past the steel and glass skyscrapers of St. Louis— may seem of a totally different order, a species irrevocably divorced from the sternwheel or sidewheel packet boat making its regular run, answering hails from a single passenger in a clearing or collecting a freight of three hogs bound for Hickman, Kentucky. Indeed, Samuel Clemens would probably stand as bedazzled in a modern towboat pilothouse as would Orville Wright in an Apollo command module. But in those technologically sophisticated pilot-houses, the direct descendants of the likes of Clemens, Horace Bixby, "Quaker Oats," Henry Nye, and Grant Marsh stand their solitary watches, learn and relearn the river, memorize the markings, calculate the risks, make the decisions, and tell their tales.[10] Tales with echoes and stories just born.

What if Mark Twain'd stayed on the boats?
We wouldn't have Huckleberry Finn . . .
you wouldn't have heard of him.

Captain Ed Winford

Life on the Mississippi is the masterpiece of the profession and the touchstone against which the words of living pilots inevitably reverberate. In it, with his usual understatement, Mark Twain said of the "marvelous science of piloting": "I believe there has been nothing like it elsewhere in the world."[11]

For a boy of Hannibal, Missouri, the loftiest, most durable ambition was to be steamboatmen. Several of Samuel Clemens's chums became clerks or

[9] See an excerpt from *The Baby Dodds Story*, reprinted in Wright Morris, *The Mississippi River Reader*, pp. 332–49.

[10] Captain Cal Blazier was nicknamed "Quaker Oats" because with his white hair he resembled the picture on the Quaker Oats box.

[11] Chapters 4 to 27 of *Life on the Mississippi*, which chronicle Mark Twain's days as a cub pilot, first appeared in several installments of the *Atlantic Monthly* in 1875 as "Old Times on the Mississippi." I have used the 1961 Signet edition of *Life on the Mississippi*, but I have noted quotations by chapter so that readers using other editions can easily locate passages.

engineers or barkeepers on the boats, but "Pilot was the grandest position of all. The pilot, even in those days of trivial wages, had a princely salary—from a hundred and fifty to two hundred and fifty dollars a month, and no board to pay" (*Life*, chap. 4). The boy who went off and became a pilot could return to his village in glory. Clemens's mentor, Captain Horace Bixby, quickly disabused the "cub" of his more outlandish romantic notions by impressing upon him that he had to learn the entire river by heart, upsteam and downstream, by day and by night. He had to know the names of towns, islands, bars, and bends; he had to learn the shape of the river as well as he'd know the shape of his own front hall. And, Bixby tutored, he must learn the shape of the river "with such absolute certainty that you can always steer by the shape that's *in your head*, and never mind the one that's before your eyes (*Life*, chap. 8).

The naive narrator allows that he had entered upon the enterprise of learning twelve or thirteen hundred miles of the Mississippi with an easy, and unwarranted, confidence, supposing that all a pilot had to do was keep his boat in the river, "and I did not consider that that could be much of a trick, since it was so wide." (*Life*, chap. 6). But then he consistently failed Bixby's oral quizzes, realized the magnitude of his undertaking, and, when rousted from bed in the middle of the night to work his watch, "began to fear that piloting was not quite so romantic as I had imagined it was; there was something very real and worklike about this new phase of it" (*Life*, chap. 6). Worklike, indeed. The pilot had to stand watch twelve hours a day and learn the shape of the river, an outline constantly altered by cave-ins and cut-offs. "Two things seemed pretty apparent to me. One was, that in order to be a pilot a man had got to learn more than any one man ought to be allowed to know; and the other was, that he must learn it all over again in a different way every twenty-four hours" (*Life*, chap. 8).

This faculty of memory, which the pilot must "incessantly cultivate until he has brought it to absolute perfection," is only one of the three requirements essential to the making of a good pilot.

> He must have good and quick judgment and decision, and a cool, calm courage that no peril can shake. Give a man the merest trifle of pluck to start with, and by the time he has become a pilot he cannot be unmanned by any danger a steamboat can get into; but one cannot quite say the same for judgment. Judgment is a matter of brains, and a man must *start* with a good stock of that article or he will never succeed as a pilot. [*Life*, chap. 13]

Characterizing pilots as "tireless talkers" who, when gathered together, talked only about the river, he remains awestruck by their company and calling. "Your true pilot cares nothing about anything on earth but the river, and his pride in his occupation surpasses the pride of kings" (*Life*, chap. 7).

Finally, the cub garners the experience that fosters confidence, but at each plateau he is once again reminded of the distance yet to travel before he can truly join the ranks of the pilot fraternity. Then, when one does, by and by, instinctively *know* rather than *see* the difference between wind reefs and bluff reefs—when he can read the river—it is a mixed blessing because glorious sunsets no longer bewitch the enraptured neophyte. "All the grace, the beauty, the poetry, had gone out of the majestic river! . . . All the value any feature of it had for me now was the amount of usefulness it could furnish toward compassing the safe piloting of a steamboat" (*Life*, chap. 9).

Besides describing the teaching tactics of his mentor, the requirements of his craft, the fickleness of unbuoyed channels, the routine activities of boating, the power of the Pilots' Benevolent Association, the catastrophes too frequently attendant to the profession, the characters who peopled the pilot ranks, the boats, the races, the demise of romance, Mark Twain told a tall tale or two along the way.

One of his best describes the remarkable skills of Mr. X, a crackerjack and a somnambulist. It was said of Mr. X that if he were troubled about some bad stretch in the river, he was sure to get up and walk in his sleep. One night a great New Orleans passenger packet on which George Ealer and Mr. X were pilots was approaching a particularly difficult crossing near Helena, Arkansas. George was on watch. Nervous and sweating from the anxiety, George was relieved when Mr. X entered the pilothouse and offered to take her through the crossing, because he had seen it since George had. George then sat back on the lazy bench and witnessed "the sweetest piece of piloting that was ever done on the Mississippi River" as Mr. X slipped the boat through to safety. George asked Mr. X to hold her for five more minutes while he went for coffee, but he hastily returned to the pilothouse after meeting the night watchman. The watchman had just found Mr. X walking on top of the railings, asleep, and had put him back to bed—the boat was "whistling down the river at her own sweet will!" Later the watchman quizzed George, asking him whether "the lunatic" had told him he was asleep. Of course, he hadn't. George, calmed now that the boat was under control again, was unflappable. "Well, I think I'll stay by next time he has one of those fits. But I hope he'll have them often. You just ought to have seen him take this boat through Helena crossing. I never saw anything so gaudy before. And if he can do such gold-leaf, kid-glove, diamond-breastpin piloting when he is sound asleep, what *couldn't* he do if he was dead!" (*Life*, chap. 11).

Looking back on years that had included the George Ealers and Mr. Xs, Mark Twain assessed the rank and dignity of piloting and proclaimed its craftsmen above kings.

> If I have seemed to love my subject, it is no surprising thing, for I loved the profession far better than any I have followed since, and I took a measureless pride in it. The reason is plain: a pilot, in those days, was the only unfettered and entirely independent human being that lived in the earth. Kings are but the hampered servants of parliament and the people; parliaments sit in chains forged by their constituency. . . . In truth, every man and woman and child has a master, and worries and frets in servitude; but, in the day I write of, the Mississippi pilot had *none*. . . . His movements were entirely free; he consulted no one, he received commands from nobody, he promptly resented even the merest suggestions. . . . So here was the novelty of a king without a keeper, an absolute monarch who was absolute in sober truth and not by a fiction of words. [*Life*, chap. 14]

Not everyone agreed. E. W. Gould, whose *Fifty Years on the Mississippi* (1889) is a compendium of unindexed river information, disputed the more grandiose of Mark Twain's claims for old-time pilots. According to Gould, Mark Twain's brief experience as a pilot on the Mississippi entitled his remarks to some consideration—"not that they are always just or truthful" and "strangers are liable to get a false impression of the facts." Gould referred to the above quotation and declared it no wonder that Mr. Twain was charmed by the piloting profession. Mark Twain, he claimed, either magnified the authority he possessed or "was fortunate enough to get on to boats under the control of incompetent milk and water masters. *Probably both.*" While he decried Mark Twain's assessment of the authority of pilots, he applauded Twain's ability to portray accurately the characteristics of his pilots. In fact, in his biographical sketches, Gould sometimes allowed Mark Twain's descriptions from "his very entertaining work" (*Life*) to carry the day. "'Mark Twain's' experience during his steamboat life on the Mississippi, whether real or ideal, portrays so much that is true to life and in accordance with facts known to many still living, no better illustration need be sought than is given in his very interesting narratives" (p. 599).

Of course, since Mark Twain's vision of the river pilot is the premiere testimony in American literature, many writers and pilots, then and now, debated and often debunked the piloting abilities of Samuel Clemens himself, with some accepting Horace Bixby's private proclamation that Clemens knew the river but lacked courage and some defending Clemens's record of having had no accidents. [12] It is fashionable to declare Mark Twain a better writer than pilot.

His [Bixby's] appraisal was accepted by rivermen generally, who felt that Mark Twain had preempted their profession and who resented the Mark Twain legend. Though Sam Clemens never had any serious mishaps at piloting, rivermen were more willing to let him have fame as a writer than as a pilot. One of them made a remark in Mark Twain's own vein—"He was a droll fellow and was always getting off something—sometimes it was a sandbar." [13]

A Mark Twain contemporary and famous Missouri River pilot who evacuated survivors of the Little Big Horn, Captain Grant Marsh, praised Clemens's courage and level-headed navigation on the *A. D. Chambers* during a dangerous ice crossing in the winter of 1858–59. [14] Captain Fred Way, Jr., puts Clemens's piloting career in perspective:

Well, here's the proof of the pudding. He was actually on the Mississippi River four years; in those four years he learned the river and he pursued his profession. This is the whole thing. Four years. That isn't hardly a college career. Two years of that was apprenticeship and two years was actually piloting. Well, in the two years he was on his own, he didn't sink a boat, he didn't get in any hard trouble I ever heard of, or somebody surely would have told. I'll give him the benefit of that doubt; I think he was getting along all right.

Though most river pilots can be nudged to offer an opinion on the prowess of their most famous colleague, the question is, of course, basically irrelevant. We recognize that he romanticized the calling, neglected some of the grubbier and

---

[12] See Dudley R. Hutcherson, "Mark Twain as a Pilot," *American Literature* 12 (November 1940): 353–55.

[13] Walter Havighurst, *Voices on the River*, pp. 165–66. A recent book by Hannibal, Missouri, native, Raymond P. Ewing—*Mark Twain's Steamboat Years: The Years of Command*—discusses in detail the boats Clemens piloted and assessments of his skill as a pilot.

[14] Joseph Mills Hanson, *The Conquest of the Missouri*, pp. 26–29.

more routine tasks of boating. But that knowledge doesn't diminish our attraction to the vision of this "mythic" exemplar of the truly independent American character. As Captain Way continued:

> I think that the reason his book was so successful, of course, he was a good writer to begin with, but the whole thing was still very much of a glory. . . . If he had stayed a little longer and the thing had got old fiddle, the book would never have been half as good, but he still had that great feeling . . . the romance, and he put it down better than anybody's done before . . . No, he was making a big glory story out of it. I think he meant every word of it because that was the way he felt. I don't think anything he ever did held a candle to the feelings of awe and majesty of bein' a pilot.

Now Twain-era tradition and space-age innovation coexist in the piloting profession. Like the river, piloting changes and it stays the same. A pilot sitting for his first-class license today does as Mark Twain did in 1852—he draws the river from memory, by hand, noting all markings, towns, islands, and bridges. Whereas Mark Twain was presented a blank sheet of paper, the applicant today sometimes receives an outline of the river, but he has to include locks and dams, more bridges, and government lights and buoys that did not exist in 1850.[15] And he is required to get a radar endorsement. Many of those aspiring pilots attend the Western Rivers Training Center at Greenville, Mississippi, or the National River Academy at Helena, Arkansas, where they receive both book tutoring and periodic practical experience with their sponsoring companies. Some old-timers argue that too much emphasis is being placed on graduation from a school and too little on whether a man can really do the job. Clearly, there have been changes in the last 130 years in the bureaucratic procedures surrounding the licensing process. Clemens received his first-

---

[15] This is a relatively recent change in the licensing procedure, within the last five years or so. The question of whether in fact pilots were required to draw the map in Mark Twain's time is still unanswered. Edgar Branch of Miami University has been exploring this question but has yet to discover a definitive, documented answer. Captain Fred Way, Jr., thinks that map drawing on examinations probably came into regular practice sometime later in the nineteenth century. Even in the twentieth century, some pilots passed oral examinations, given them by rivermen who knew whether the answers were correct or not (see p. 244). Prospective pilots have always had to secure the recommendations of pilots who knew their abilities, regardless of whether they drew a map or told an examiner how they would run a certain stretch of the river. At any rate, Mark Twain's account reinforces the extraordinary amount of detailed information required of the prospective pilot in order to be officially admitted to the regular pilot ranks.

class license from the U.S. Steamboat Inspection Service. Today, licensing is handled by the Coast Guard. And today a pilot of diesel towboats need not draw the river at all; he can be examined for what is called a towboat operator's license, which allows him to operate on the western rivers rather than on a certain stretch of the river over which he has shown competence.[16] But basically, the twentieth-century pilot, like Samuel Clemens, must meet the requirements of memory, nerve, and judgment to master his craft.

Perhaps the strongest echoes rebound from those stories of boyhood ambition and cub pilot initiation—what one must learn and *know* in his head before he can make it as a pilot. Likewise, the tall tales and the stories of pranks, accidents, and unforgettable characters are familiar to readers of *Life*. Mark Twain gave us Mr. X, his somnambulist wizard of the wheel. George Merrick, a former riverman (1854–63) and Twain contemporary whose river column ran in the Burlington, Iowa, *Saturday Evening Post* from 1913 to 1919 and featured both his documentation of boats that had run on the Upper Mississippi and letters from veteran rivermen exchanging information and stories, repeats in the August 13, 1918, edition the undoubtedly apochryphal tale of a pilot named Old Bill Cupp. A boat from Pittsburgh, bound for the upper river with a mixed cargo, had arrived in St. Louis. The nervous captain interviewed Cupp as a prospective pilot and inquired if he knew the river, especially the rapids. Cupp answered that he thought he did, that being his business. "But do you know every rock in the rapids?" persisted the captain. The laconic Cupp allowed that he did. When the boat reached the lower rapids (Des Moines) and began the ascent, the boat bumped a rock. "The captain rushed up to the roof and asked Bill if he knew he had hit a rock. 'Yes,' said Bill, 'That is one.' Very soon she hit another and the captain was wild. 'I thought you said you knew where every rock was?' 'I did and I do,' said Bill. 'That was two. There are seventy-five more and I will find them all.' The captain realized his error and retracted. 'But do you know where rocks ain't?' 'Sure,' said Bill, 'I generally aim to miss them; but I thought you wanted me to find them. I always aim to please my employers.' After that he found no more rocks."

In his book, *Pilotin' Comes Natural*, Captain Fred Way, Jr., recounted pilot Dayton Randolph's yarns of the remarkable feats of the steamer *Hurronico*.[17] One will suffice to suggest the nature of the fabricated *Hurronico* legend. On one

---

[16] The effect of the institution of what many veterans claim to be an inferior license on the pilot profession as a whole is discussed in Chapter 7.

[17] Frederick Way, Jr., *Pilotin' Comes Natural*, pp. 243–44.

occasion, Randolph, approaching the Marietta, Ohio, bridge in high water with a nervous captain hypnotized by the imminent tight situation, began telling a tale to fit the occasion. The anxious captain stood "bored to exaspera-tion" by Dayton's endless *Hurronico* extravaganzas, stories about a boat so big she carried eighty clerks who rode around on bicycles to collect deck fares, and so fast she'd "run from St. Louis to New Orleans and meet the smoke she'd made going down on the return trip clean back to Memphis." Dayton, who knew they would clear the bridge, taunted the captain by remembering that one time in much higher water, the *Hurronico* had no chance of making this very bridge.

"But there's where her rubber gangplank came in handy," said Dayton. "They eased the *Hurronico* down to the bridge and fasted the shore end of the gangplank right to the center span. Backed full head on her and that rubber gangplank stretched back like a rubber band until you'd a swore it would'a snapped—but it didn't—and the captain kept hollering 'Back 'er!' until we were a quarter of a mile from the bridge with that gangplank shrunk about half normal size and tight as a fiddle string. 'Stop 'er!' yelled the captain—and the *Hurronico* leaped forward and up like a blamed jack rabbit and heaved herself clean over the top of the superstructure." [P. 237]

Extraordinary pilots, remarkable boats, and even obliging critters furnish the tease of tall tales. In *Big River to Cross* (1940), Ben Lucien Burman repeats a popular yarn about a famous mate on the *Gordon C. Greene* who met the challenge of a stubborn sandbar in unique fashion. Standard methods of working the boat off the bar had failed. The lower deck was loaded with turkeys going to market, so the mate freed them from their coops, stapled their feet to the deck floor, and ordered the roustabouts to stand by with towels, aprons, and rags. At his whistle, the rousters waved the cloths over their heads and yelled. The turkeys flew up and lifted the boat over into deep water. In the late 1950s at least two other versions of that story were current among veteran Ohio River pilots. One pilot claimed to have been present when the original version was told by a captain to his curious son. The boat was the *Katie Frazer*, and some man had thousands of turkeys up Wagner's Ripple he wanted to ship out. The turkeys filled up the deck space, so the mate ordered the rest taken to the roof, where he stapled their feet so they wouldn't fly away. All had been stapled except a great big old gobbler. Then one of the boys drove a staple too far in and the old turkey gobbled his protests, raised his wings, and flew. All the other turkeys followed his lead, and the *Katie Frazer* went up with 'em—and that was the last of the *Katie Frazer*[18]

Yet another version is similar to the one Burman published, except the old mate tacked their feet, pulled out his pistol, and shot at 'em; they flapped their wings and raised the boat over the shoals. This time the story, told among a gathering of three or four rivermen, is a Tennessee River story, the boat on its last trip of the season. When the teller reached the punch line, one cagey listener protested: "You can't fool me on that. That was the *Katie Frazer!*"[19]

In subsequent chapters many narratives will illustrate both continuity and change, tradition and innovation. I heard stories of a crackerjack pilot who was also a kleptomaniac, pilots who purportedly steered better when drunk than sober, a young cub who fastidiously scrubbed clean pilothouse windows in order to be there to learn the river. Some became rivermen totally by accident; others fulfilled boyhood ambitions. One pilot rang the bell for dead slow so he could watch, enchanted, as a deer swam in a moonbeam across the boat's bow; another spotted a deer and pursued it as game. There are stories of men who learned to pilot from crusty old masters and pilots tutored by even-tempered craftsmen. Some pilots cling to that dash of romance; some primarily articulate the routine.

In 1882 Mark Twain bemoaned the lot of steamboats and steamboatmen. "He [steamboatman] was absent because he is no more. His occupation is gone, his power has passed away, he is absorbed into the common herd, he grinds at the mill, a shorn Samson and inconspicuous" (*Life*, chap. 22). Few steamers—only two overnight and a few daylight excursion boats—still ply the inland waterways of America. Pilots and captains who began their careers on steamboats and finished their working years on diesel towboats are generally in their

---

[18] In 1957 and '58, John Knoephle interviewed many river-connected people, primarily in the Ohio River Valley around Cincinnati and Louisville. These people included pilots, lockmasters, roustabouts, cooks, clerks, boat agents, newspaper writers, engineers, deckhands, and musicians. Duplicate copies of those tapes are deposited in the Inland Rivers Library at the Cincinnati Public Library. Since no release forms were obtained in that less-legal era, I will cite no individual names in stories taken from this collection. Hereafter, the notation will simply read Knoephle Collection.

[19] Knoephle collection. Folklorists will recognize the *Katie Frazer* stories as a version of the "bird that flies with man to safety," entry B 542.1 in Ernest W. Baughman, *Type and Motif Index of the Folktales of England and North America* (The Hague: Mouton & Company, 1966 [1967]; Indiana University Folklore Series no. 20). A western-American variant involves a man who has fallen in a deep hole and cannot get out. He lassos buzzards flying overhead and they carry him to safety.

late sixties, seventies, and eighties now, and eager, I found, to share their memories and perceptions of sometimes a half century on the river.[20] As one might expect from men who have learned up to five thousand miles of river, their memories, as a group, are extraordinary. Although the absolute monarch that Mark Twain eulogized has retreated to history's shelves or imagination's fancy, the river pilot's occupation is not gone, he is not "absorbed into the common herd."

Despite all of his romantic hyperbole, Mark Twain nevertheless suggested a composite portrait of the steamboat pilot while still delightfully preserving the individuality of those he sketched. In presenting modern-day pilots who tell their own stories, I strive to do likewise.

[20] Some veteran steamboatmen are spending their "retirement" years by "going back home" to those few steamers like the *Delta Queen*, the *Mississippi Queen*, the *Belle of Louisville*, the *Natchez*, and the *Julia Belle Swain*, all twentieth-century boats whose very existence on the rivers confirms the tenacity of the romantic vision we still hold of nineteenth-century steamboat America.

You could learn how to be a brain surgeon, I'm sure, just by continued exposure. Contrary to all the things that higher education folks would have you believe, exposure is the real criteria for any kind of education. You can make it concentrated or very lackadaisical, but . . . if you watch something for long enough, you'll know how to do it.

Captain Donn Williams

Now let's get this straight. I never did have an ambition to be a pilot. No, I thought that was completely beyond my comprehension. To stand up there and watch those men steer those things—all hand steers in those days—that enormous boat from such a little room. I was absolutely afraid of it.

Captain Fred Way, Jr.

The phonies don't make it out there.

Captain C. W. Stoll

When I was a boy, there was but one permanent ambition among my comrades in our village on the west bank of the Mississippi River. That was, to be a steamboatman.

Mark Twain

CHAPTER ONE

Beginnings

Captain Walter Karnath (left) and Captain Rudolph "Red" Karnath on *General Allen*, 1938

As a boy Samuel Clemens dreamed of one day returning home in glory as an honored steamboat pilot. But his eventual experience as a cub pilot was, by and large, a result of serendipity and necessity. Having received a "cold shoulder and short words" from mates and clerks on steamboats, the young Clemens reluctantly gave up his original ambition but was too ashamed to return home. So in a plan remarkable for its inattention to practical detail, he determined to travel from Cincinnati to New Orleans on the *Paul Jones*, "get a ship" for South America, and join a government expedition exploring the Amazon—all of this on the princely sum of thirty dollars! However, when he arrived in New Orleans, he soon discovered two insurmountable difficulties: "One was that a vessel would not be likely to sail for the mouth of the Amazon under ten or twelve years; and the other was that the nine or ten dollars still left in my pocket would not suffice for so impossible an exploration as I had planned, even if I could afford to wait for the ship."[1] It was then that he contrived to hire aboard the *Paul Jones*, strike a deal with the pilot, and enter upon "the small enterprise of 'learning' twelve or thirteen hundred miles of the Great Mississippi River."

Pilots of today got their start on the river for various reasons: a boy's ambition, family tradition, accident or luck, financial necessity. Many boys, especially those who lived in river towns, dreamed of being crew members on the boats that blew for a landing. Some of those boys never considered any other kind of work because their fathers, uncles, grandfathers, or brothers had worked the river before them. Captain Roy W. Boyd, who eventually spent nearly eighty years on the river (one way or another, as he says) and was a carpenter as well as a pilot and master, remembers the idyllic island his family owned near Louisiana, Missouri—in Mark Twain country not far from Hannibal—and his boyhood days tuned to the sounds and sights of the river.

[1] Samuel Clemens, *Life on the Mississippi*, Chap. 6. Subsequent quotations will be cited in parentheses following the passage.

That river was home to me. I've been on the river practically ever since I was
six years old! All that time I was ridin' with my dad, or somebody else. Then
when the motorboats come along, why I was the big chief on that.
[Laughs.] . . . I was a river rat from the time I was big enough to
walk . . . Every time a boat whistled, 'fore I went to school, if I was around
home, whish, up on a hill, to see the boat go by. . . . And, when raftboats
was goin', I used to spend the biggest part of my time up there on that hill, if
it was a nice day, watchin'. You could see up the river and you could see the
smoke from as far up as you could see, to as far down as you could see,
and . . . you could count the smoke of 'em or see 'em—eight or ten boats at
one time, most any day. There 'as that many boats a runnin'. . . . I got so I
knew the whistle of practically all of 'em.

Laughing, Captain Boyd acknowledged his kinship to Mark Twain: "I guess
we was bit by the same bug."

Many say the river "gets in your blood." One young Memphis boy, Arthur
McArthur, sold newspapers and magazines on the boats at age ten, ran errands
for crew members, cashed their checks, bought them tobacco, and generally
hung around the boats hoping one day to be a pilot. Captain McArthur
remembers nearly drowning at age seven or eight when he went under at a
"step-off" in the river. "I took in a lot of river water, and as they say, if you ever
get a drink of this old Mississippi River mud into ya, it's always there. So, I
guess that's where I got baptized by the river." Though his dream had always
been to work on the river, the immediate impetus for sixteen-year-old Arthur
to hire on to the *Minnesota* was financial necessity. His father had lost
everything in the Depression and the family needed help. "'Course I was just
lucky because there was so many men out of work and standin' on the bank
there waitin' just to go to work there, and they were actually willin' to go on the
boat and work for nothin' but just the food back there in 1934. That's how
many people you had unemployed."

Like Samuel Clemens, young William Tippitt of Cairo, Illinois, thought
that steamboats were the most exciting visitors a small town could have.

I was born June the 8th, 1900, and down there every kid in our neighborhood . . . could tell you the name—the boys especially—of practically
every packet boat that landed at Cairo by the time they was five years old
because that was the, well, you might say the most exciting place for a small
boy to be is up on the levee looking down that long slope to the wharfboat

and looking at all these steamboats come in, the people on them. The people coming off and the labor working there, carrying the freight on and carrying the freight off.

And the boys knew firsthand that steamboatmen were classy.

They lived down there in our neighborhood, so us boys knew all the steamboatmen. And another reason we knew them, they was the richest folks in town. They always had money and they was liberal, too, with it. They'd give a kid a penny anytime for a piece of candy or something, and they all had diamonds. You see a man goin' down, has a great big diamond in his shirt stud, big gold watch chain across that overport stomach of his, and big gold pilot wheel on there about the size of a fifty-dollar gold piece shinin' there—why, all duded up. That man was something, when he walked down the street! And every kid wanted to be a steamboatman.

Though he will tell you that he did not make good grades in English, Captain Tippitt took pride in knowing what mattered: "I could tell you the name of every steamboat on the river and I could tell you who was captain and pilots on 'em and who was engineers on 'em. And I could tell by the whistles, even if I was sittin' in school, I could tell ya what boat was comin' in."

Born in 1904, Captain Ben Gilbert grew up in Paducah, Kentucky, half a block from Tennessee Chute, where his father built barges for the West Kentucky Coal Company. During summers he was a water boy at the barge plant, and at age fifteen took his first trip as galley boy on the *Eagan*. He too had always wanted to be a pilot. Captain Walter Karnath first steered a steamboat at age eight under the watchful eye (and, no doubt, with assistance from) his father. Karnath says he was lured by family tradition, the scenery, and the changing character of the river. Or, more simply: "Of course, the river more or less grew on me." Gordon Nelson, born in the late 1930s, had working on the river set in his mind from the time he was about nine. Born too late to have witnessed the steamboat spectacles Tippitt describes, Nelson sat at the knee of his Norwegian grandfather listening to his tales of life on a whaling ship. "I always wanted to go to sea. That's what I wanted to do when I was a little kid. And we lived in North Dakota at the time. We left there and moved to Iowa. And I got to see these towboats goin' up and down the river. And I thought, 'Why . . . that's the thing.'"

Such ambitions led some young boys to forsake school and hire on as deckhands, mess boys, mud clerks, cabin boys, cooks, dishwashers, and the like to fulfill their dreams. Captain Lester "Whitey" Schickling of Prescott, Wisconsin, left high school with only six weeks to go until graduation. He now laughs when he recalls that his physics teacher said he was going to flunk him. Whitey responded with a flourish: "Go ahead and flunk me. I'm going to the steamboat!"

Others, however, nourished no childhood fantasies of life as a river pilot nor carried on a family tradition. When one asks Captain Harry Louden his reasons for getting started on the river, his terse reply is devoid of glory-day romance. "Oh, my God, out of necessity. Mainly." Somebody got him a job "warshin'" dishes. Fifteen-year-old Clarke Hawley "just went on the river by accident" for a summer job in 1950, after visiting the old *Avalon* with his brother's school class. They needed a calliope player; he figured he could play it since he "played by ear" and had a pump organ at home. Today he is master of the steamer *Natchez* in New Orleans.

Many rivermen came from farm backgrounds. Captain Loren "Shorty" Williams did not take to farming because "there's a lot of hard work connected with it," but he had no particular visions of river work.

> And, one day I was out plowing corn, and it was hot and dry and the team was kind of frisky, and horseflies were bad, and the harness and the cultivator were in poor shape, so . . . going along the field there one of the horses was very allergic to these black horseflies and one of 'em got on him and he switched around and squirmed and twisted and bucked, and everything else, broke the tongue of the cultivator. . . . When I went to unhitch the horses, why he wrapped that tail full of cockleburrs around my neck, and I thought that was enough of farming. So I left that cultivator in the middle of the field, and as far as I know, it's still there! But I went over the levee and there was a dredge boat working there—a government dredge—and I got a job as a deckhand.

Captain Ed Winford also started on the river by accident—and doubled his salary in one day. "July 23, 1928, I worked all day for a farmer, plowin' with two horses, and made a dollar. And a friend of mine came and got me that night, and I got a job on that dredge for two dollars a day. See, I was really goin' up in the world." Captain Arthur Zimmer had been a motorcycle policeman in St. Louis for twelve years before going on the river full time because the money was better than on land. Captain Carroll "Rip" Ware had been a soda jerk at the drugstore when he hired on a boat in May of 1930. [2] Born in Sullivan's Hollow, Mississippi, Ware had watched the steamers *Ouachita* and *Murphy* come in and out of West Monroe, Louisiana, when he was a boy. "Times was hard" in 1930, and Carroll Ware got started on the river because a "man give me a job during the Depression for two dollars a day and three hots and a flop." Likewise, others who would eventually become pilots and masters and spend nearly a half century following that profession started out by accident—a "matter of luck" for men happy to get a job.

INITIATION

A river pilot is born, not made, and
if he does not have that sixth
sense, he had better plow corn
or nowadays ride a tractor.

Steamboat Bill Heckman

Once on the river, the men underwent similar initiations enroute to the pilothouse. Samuel Clemens did not arrive via the path followed by most would-be pilots. He never worked as a deckhand. He was taken on as a steersman, a cub, in consideration of the sum of five hundred dollars to be paid to his mentor out of future wages. While it was common for some captains even in the early twentieth century to extract percentages or flat fees from steersmen in return for their tutelage, most pilots began their careers as deckhands or galley crew or clerks and eventually worked their way up to the wheelhouse.

In his memoirs of sixty-nine years (1875–1944) on the river, *Lore and Lure of the Upper Mississippi* (1945), Frank Fugina described one prank pulled on green rivermen by their seasoned colleagues.

Suspended from the bow flagstaff at about half-mast and in line with the pilot's vision was placed a large metal ball. This the pilot could see at night and could use to line up with a shore mark. The ball was called the "nighthawk."

Some boats had a metal eagle on the pilothouse. The first assignment of

---

[2] "Them good lookin' girls would come in there; I'd reach in there and get that ice cream out with that scoop . . . and I'd take that scoop and throw that ice cream up and catch it with that thing. I kicked a many a scoop of ice cream under that soda fountain."

many a "landlubber" when he joined the crew of a river boat was to feed the nighthawk and the eagle. [Pp. 19–20]

Captain Charles White, Sr., laughed when he recalled jokes played on new deckhands who did not yet know that pilots require absolute darkness at night so they can see their marks properly.

They'd get a new deckhand, they'd tell him, "It's awful dark up in the pilothouse, there. I believe it'd be a good idea—light a lantern, take it up there, and set it along side of 'im." Or, take two of 'em—one on each side of 'im—so he could see. And, oh, that deckhand'd get run out of there so fast!

Or pranks on gullible hands unfamiliar with technology:

One incident, we come up to a lock. They had a new deckhand on there and the mate told this new deckhand, he says, "Anybody bring the key to the lock on there?" "Nope," he says, "No, didn't—I forgot it, I didn't bring it out." So he told that new deckhand, "Go back to the engineer and ask him for a key to the lock." The engineer knew what was up, so he gave him a wrench. I guess it was almost as long as this room (about eight feet); it was a wrench that they used to take the end of a cylinder off—great big wrench. And he dragged and pulled and he tugged and he tugged that all the way out to the head of the tow to open the lock. [Laughs.]

Captain Allen Fiedler and cronies used to "help" the neophytes along. "We used to send him up to the pilothouse with a crowbar and tell him to help the old man get around the bends.[3] . . . So he'd get up there and open the door up. And he said, 'Well, Captain, what do you want with this?' 'With what?' 'Crowbar.' He said, 'Get the hell outa here.'"

That first trip after hiring on a boat could be grueling or embarrassing for young men eager to make a good impression. Young Arthur McArthur was only sixteen when he persuaded Kentucky Red, mate on the *Minnesota*, to give him a job. Delighted that he had succeeded, Arthur ran home to get his clothes.

So I ran home and told my mother I had to get back down on the boat and everything. I said, "Captain wants me to bring a note back sayin' I'm nineteen years old." So she wrote me one out and cried, and my sister and all them cried. I ran out the door to get down on the boat. . . . It was so hot on

---

[3] Traditionally, the master of a river boat is referred to as "the old man"—regardless of his age.

June 23, 1934, I'll never forget it. That sulphur, we had some sulphur barges makin' up and just a little bit of wind blowin', and it got in my eyes and was burnin' me. And I had my shirt off and I didn't have sense enough to look at those other men out there, those old-timers, they had these big heavy jackets on 'em, see. And they had caps on . . . and hankerchiefs up here [neck], and what they'd do is when you're workin' like that you put on kind of a heavy jacket and you workin' in hot weather like that, you sweat, and that sweat keeps you cool. And there I was, burnin' myself up. And I'll never forget, we were goin' by Beale Street and I was runnin' out there with those big lines . . . they weighed pound and a half to the foot and they were sixty-five feet long. . . . So when we were goin' by Beale Street, I looked up at Beale Street and could see those lights up there and everything, and I thought, "My God, if I could get off here, I'd never ride another boat."

And so I done put in my whole afternoon there helpin' make up that tow, and that was when I was 'sposed to be off watch, still workin', and I went up and I finally took a shower when they knocked me off. And at midnight I went out there and the lead line was goin'. I had to go out there and relieve a man. They told me, "You get up on the top and pass the word." And I couldn't sing or carry a tune in a basket.[4] I still can't. . . . So we got up around Dean's Island at three o'clock in the mornin' and a double crossin' [a place where you have to break the tow and make two trips through], a bad crossin' there, that'd break your tow in half and just take half of it over. So Kentucky Red told me, he said, "Well, you stay on the barges." And there I was; here I was in these damn woods and I'm gonna have to stay on these barges. He said, "We'll be back in three, four, five hours. Stay on the barges and watch 'em while we're gone." I was supposed to go off watch at six o'clock. So I said, "OK."

So they knocked out with that barge and left about four o'clock in the morning. So about nine o'clock in the mornin' the boat got back and I had to help 'em hook her up, hook the boat up. . . . Then he told me to go on up and tell the cook to cook me some eggs. I went up and he cooked me some breakfast. Then it was time for me to lay down for a little bit, and it wasn't long before that bell was ringin' "dingalinga, dingalinga, dingalinga, dingalinga." I run out there and it was time we were gettin' into eatin' and

---

[4] Instead of yelling the marks on a lead line, the leadsman would sing it and intermediaries would pass that along the barges so the pilot could hear the sounding. See Chapter 2 for a more detailed discussion.

gettin' up there ready to make up to the rest of the tow. And all that afternoon we was out there soundin' the barges and layin' steam lines and pumpin', and there I'd prac'ally been up from the day before and here it comes along almost six o'clock in the evenin', and then I went to bed and I slept to midnight that night. Oh, God, I slept. . . . I was tired. Oh, yeah, I thought many a time, if I'd a got off at Beale Street, I don't believe I'd a rode another boat back in those days.

Still enjoying a hearty laugh after all these years when he tells the story, Captain Fontain Johnson remembers his first trip as steersman. Steersmen made $47.50 a month—no vacation, no time off.

When I worked it out and finally got a steersman job on the Federal Barge Line, the first boat, it was in January right after Christmas. I got on the steamer *Natchez* in Helena, Arkansas. . . . I went up to the pilothouse, and to get the picture so you'll understand it, the winders in the pilothouse— you've seen these little bitty square plates, built like a house, you slide 'em. . . . Had a pilot on there, on watch, named Ed Rucker, who lived in New Orleans. He was a Frenchman with an old mustache and wore white suits, white gloves to work. . . . Yeah, old packet boat pilot. . . . So I came up to the pilothouse, and Captain McCaffrey introduced himself and he said, "Say, boy, I understand you'as supposed to be the steersman." I said, "Yes, sir." He said, "Well, the first thing I want to know if you know anything about oil stoves." I said, "Yes, sir." He said, "Well, we just put this on here. We had an old coal stove on here, and just at New Orleans last trip they put the oil burner on." So I said, "Yes, sir." He said, "You know how to light it?" I said, "Yes, sir."

So I went over and got me some paper and I pumped the oil in there and I throwed the match, lit a match and put a piece of paper and throwed it in there, and when I did, that thing blew. And when it—that little thing that pushed in—when it came out, it went through that window like a bullet—bloop. When the soot all settled, Captain Rucker was standin', and the only thing white on him was inside of his gloves. I didn't know they'd been pumpin' oil in since they left New Orleans, you know. I mean, they didn't tell me. Anyway, . . . he started raisin' some cain. He says, "You no good so-and-so, you don't know what you're doin'." This is the way they talked in those days. I said, "Yes, sir." And I was 'bout shakin' in my boots; I didn't know what to do. So he said, "All right, go on and go to bed."

So in the meantime they'd switched captains, transferred captains, and put a Captain Powell over there on that boat and put Captain McCaffrey on his boat, the *Cairo*, which was goin' back . . . Captain Powell was on there: "Take a lead line and go out and see how much water's around the bar." Well, I'd never been involved in that too much before. I took the lead line out there, and I throwed it over there, and it kep' on goin' and goin' and goin' till that thing was gone!

He says, "How much water you got down there?" I said, "Captain, I lost the lead line." "What!" I thought the thing was aground; I didn't know there was eighty feet of water on this side. So he said, "Well, God damn, get out on the head of the tow with the spike pole. See how much water we got." So they sounded around the barges. . . . Mate on there by the name of Tupalo Red. . . . So they got those big high cargo barges and I'm down there with this spike pole, and I stick it in the water and Tupalo says, "Fontain, the Captain's ready"—they didn't have but a big megaphone on there, you know—"How much water you got?" I said, "Tupalo, I don't know; the thing's not marked; I can't tell!" He said, "Got to tell him something." I said, "Well, tell him way up on the spike pole!" The next thing I heard, the captain said, "Tell that so-and-so to get his so-and-so back in before he drowns all of us!"

Having weathered such initial hazings, unusual rigors, or general ineptitude, these new rivermen performed their assigned duties and then often started learning the river on their off-watch to prove their eagerness to advance. Some veteran pilots recall their early days when river traffic was dying and crusty old masters refused to "make new pilots" for fear their jobs would thereby be threatened. Some pilots remember the help proferred by kindly teachers; others remark the obstacles constantly thrown in their way. One way or another, like Sam Clemens, they all had to learn the river.

The cub Sam Clemens initially paid little heed to Bixby when he called attention to Six-Mile Point or Twelve-Mile Point or the slack water by the China trees where it was safe to make a crossing. Everything looked the same to young Sam, and he didn't bother to clutter his mind with such details—until, that is, Bixby roared his disapproval and called Sam the "stupidest dunderhead" he'd ever seen. "The idea of *you* being a pilot—*you*! Why, you don't know enough to pilot a cow down a lane." Clemens said he thought Bixby had told him the points "to be entertaining." Clemens then learned—to his everlasting consternation—that he would have to keep a memorandum book, put everything down that Bixby told him, and then "get the entire river by heart." "That was a dismal revelation to me; for my memory was never loaded with anything but blank cartridges." His hopes that Bixby was "stretching it" were in vain.

> Now, if my ears hear aright, I have not only to get the names of all the towns and islands and bends, and so on, by heart, but I must even get up a warm, personal acquaintanceship with every old snag and one-limbed cottonwood and obscure wood-pile that ornaments the banks of this river for twelve hundred miles; and more than that I must actually know where these things are in the dark. . . . I wish the piloting business was in Jericho and I had never thought of it. [Chapter 7]

Nevertheless, he went about that formidable task of learning the river by heart, developing judgment of distance and speed, and exercising the courage to navigate what he knew rather than what he saw.

Though a few pilots say they can tell "pretty quick" whether a man can do the work as a pilot, others contend you cannot predict ahead of time. Captain Fred Way, Jr., recounted his cub pilot experiences in *Pilotin' Comes Natural*. Dayton Randolph said to his new cub, Way:

> I always kind of hate to break in a youngster to piloting—especially a fellow who really likes the river: it's a treachery, for it's apt to take the confidence right out of him, and make a coward of him. Can't never tell. About one in thirty have the right stuffings in him. The dickens of the whole proposition is that there's no predicting about it; you can't tell by looking at a fellow what sort of a pilot he'll make. Some of the big, husky fellows I've took on to learn never were any account—wasted four years at it—all for nothing. Then again, some little puny fellow who don't look like he could whip a cat, just up and comes in a winner. No telling about it. [Pp. 210–11]

Neither the husky nor the puny fellows who did have the "right stuffings" will forget the task of learning the river or the men "who learned 'em."[5] Most recount their experiences in some detail and accent the difficulty of the project. However, Captain Jesse Reed of Memphis, when asked about his apprenticeship, replied with quiet understatement:

> We just lived from day to day and soaked up what you could and, finally, you decided, "I believe I'll get some books and study up for the examina-

---

[5] Mark Twain, Fred Way, and others note that the word "teach" is missing from a riverman's vocabulary. This is not altogether true; it crops up every once in a while.

tion," and that's what you did. Mostly, you watch the pilot operate, and steer for him, when he was in good humor and wants to let you. Some of 'em would be a little jealous and didn't want you to learn much. Some of 'em democratic like.

Captain Walter Karnath of Winona, Minnesota, who retired in 1976 after fifty-four years on the river, remembers learning to read the water and making a mistake that could have been costly indeed.

Well, first thing you had to learn was how to steer the boat. In the early days when I was steering the boat, it was steered by hand with a big pilot wheel. . . . But you stood on one side of the wheel and kept turning it one way or the other, and if you had it over where you wanted it, there was a foot brake on the floor. The brake was underneath the pilothouse and it would brake the wheel, see. You'd step on that and you'd hold the wheel instead of holding the spokes all the time. Then, especially when you were backing up, if you're backing up and you'd turn the wheel all the way over one way, you had to step on the brake in order to hold. Well, the main thing was to learn to steer the boat, and then you had to learn where to go.

Then, of course, another thing about learning where to go is you had to learn where the wing dams were, and also you had to learn how to read the river, especially when there was a sandbar underneath the water. I know one time I was in the hospital down at LaCrosse when I had a back operation, and I met a psychiatrist there and I was telling him about running on the river. And I says that he had to learn to read the river. He thought I was nuts.

Yeah. Well, when you see all these little ripples on the river, you know, there's a little sandbar underneath, that's a reef. If there's one jutting out here and another one jutting out here, you run in between them; you got the deeper water, see. But if you miss one . . . it all depends upon how severe those ripples are. If they're higher, why then the sand is closer to the top. If they're smaller, then the sand is further down.

Well, during the daylight you'd make your marks and at night—well we didn't run that much at night at first. . . . Up until the middle twenties I don't think we ran at night at all. It was all daylight. Oh, I remember one time, we were just daylight boats and we went down the river on the *Fury*, and we had to deliver something down at LaCrosse, and on the way back somebody threw a line overboard, or a line was floating in the river, and it caught the wheel.

It got in the cams of the boat and the boat wouldn't go right. So it tied up, and they got that line out of the wheel. . . . And we got kind of behind and we had to run all night to get back to Fountain City and pick up a barge of rock and go up the river with it. The next morning we left Fountain City and went up the river, and Dad called me up in the pilothouse. . . . He said, "Why don't you steer now? I'm going to sleep for awhile." He thought I had slept all night. And I was half sick that night. . . . He thought I was sleepin'. So I went up in the pilothouse and I steered the boat and I got up there, just below Fisher Island, and I went to sleep . . . steerin' the boat. The boat headed for the bank. The engineer saw what was happening and he slowed her down a little bit. And we were just lucky the boat hit the bank; the barge hit the bank and it twisted the barge like that. The barge number was 322. Boy, did I catch hell! That's the only time I went to sleep working in the pilothouse.

Captain Ray Prichard of Prescott, Wisconsin, like many of his colleagues, believed there was something intuitive, something natural about those who made it as pilots.

A judge of distance, possibly, . . . and speed, is a primary requisite of piloting. Now, I knew just an awfully good pilot, but his nerves, so to speak—if that's what you want to call it—overlapped his judgment. He was out to make time and wanted to make some points, I suppose, with the company, and he does an awful lot of damage. But he had a nerve and would try anything. But his judgment was poor . . . especially his speed judgment in relation to the tonnage that he had out in front of him. And as soon as you get that down, he's got it made. I think. . . . You can tell in a week, if you let that man work, and watch him carefully, you can tell in a week if he's going to make it or not. And if he isn't going to make it, then the company's wasting their time and their money. They might as well put somebody else up there.

Cap'n Wethern probably taught me all that I know in regard to this work. Now I don't know, of course, I had to have something, other than what he would tell me, too. Now you see, to be a pilot, any kind of pilot . . . if it's on this boat [*Delta Queen*] or on those larger coal tows, or something . . . you might say you have to learn the river four ways, a piece of river. You have to learn at night—up; night—down; and day—up; and day—down. That gives you four different rivers to learn. Because the bank lines and channel lines are different. I don't know—I can't explain that and it's not written. You just know, that's all, and it comes to you . . . just like practicing a piano. . . . But some make it, some don't.

At times [Cap'n Wethern] was pretty rough. Yes. He was of the old school, and when you were working for him, you didn't sit down. You stood up . . . if it was for six hours. Now, when I went to work as steersman, the first thing in the morning was to clean the windows. That was the first thing. And then you had to clean up your pilothouse. That had to be pretty spotless. Shine any brass that was around and, of course, we had the old-style spittoon, and that had to be cleaned out. Every morning that was it, and then you went down and you changed from your working clothes into your steering clothes, if you want to call them such, and you came up and if the weather was decent, why he handed it over to you. And the first year, he paid pretty much attention to what I was doing. That is, he would sit back there on the bench or at his desk there, if that bridge didn't look just right to him, I mean, we had adverse conditions, the weather or something, why he would probably do that work. Now the second year I worked with him, I hardly saw him. I did all the work.

Because whenever I wanted him, if for some reason I thought that I might not be capable of making this bridge or that lock, or something, and conditions weren't just right, why I could always get ahold of him in the engine room. He would always be down in the engine room talking to the engineer. Cap'n Wethern had an engineer's license also. He was what we call a "double-ender." There's not very many of those any more, that is, with two licenses. Engineer and pilot license. But he . . . took care of me and he saw that I was going to make it and he spent a lot of time with me. And he told me how to do things and where to hold the head of that tow on a certain thing, you know. Because you're going to get a draft here or the current's going to set you over there, or something. He taught me all that stuff and I remembered it. And the last few days I went to see him in the hospital and—well, he always called me "son"—and he said, "Son, I'm not going to make it this trip." And I said, "Well, I'll do all I can. What do you want me to do?" "Oh, just blow a salute when you go by." At the cemetery. And that's what I always do.

Some recall crusty old masters who made it rough on young steersmen, and others, like Captain Prichard, speak fondly of men who were like fathers to them. Captain Fontain Johnson of Greenville, Mississippi, says he became a pilot in spite of many obstacles put in his way by others who told him he couldn't do it. As a steersman, he had an "investment" in learning the government lights.

Cliff Norton, pilot on the *Cairo*, used to bet me a Co-Cola—in other words, every light I could name, he owed me a Coke . . . that was correct, and every one I couldn't name, I owed him one. So I went down there and memorized every light from . . . New Orleans to Memphis. He didn't win one Coke! And I won the whole match. But that's one way, that didn't hurt me, that helped me.

Captain Ed Winford of Memphis claims those old captains "played hoot and holler and raised hell" but that he later realized it was just a lot of bluster. At that time, he would get mad and quit, but often wouldn't even miss a watch before returning to work.

Captain Campbell, he was a rough-and-ready old gentleman. He'd take these young fellas like myself to make pilots out of. He'd let us go, you know. When you're young and startin' out you do a lot of beatin' and bangin' and gettin' around and doin' things awful. And he never would lose his cool. No matter what you did, he wouldn't get upset about it. Well, he had his peculiarities; he left out of Engineer's Depot one time, that was on the *Russell Coiner*. Captain Campbell was the captain on her, and the steamer *Mississippi* left out at the same time goin' down the river. Well, we started out at the same time; we actually started racin'. And I called down to the engineer and told him to speed her up a little bit, and they did the same thing on the *Mississippi*. And we kept neck and neck. Captain Campbell was up there watchin' all the time, makin' comments. And we went ten miles down the river, couldn't gain on either one, and got to a narrow place where there wasn't room but for one boat. So I didn't care whether I won or lost, so I slowed her down and let the *Mississippi* go on down river. Captain Campbell said "a dirty word," and he got up and left. That's all he said, "a dirty word" . . . He wanted to win the race.

QUESTION: But if you'd gotten into trouble, he'd . . . .

WINFORD: No, he wouldn't a cared; he didn't care. The old man never lost his cool—things get to poppin' and a crackin', timberheads a flyin', barges get aground—old man, he didn't say a word, he didn't fuss at ya.

Captain Carroll "Rip" Ware was nineteen when he started his river career in May 1930, on that "little old boat," the *City of Monroe*.

And I mean times was hard. I didn't finish high school, so I was green enough that I thought the captain bought his license, and when I walked on that boat, the diesel engineer, he was wheezin' and smelled like diesel oil and all. And I looked up there and the old captain settin' up there and that wind was blowin' through his hair, you know, his grey hair, so I found out right quick I didn't want no engineer license on account of gettin' dirty, so I asked that old captain, I said, "How much did your license cost?" He said, "Well, you start out as a deckhand, you got to work three years, serve three years' time, and if you apply yourself, the captain will give you a letter and you go take your examination." That's when I buckled down.

The name by which he is known on the river, "Rip," was given to him by his mentor, Captain Leto Lopez Lanius, "the man I loved next to a daddy." In fact, Rip later named one of his own sons after Captain Lanius.

And on this little boat me and him was on—it was a little paddle-wheel diesel boat—they had hot-water radiators. And I'd nearly freeze to death up there in that pilothouse. So what I'd do, I'd put me some newspaper down, I'd lay down on that floor by, so I could get the whole length of myself up against that heater, see. [Imitates the old captain by using very old man's voice and clipped delivery.] "Git up, git up, my old head's killin' me. You'll never learn a damn thing! Rip Van Winkle, slept twenty years, stock handle rotted out!" Man, I heard that a zillion times. "Git up from there, my old head's killin' me." And I'd get up and steer.

See, I never steered in the daytime 'cause we worked. I done all my steerin' at night. When I brought his coffee at eight o'clock at night, he'd set in the chair till eleven o'clock. Then I went down and made coffee and cleaned up the galley. I always worked from eight to eleven. . . . I tell you somethin' you ain't gonna believe it. . . . I carried him enough bakin' soda, Arm and Hammer Bakin' Soda, in this hand and my broom in this hand. But I knowd if I didn't bring that Arm and Hammer Bakin' Soda up there to him, he'd send me back to get it. So I said, "Cap'n, what you eat them old hotcakes for?" He said, "Dammit, Rip, 'cause I like 'em!" [Laughs.]

And I would scrub that floor so much where that chair set. . . . See, I'd mop that and I'd pull up a splinter, it was a hole wearin' in it—so one mornin' I set his chair back up there and he set down in it and a chair leg fell through it. I said, "Well, one thing I can brag about the rest of my life. I scrubbed one damn floor enough that I scrubbed a hole in it!"

Captain Ware explains Captain Lanius's technique, one not unlike that of Captain Horace Bixby in the 1850s.

The way old Captain Lanius drilled me over there on the Ouachita River and the Mississippi River from Angola to New Orleans was, he would tell me the name of a place. At one time this whole river looked just alike, just the same. I know how it looks to you. Everything looks just the same to you. All right. But the way he would do, he would say, "This is Alligator Bayou." Over there on the Ouachita River that was a little bayou that come into the river. All right. Then he'd go on and wouldn't say nothin'. Well, maybe when we went back down the river and we went by there, he wouldn't ask me and I'd be just dyin' for him to ask me. But when he would ask me, it would be unexpected, so that way I had to keep all of it in my mind.

Now the first place that I learned on the Mississippi River was down there across the river from St. Francisville. It was a water pump and a rice farm down there, had a big ole concrete foundation with a round hole in it. So we went by there one day; he told me that that was Bayou Sara. So when we'd leave New Orleans I'd start lookin' for that big old piece of concrete foundation with that hole in it and I'd run up there hopin' that he'd ask me where we was at. Well, sometimes he would, sometimes he wouldn't. But, he would ask me, and if I couldn't tell him, he would shame me-like, you know what I mean? So that made me keep whatever he told me, it made me keep sayin' it over and over and thinkin' about it. And that's the way it was. And so that's the way he done it.

Yeah. Like, before we got out on the Mississippi River, he would ask me the name of the "govamunt" lights, things like that. So when I had my three years in, I was ready to go get my license, Monroe, Louisiana, to New Orleans. Back in them days they was steamboats, and you had to get steam licenses. And the first license they give you was second-class pilot license and that would keep you off a steamboat over one hundred and fifty tons. Then you worked on that license a year, and I went back and they give me the exact same examination over. But I had to show 'em that I had done worked a year before I got a first-class license and then I kep' that first-class license awhile and then I got my master's license. And the way my license reads, they don't make 'em read that way now; my license reads that I'm first-class pilot and master on the waters that flow into the Gulf of Mexico. That takes 'em all, see. . . . Now, for years I didn't work on nothin' but paddle-wheel boats. Then when I went mate out on the river, went deckin', I'd get on those twin-screw jobs.

No longer the green deckhand who thought he could buy a pilot's license, Rip became pilot on that little old boat and revelled in his new status. With a crew of only seven, everyone had pitched in and become a little bit of an engineer, a little bit of a deckhand, a fair hand at brewing coffee. But being pilot is top dog.

Yeah, when I got to be pilot, we got up there, and I was relievin' that old pilot, see, I was relief man. So the water was so high they couldn't unload the stuff, so they told 'em, they said, "Overhaul the engines." I wasn't makin' but five dollars a day pilotin'. So now I walked around them streets there all that week drinkin' that dime beer; I think beer was a dime when it first came out. So the chief told me, he said, "How 'bout takin' a time [book] and let's go back and get our money." I said, "Yeah." Took that time book to a little fella in the office, I never will forget. Old fella grabs me and he says, "How come you ain't down there heppin' . . .?" I says, "Man, I'm *pilot* this trip. It ain't customary for a pilot to work in the engine room." He said, "You mean, you been down there all that week and you ain't hepped 'em?" I said, "No, man, I'm *pilot!*" And he said, "Come back in about thirty minutes."

He run down there and he grabbed old Captain Lanius and he said, "How come you didn't tell me Ware wasn't heppin' in the engine room?" "Well, he ain't 'sposed to; he's pilot." Then he run after the engineer. He said, "How come you didn't tell me?" "Well, I ain't got nothin' to do with it; he's pilot this trip." That made him mad, so when he come back up there—that was on Saturday and we was gonna leave Monday—and he come back up there, and he said, "If I'd a knew you hadn't been workin','"—now that was after bein' there almost six years—" . . . I'd a laid you off this week." I said, "Well, I was just doin' what the other old pilots done." He said, "I tell ya, since you ain't gonna work in the engine room, how 'bout stayin' on just twelve hours?" I said, "I'll sure stay on it twelve hours." So I stayed out all that night, and all that Sunday I slep'.

But, see, I done already told that old captain, I said, "If I ever get to be pilot . . . if I *ever* get to be pilot, they gonna expect me to work in that engine room." Sure enough, they did.

I called 'em down river and got a man to git me another job. That old captain, he said, "Git off here in Baton Rouge and go down there, and if you don't git the job, catch me back here in Baton Rouge and they won't know nothin' about it up at Monroe." So I got off at Baton Rouge, and I knew a pilot on the Canal Street Ferry. I didn't have no money, so I rode that old ferryboat all night. The boat I was lookin' for was tied up there where it docked, used to call that Third District, big old five-boiler steamboat . . . haulin' molasses from New Orleans to Peoria, Illinois. And I thought I was goin' clean across the world!

Though he subsequently got licensed from Cairo to New Orleans, Captain Ware couldn't get a pilot job in the late 1930s, so he went decking and tried to learn more of the river. Sometimes, he would get on as pilot for the stretch until his license ran out, then he would deck until they returned to that stretch.

I was deckhand. See, they wouldn't even let you come up to the pilothouse back in them days. No. I was on one little old boat in the barge line and I was pilothouse horse; I would clean up the pilothouse. So them pilots knew what I was tryin' to do, and old Harold Bruce . . . I said, "I sure wished I could see that piece of river up yonder." He said, "Well, warsh them windows. I can't see nothin'!" And there wasn't a speck on 'em, but I was warshin' them windows to get to stay up there.

Captain Ware eventually went pilot for the Pure Oil Company in 1941, stayed with them for thirty-one years and two months, and, he proudly claims, wore out three pilot chairs in the process. When Captain Lanius was an old man, Captain Ware carried him as a guest on his boat for a few days.

I would never let him steer at night 'cause I knew his sight was bad. Anyway, that day, I said, "Captain, you want to work some?" He wasn't used to that nine feet out there; I made sure we was in a good piece of river. And so I eased up to him over there and I said, "Captain, I didn't think this would ever happen, but pull over just a little bit." "Damn, you think you're smart, dontcha?" [Laughs.] He done drilled me for years, you know, tellin' me where to run and all.

Other pilots recall their mentors. When asked who he cubbed for, Captain Roy Boyd of Rock Island, Illinois, answered:

He was an old government man—he was carpenter on the steamer *Lilly*— the lighthouse boat. . . . And he learned the river—see, she was a sidewheel boat, and the carpenter shop was on the back end, and he learned the river by watchin' where the boat had been! [Laughs.] He got to be a pilot . . . and a most cantemperous old man you ever saw in your life!

Captain Loren "Shorty" Williams learned from a second-generation pilot whose father had owned steamboats as well—Captain Ray Fugina, a "wonderful fellow and very good pilot."

Of course, Ray grew up on steamboats and there were very few available pilots when Federal Barge Line started running steamboats up here on the upper river. And this, of course, was preliminary to the nine-foot channels. . . . But with Ray Fugina, he was the kind of fellow that was . . . interested in making pilots. And he gave me a lot of good instruction and let me do the work. There were many days—nights and days both—that he would sit back on the bench and never touch the wheel, but just let me do the work, and he'd let me get into a little trouble as long as he saw it wasn't going to be serious. And then let me figure a way out of it, too. But he *was* a good master, and he strictly went by the regulations. He had his fire drills, at exactly the right time once a week, just as required by law, and entered it in the log, and he never left the pilothouse when I was working.

There was one time that he did go to sleep that I remember. . . . We was landed at Winona to handle freight, and his wife was there, so he . . . spent the time when he would have normally been sleeping . . . with her and his folks, who lived at Winona. And so when we came out of Winona, he dozed off on a bench back there. And there was one place, right below LaCrosse, where—you can call it Sand Slough—is a real sharp bend. And it was almost impossible to get by there with these old sternwheel boats without, what we call landing, lighting. . . . And it was pretty close. You had to get down into the bend about as far as you could to have water enough to go by, and he was snoozing back there and I didn't know it. Well, I decided, now this time, I'm gonna steer this place and not light in the bend. So I overdid it! And I hit the end of a wing dam, and of course that brought him awake, right quick, when he felt her bump. It didn't do any damage, but we had quite a little trouble gettin' offa the wing dam. So he named that "Shorty's Shortcut."

Though he learned primarily from Captain Fugina, Shorty on occasion steered for other pilots.

That was the attitude of a good many pilots or masters—that they didn't want to make pilots; there was a surplus, originally, of pilots left over from the packet boat days that couldn't find pilot jobs because there were no packet boats. And they acquired that attitude that any time you made a pilot, you jeopardized your own job. . . . But Roy Wethern, I think, was farsighted enough that he saw that there was going to be a shortage of pilots in time to come. And, well, I'll tell you a little experience I had—and you may have run into his tracks too—Walter Hunter?

Well, he was an old log-raft pilot, and later went on towboats, and he would *not* make a pilot. He wouldn't help a cub, and it just happened that one time . . . they put Captain Hunter as master of the *Mark Twain*. And so the boys all told me—that had worked with him before—said, "You're not going to do anymore handling now while he's here, because he don't make pilots." And I had known the old gentleman for several years, because I got acquainted with him when I was with the Corps of Engineers and he was on the Streckfus . . . boats.

But I'd go to the pilothouse and he wouldn't say a word. I'd keep the log and I'd wash the windows and I cleaned the cuspidors, swept the floors, and then I'd sit on the bench. And he'd never say a word to me or even appear to know that I was there, except once in awhile at night, he'd turn around and he'd say, "You know where you are?" And, of course, I knew the river very well—this part of it in the Rock Island district, especially, because . . . Ray had taught me about it and I'd been on the survey for the nine-foot channel to St. Paul. . . . One of Walter Hunter's big gripes was that they changed the names of the locations along the river. The names of lights. And we were comin' down below Bellevue, one night, and he turned around and he said—it was black as pitch—he says, "You know where you are?" And the name of the light, as well as I could remember, had been Pleasant Creek, but I knew that many years ago—I had always been interested in history— and I knew this. . . . Well, he turned around and he said, "Do you know where you are?" And I said, "Yeah, Captain, that's Goldwin Woodyard-." . . . That had been a woodyard in the packet boat days where some people named Goldwin cut wood for the packet boats. And he said, "Whoo! Haven't heard that for a hundred years!"

And you know, the next morning . . . when he came on watch, he said, "Hey," he said, "you want'a steer?" I said, "Captain, that's what I'm here for." And he let me between the handles and he never touched it again, as long as we were together. And he'd sit back there and tell Irish jokes and laugh and have the best time! It was just because I knew the old name of Goldwin Woodyard light. But he was a real character.

Captain Clarke "Doc" Hawley, currently master on the steamer *Natchez* in New Orleans, felt fortunate to have learned the river (in the 1950s) from several old captains still working when he was steering.

Some of them were just crusty as they could be, but it was a defense mechanism on their part, and they weren't really so crusty down deep. Also, a lot of old-timers took pride in training a young fella, if they liked him. Had to like you a little bit, you know. If the company sent somebody in there and said, "Train this man," that just didn't work. Just didn't work at all. And he'd, the trainee, would meet nothing but animosity, but if the pilot sort of figured that you wanted to learn and wanted to learn from him, he was flattered and he would teach you.

I'll never forget, I was at Pittsburgh and I was captain of the *Avalon* then; I was relievin' Captain Wagner. I was about twenty-four years old; I looked like I was about nineteen then. And Captain Emory Edgington . . . was eighty-seven or eighty-eight at that time and was on watch in the pilot-house. Well, I was out on the bridge givin' the landing instructions, tellin' him when to come ahead and when to back up and all that business, and so we had a reporter from the *Pittsburgh Post* in there. And the repoter said, he asked Captain Edgington, "How can you take orders from a young whipper-snapper like that? You're eighty-eight and he's twenty-four." Captain Edgington said, "Huh, don't know why I shouldn't. Taught him all he knows!"

But even though he cleaned spittoons, washed windows, mopped floors, and stoked stoves, the young cub felt elevated when he became a steersman.[6] Captain John Skidmore, originally from West Virginia, started out in about 1926 on such steamers as the *Minnesota*, the *Iowa*, the *Illinois*, and the *Missouri*—commonly called the "state boats."

I was a fireman; I was a striker; I was a daylight man; and then I was advanced to a steersman, or a cub pilot. And that's apprenticeship to become a pilot. And I was very proud of that; I was gettin' $89.24 a month at that time. And I never *shall* forget it, the first payday I got, I was gonna dress up like a pilot. I bought me some silk shirts and silk socks and ties, and so forth and so forth. Because back in those days, I worked with this one pilot— Captain Harry Silvernagle, he was a top-flight pilot—and they stood a watch from six o'clock [evening] till eleven o'clock, one pilot did; then the pilot would come from eleven until three, and the other would come back on and work three to six.[7] Then it alternated. So therefore, every other night

---

[6] Captain McArthur speaks of spittoons with particular disgust: "They spit tobacco juice in 'em and that dern kind of stuff all over and I sure hated to clean the damned spittoon. I'd take 'em downstairs, put a line on 'em, you know, and hang 'em overboard, and wait. A lot of times, the line'd break. . . . I hated to clean those suckers."

[7] This was called the dog watch.

you worked eight hours. But Captain Silvernagle, if he got up at three o'clock in the morning or eleven o'clock at night, he put on that stiff collar and tie. Those pilots back in those days had a lot of dignity to 'em. They considered the profession somethin'; they were just a little bit higher than everybody else. Well, anyway, I was advanced to steersman on the boat . . . and, man, I was a big shot! [Laughs.]

And the duties of a steersman back in those days was just about everything. These old pilots, they didn't want to make any new ones, and they knew I had an uncle who was rather influential with the officials, and I might become a pilot. And they gave me a hard way to go. In other words, the duties of a cub pilot—I had to keep the 'fahr' burnin' in the . . . I mean carry the coal up to the pilothouse. . . . And I had to keep the pilothouse clean, had to clean the windahs, and if the pilot wanted a cup of coffee, I had to go downstairs and git him a cup of coffee. And one old pilot—I had to warsh his back for him! [Laughs.]

MAKING IT

Finally, the apprenticeship over, the steersman secured letters of recommendation from pilots he'd worked with (and for some, one engineer as well) and sat for his license examination, which entailed answering questions about rules of the road, safety, boating equipment, and technique, and the like.[8] For a first-class pilot license, he had to draw from memory the particular stretch of river for which he was making application. Captain Fred Way, Jr., in *Pilotin' Comes Natural*, proclaimed the written exam required by the Steamboat Inspectors to be a notable achievement.

> It pries into all the piloting knowledge a man possesses, and unless he has his bunkers full of fuel he is apt to lose considerable steam pressure when confronted with the first question. It is roughly, this: "Draw a map of the portion of the river over which you desire license, making it on a scale amply large to clearly designate all the cities, towns, and tributary streams along

[8] This apprenticeship lasted at least thirty-six months. Applicants for a first-class pilot's license were required to have deck and steering experience and to have made at least ten trips over a particular stretch of river they were to draw. Some spent several years on deck or in other positions before advancing to the pilothouse, the amount of time often depending on external circumstances, such as willingness of pilots to "make" other pilots, wartime needs, shortages, and demand within a particular company.

either bank: all bridges (giving heights above low water and the width of the channel spans): all locks and dams, indicating the length of the locks, their width, the breadth of the navigable pass, the number of beartraps in each: all islands: all sandbars, gravel lumps, rock reefs, and other natural hazards to navigation: draw a line indicating the channel: give distance in miles and tenths between principal cities: name and locate all the government lights, day-marks, and other aids to navigation: locate ice piers, piling clusters: describe the nature of the shores . . ." and so forth and so forth. It is a good idea to become a map maker before attempting your pilot examination. [Pp. 243–44]

Today many towboat pilots earn what is called an operator's license. To receive this license, they are not required to draw the river but must have accumulated a certain amount of time on the river before applying. (See Chapter 7 for pilots' views of these respective licenses.)

In the January 10, 1914, edition of the Burlington *Saturday Evening Post*, George Merrick ran this story in his continuing river column:

There was Wm. W. Slocumb, known as "Old Bill" and Wm. R. Slocumb, his nephew, known as "Young Bill." They ran together many years in the employ of the Knapp, Stout & Company. . . . "Old Bill" had a very heavy voice—one of the "foghorn" variety when he so desired. A story is told that when Wm. R. was being examined for his pilot's license, he was asked what he would do if his boat was broken down at night, and had no steam up, and he wanted to hail a passing boat, to which Wm. R. replied he would ring his bell or swing a light, etc. The inspector said: "Suppose you did not have a bell or a light?" and seemed to be getting him fairly well cornered, when he said, "Oh, I'd just get Uncle Bill to whisper to 'em." He passed all right.

In his collection of *Mississippi River Folklore*, B. A. Botkin reports the experience of Captain Jerry Webber when he was being examined by the U.S. Steamboat Inspectors. He was asked, "Captain, what would you do if your boat was moving along and you suddenly saw a big rock sticking up out of the water right in front of your boat? You could not go back." "By———," said Captain Webber without a moment's hesitation, "I'd bust into it." The examining officer agreed that no one could do otherwise.[9]

Captain Skidmore got his license and then paid three dollars a day to a pilot

[9] B. A. Botkin, *A Treasury of Mississippi River Folklore*, pp. 79–80.

who helped him get started. If you were not good, you would lose your job, he said, so it was worth the investment.

I got my first issue of pilot license, think it was in 1926 or '27, and I took my examination in St. Louis. I had memorized the pilot rules. And this inspector that gave me these questions—I wrote 'em out word for word—he said, "You cheated." I said, "No, I haven't." He said, "Well, you got these pilot rules written out just like they are in the rules of the road." I said, "Well, I know 'em that well." And he tried me out and he found that I did. So I got my pilot license and I was proud of 'em. I went downtown and I got me a gold frame—looked like gold—and took 'em down and put 'em in my room and everything, just like a kid, you know. [Laughs.] So anyway, I got up one morning and my pilot license had disappeared. I thought, "What in the world has happened to 'em." But this is an actual fact—I went into the toilet and somebody had taken and put 'em up on the wall and drove a *nail* through 'em . . . and I was *furious*. . . . . We was always playin' jokes on people.

Pilots rarely forget the first trip they steered as a regular, full-fledged pilot. In *Old Times on the Upper Mississippi*, George Merrick described his first trip from Prescott, Wisconsin, to Stillwater, Minnesota, in the mid-nineteenth century. Since the reputation of every man was, he said, "common property" over the length of his run, it was important that a new pilot prove his mettle. He proved his by taking the boat to Stillwater in the teeth of a terrific storm.

I had a great deal of pride in those days, however, and a fair allowance of inherited courage, with perhaps a dash of pig-headedness. I did not wish to have it bulletined from one end of the river to another that the first time I was left in charge of a steamboat, I had hunted a tree to tie up to because it happened to thunder and rain a little. That would have been the popular version of the incident, in any case.

With a glass of brandy to "take the chill off," young Merrick guided the boat to a safe landing at its destination. His reward: the mate confided to him that the "Old man says you're all right. He says that you've got nerve enough to last you through."[10]

In an August 8, 1914, column of the Burlington *Post*, Captain Henry B. Whitney described his first trip alone.

[10] George Merrick, *Old Times on the Upper Mississippi,* pp. 106–9.

My first trip alone as a pilot was to take a small steamboat and barge from Rock Island to the head of Horse Island, a trip at that time considered dangerous because of boulders that made no clear break. On landing at Horse Island I went aboard the steamer "Prescott" to get Captain Peel's [man who taught him] approval of the manner in which I had run the marks. After I had recounted how I had ran them he said: "Well, you can take the boat back to Rock Island any way you want to go. Any pilot that can take a boat where you did on this stage of water and not hit, is safe to go anywhere. You might even try it over land."

Captain Gordon Nelson of Guttenberg, Iowa, currently master on Mv. [motor vessel] *Ann King*, had worked maybe an hour to an hour and a half of his first solo watch when he "knocked a hole in the end of the barge big enough to drive a truck through." And some first trips feature a variety of discomforting difficulties. Captain Arthur McArthur testifies:

Well, my first trip startin' down the river as a pilot I got aboard the *Baton Rouge* in Memphis in 1942. . . . So we went on up the falls, about fifty, sixty miles above Memphis, and we turned the *Illinois* around. Just to be old Arthur's luck, at three o'clock in the mornin' they done got the tows exchanged and was ready to depart down the river and here I'm comin' on watch at three; we dog-watched in those days. So, captain said, "OK, all ready to go." And we had tows exchanged . . . and I wasn't used to those round knuckle barges, there in those close places. So I started down the river and boy she started settin' in that derned bend at Island 34. . . .

Captain was settin' up here. I started to back her, you know, to keep from hittin' the bank, just got out of that scrape and Captain Gentry Lowe was the mate on there . . . so he said, "You got it made, Arthur, you got it made . . . " About that time, she hit and took that whole four string of barges off. Whoom! Here they come flyin' down the side of her. Gentry and them was out there catchin' 'em, you know, as they were comin' along. So after we finally got those barges back in tow and rounded up again with 'em, turned completely around . . . I finally got her cranked out of that and I went down a little bit more and she slid and I backed up again. Then I went on down a little bit and I had her hard down and she clipped the rocks at Lookout at the foot of the bend. She headed over there for that towhead [small island] across the river, and I pulled her hard down and it didn't look like we were gonna make it, so I set her to backin'.

There were two or three boats comin' down there at Point Lookout above

Randolph Bluff. I was lookin' at 'em, had those searchlights on, and I couldn't see too good and I kinda run up on the rudders, and first thing I know, I looked in there and I got too close to the sand and I started backin' her up again in an old sandbar and we sat down on it. I backed up there and she started to turn around and the captain was hollerin', "Oh, Lordy, Lordy, how we ever gonna get to New Orleans!" And I was so busy ringin' bells, I said, "Hell, captain, I don't know myself!"

That was the truth. And when I went off watch at six o'clock I was roundin' her up again. In three hours I hadn't made no miles at *all* down the river! And I said, "Shoot, this is a different kind of pilotin'; I'm gonna have to start doin' it."

So I went downstairs and come back on watch and we were gettin' close to Memphis and that's when I started gettin' ragged. I said, "Well, I'll hold her wide and high and handsome after this." That's the way I started pilotin'. I come on to New Orleans and didn't have no more trouble. Except one time, yes, I did have one time. We was just comin' down and I was 'sposed to be comin' on watch at six o'clock in the mornin'. The fog started shuttin' down at right off of Rifle Point over to Magnolia Bluffs. And so I started backin' and rounded up there . . . and I got into the bank, and in a little while the captain come up and she [fog] started blowin' off a little bit. He was hell-bent for Georgia to go down the river and he said, "Let's go, let's go, let's go!"

So, of course, me bein' a new young pilot, I didn't know what to do. But I rounded up; I figured, hell, he's here to back me up, you know. So I started goin' down the river, and I got down and headed over to Natchez, and that fog shut me out and everything, and I set her to backin' and he said, "Well, well . . ." "Hell, you know more about it than I do; I don't know." We had men out there on the head of the tow. . . . Said, "You see anybody, anything?" He said, "Well, back into the bank." I said, "You tell me where the other bank is, Captain. I don't know." I said, "One thing about it—you'll never get me out in no more fog long as I'm on a boat. You take and back her into the bank. You got me out here!" [Laughs] . . . That taught me a lesson. After that, nobody caught me out gettin' out in no fog anymore.

An apprentice pilot today need not wrestle the huge pilot wheel or learn the handling differences between a sidewheel and a sternwheel steamer, but he has to learn to handle his powerful towboats and to maneuver bends, bridges, and locks with a long string of barges in front of him. He has to learn the river, make his mistakes, gain confidence, earn his license, and start that first trip alone in the pilothouse when the mate yells out, "All gone, sir." And, like the young George Merrick who showed his pedigree by navigating his first trip through "torrents of rain, and incessant lightning which took on the appearance of chain-mail as it shimmered and glittered on the falling rain drops," he will establish a reputation—perhaps as a crackerjack, perhaps as a bridge buster—that will be "common property" the length of his run.

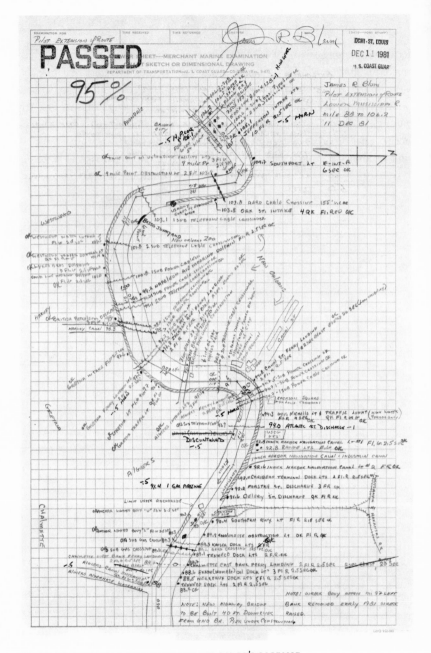

HAND-DRAWN MAP FOR FIRST-CLASS PILOT'S LICENSE

Captain James R. Blum drew this map for his pilot extension-of-route examination on the lower Mississippi River from Mile 88 to Mile 106.2, December 11, 1981. Note that he drew freehand the shape and the numerous other details of the 18.2 miles of river. Note also the accuracy required by the examiners. See Chapter 1 for Captain Fred Way, Jr.'s description of the examination for first-class pilot's license. Courtesy of Captain James R. Blum and the U.S. Coast Guard.

*With these abundant beacons,
the banishment of snags, plenty
of daylight in a box and ready
to be turned on whenever needed,
and a chart and compass to fight
the fog with, piloting, at a good
stage of water, is now nearly
as safe and simple as driving
stage, and is hardly more than
three times as romantic.*

Mark Twain, 1882

*Now there are new different
queens on the Mississippi,
magnificent towboats of enormous
power, equipped with every
comfort of sophisticated living
and manned by young, unso-
phisticated rivermen from the
sleepy towns and villages along
the shore. . . . I have seen
how when the new paint on the
towboats has flaked in faint
patches and the young men have
mellowed a little with age and
watery wisdom, the river once
more acquires its earlier charm
and fascination. It is the old
river, in a new reincarnation.*

Ben Lucien Burman, 1973

*Let's see now, wooden boats and
iron men back then's what they
say. Now it's iron boats and
wooden men.*

Captain Ed Winford, 1977

*They built this boat in '29. Of
course, come out in the spring of
'30. And the wonderful thing
about that is—the boat was
700 horsepower. And they took
that boat to St. Louis and tied
it up there . . . just for people
to look at for a couple of days.
That great big powerhouse. It
wouldn't make a yawl for some
of 'em now. Some of 'em have
10,500 horsepower.*

Captain E. L. "Wamp" Poe,
1980

CHAPTER TWO

Technology

Packet *Queen City* pilothouse, 1923

In their memoirs, either spoken or written, pilots inevitably see the glamour age of riverboating as about a half century ago. From the vantage point of the 1880s, Mark Twain looked back to the 1850s as the golden age of steamboating, before government snag boats had "pulled the river's teeth" and taken away the romance of a pilot's calling. In 1908, Mark Twain's contemporary, George Merrick, who never actually finished his pilot apprenticeship because he left to fight in the Civil War, eulogized the halcyon days. And in 1915, in the columns of the October 30 Burlington *Post*, a riverman notes the rise of "modern contrivances" and the demise of the "old snag and sandbar dodging days." "The mightiness of the Mississippi which can move the commerce of a nation on its bosom will come back, but the days of river romance are gone forever."

Thirty-five years after Mark Twain's pronouncements, and at a time when steamboats were still the rule on the river, the *Post* writer was prophesying the river's commercial comeback while bemoaning what it had lost forever. Even among veteran boatmen today, one hears regrets at the passing of the steamboat age. For many of them the "old days" are the early 1920s, before the big locks and dams, regular buoys, bank revetment, and revitalized commercial traffic. Mark Twain looked back to a time devoid of government lights, river charts, and pilothouse searchlights. Today veterans look back to a time devoid of sonar depth finders, two-way radios, and radar scopes. To Mark Twain, the improvements made piloting easier and safer but robbed it of its romance. On his return to the river in 1882, he observed the new conditions.

As we approached famous and formidable Plum Point, darkness fell, but that was nothing to shudder about—in these modern times. For now the national government has turned the Mississippi into a sort of two-thousand-mile torchlight procession. In the head of every crossing, and in the foot of every crossing, the government has set up a clear-burning lamp. You are never entirely in the dark, now; there is always a beacon in sight, either before you, or behind you, or abreast. One might almost say that lamps have been squandered there. . . . Lamps in such places are of course not wasted; it is much more convenient and comfortable for a pilot to hold on them than on a spread of formless blackness that won't stay still. . . . But this thing has knocked the romance out of piloting, to a large extent. [Chapter 28]

While many contemporary pilots contend that in their "old days" one had to be a more skillful pilot than he does now, with all the new gadgets, as a group they rarely yearn for those hardships of an earlier time. Still, there is pride in knowing they were pilots when steamboats and first-class licenses and running rivers and irregular markings were the norm. Ben Burman, who had cubbed on the *Tennessee Belle* in the 1920s when he was a young man, returned in the early 1970s for a trip on a diesel towboat pushing thirty-three barges. In *Look Down That Winding River*, he transcribed the pilothouse observations of an old deckhand and a young pilot. Long Jack, the deckhand, says to Burman: "It ain't the same Mississippi you knew noways . . . ain't no more like she used to be than a old Ozark mule's like a ten-thousand dollar automobile." The young pilot agreed: "Forty years ago all you had in a pilot house was a big steering wheel broke your back to turn and a speaking tube to cuss out the engineer. Now we've got as many gadgets as the astronauts going to the moon." A wizened, snowy-haired old man sitting near the pilot provided a tart rejoinder: "One of them old ladies used to drive them electric automobiles could run a towboat nowadays."

Later, when the boat on which Burman was riding was hit by another boat and rendered helpless by the Mississippi's current, he seemed actually reassured by the changeless quality of the river.

Despite the complex instruments in the pilot house, the perfection of all that modern marine science could devise, despite the massive engines designed to meet such crises with the strength of 5,000 horses, the boat continued on its headlong way. Some hidden current seized the hull like the grip of a giant hand and left the pilot powerless. The river, not man, was still the master. [1]

That river, the Mississippi, as well as the Ohio and other tributaries, has been transformed in its physical characteristics if still recognizable in its less tangible, spiritual qualities. In 1940, Burman remarked, "For the river remained and still remains basically as it was in the olden days: beautiful,

[1] Ben Lucien Burman, *Look Down That Winding River*, p. 192.

fascinating, terrible, always unpredictable." The "temperamental, almost demonic" quality of the river continued to give the steamboating of 1940 its picturesqueness for Burman.

The rivers have changed since the 1850s from unmarked, free-running streams to charted pools separated by huge locks and dams. Only the lower Mississippi from St. Louis to New Orleans remains free running. The upper Mississippi from St. Louis to St. Paul has twenty-six locks and dams; twenty-two such structures dot the Ohio from Pittsburgh to Cairo. The U.S. Army Corps of Engineers is charged with channel maintenance for navigation and for flood control. Historically, several methods, alone, or in combination, have been used to guarantee first the four-and-one-half-foot channel authorized in 1878, the six-foot channel authorized in 1907, and the nine-foot channel authorized for the Ohio in 1910 and the upper Mississippi in 1930.

The removal of snags, Mark Twain's "pulling the river's teeth," and the building of wing dams were initial efforts at improving conditions for navigation. Wing dams purportedly deepened the channel by directing the flow of water into a relatively narrow stream thus allowing the water to scour its own channel. Later, wooden pile dikes, then concrete dikes would be used. The Corps has used maintenance dredging, shore revetment, and cutoffs in the lower Mississippi to, as Mark Twain said, "try to bully the Mississippi River into right and reasonable conduct." Revetment techniques have progressed from Walter Blair's days when it meant clearing the bank of trees and stumps, grading it to a 30° slope, covering it with long, wide (100 feet by 300 feet) mattresses of willow and loading it down with layers of eight to twelve inches of broken rock (riprap) to keep it in place.[2] Later experiments with fascine-type mats (willows held by cribbing poles and wire), cinder slabs, lumber mattresses, and concrete-slab paving gave way to the articulated concrete mattress still in use today. The cutoffs served to shorten the river and were primarily a flood-control measure, one that was not unanimously popular among pilots who had to wrangle with the faster currents through certain spots that had previously been nearly slackwater oxbows.

The construction of locks and dams and diversion canals has eliminated both the old-time dependence on natural water levels and the hazardous rapids at LeClaire and Davenport, Iowa, the Falls of Louisville, and the Chain of Rocks near St. Louis. The current is still a worthy and cagey adversary on the lower Mississippi, but when the water is pool stage on the upper Mississippi and on

[2] Walter Blair, A Raft Pilot's Log.

the Ohio, the numerous locks and bridges provide the pilot his constant challenges.

The boats, too, have evolved beyond the creative imagination of even a Samuel Clemens. In his day, wooden, steam-powered packet boats carried freight and passengers; log rafts floated downstream, the "barge" and cargo a synonymous entity. Now, steel, diesel-powered towboats regularly push fifteen to forty-five barges loaded with thousands of tons of cargo.[3] The packets stopped frequently for landings, fog, repairs; the diesel towboats are constantly on the move. Boats have been fueled by wood, then coal, then oil. The crew accommodations have changed to reflect the amenities now enjoyed by land people—air conditioning, color TV, and comfortable beds. Unwieldy pilot wheels have disappeared; hydraulic steering levers have taken their place. Communications have advanced from megaphones to intercoms, lead lines to fathometers, hill marks to radar, post boxes to two-way radio to VTS (Vessel Traffic Service) computerized sophistication.

It is perhaps in the area of technology—as applied both to the river and to the boats—that the changes in the pilot profession are most profound and most obvious. In this chapter, pilots from several eras describe the river they knew and the boats they steered.

To proclaim that a pilot is "of the old school" is generally to acknowledge both his considerable accomplishments and his dependence on his own skills in a more primitive piloting era. Or, as Captain Fred Way, Jr., puts it, he seemed to know nearly everything and had "all the present-day troubles, but none of the modern aids." For Mark Twain, the old-school pilots were the Horace Bixbys and Grant Marshes of the mid-nineteenth century; for John Skidmore, William Tippitt, and Ben Gilbert, the old school means men like Henry Nye, Bill Haptonstall, and "Quaker Oats" of the early twentieth century; for a ten-year man on a high-powered diesel towboat, the old school includes men like John Skidmore, William Tippitt, and Ben Gilbert, who came of piloting

[3] Depending on the stretch of river. In the upper Mississippi, for example, a normal load is fifteen barges because of all the lockings to be made. In the lower Mississippi, thirty to forty-five-barge tows are not uncommon. The May 9, 1981, issue of *Waterways Journal* reported a record tow set for the lower Mississippi by the Flowers Transportation boat, *Miss Kae-D*, which pushed a seventy-two barge tow that was eight barges long and nine wide, measuring 1,580 feet by 315 feet. A normal tow for the *Kae-D* is reportedly about forty-two barges.

age in the 1920s, '30s, and '40s, when steam was still common and buoys still rare.

Earlier in the initiation chapter, Samuel Clemens detailed the task laid before the young cub who wished to "learn the Mississippi River." The older Mark Twain in 1882 could announce disdainfully that the lights made the Mississippi a two-thousand-mile-long torchlight procession, and the removal of snags took the anxiety and thrill out of piloting. But the younger Clemens featured in the first part of *Life on the Mississippi* bemoaned that "there is neither light nor buoy to be found anywhere in all this three or four thousand miles of villainous river." George Merrick also regarded the mid-nineteenth century pilot's feat with awe.

Compared with those days, the piloting of today [1909], while still a marvel to the uninitiated, is but a primer compared to the knowledge absolutely necessary to carry a steamboat safely through around the reefs, bars, snags, and sunken wrecks which in the olden time beset the navigator from New Orleans to St. Paul. The pilot of that day was absolutely dependent upon his knowledge of and familiarity with the natural landmarks on either bank of the river, for guidance in working his way through and over the innumerable sand-bars and crossings. No lights on shore guided him by night, and no 'diamond boards' gave him assurance by day. No ready search-light revealed the 'marks' along the shore. Only a perspective of bluffs, sometimes miles away, showing dimly outlined against a leaden sky, guided the pilot in picking his way over a dangerous crossing, where there was often less than forty feet to spare on either side of the boat's hull, between safety and destruction.

Today . . . he knows that the government engineers have sounded every foot of the crossing within a date so recent as to make them cognizant of any change in its area or contour. Constantly patrolling the river, a dozen steamboats, fully equipped for sounding, measuring, and marking the channel, are in commission during the months of navigation. . . . If a snag lodges in the channel it is reported at the nearest station, or to the first government steamer met, and within a few hours it is removed. Dams and shear-dykes direct the water in permanent, unshifting channels. Riprap holds dissolving banks, and overhanging trees are cut away. Millions of dollars have been spent in the work, and its preservation costs hundreds of thousands annually. All this outlay is to-day for the benefit of a scant score of steamboats between St. Louis and St. Paul. Forty years ago two hundred men, on a hundred boats, groped their way in darkness, amid known and unknown terrors, up and down the windings of the great river, without having for their guidance a single token of man's helpful invention. [Pp. 78–79]

Of course, the "tokens of man's helpful invention" Merrick refers to have since been superseded by new materials and advanced procedures. But even long after Merrick's 1909 observations, pilots still relied on "hill marks," familiar noises, and techniques of sounding the river's depth that would not have seemed foreign to George Merrick's or Mark Twain's old-school pilots.

When Captain Walter Karnath started on the river in the 1920s, there were government lights, but one still depended on the old marks as well.

In the early days before they had lights, they used to run by the sight of the brush up ahead, or the trees, or the hills. They had to always run by a certain direction. That's why a lot of these piers in the river now are so constructed that you have a definite pointing, see. There might be a light way down here . . . but maybe there might be a two-mile stretch, there might be another one way up here about a mile away or two miles away. And you get in line with those two and you can stay right on course. . . . [Before lights] we did that by bushes and the trees and the contour of the trees and the contour of the hills, see.

QUESTION: You were running the river before there were any lights?

KARNATH: Well, they had some lights, to a certain extent, but nine times out of ten the lights were out . . . either the lamplighter forgot to light them or he lit them and they blew out, or something. . . . They were kerosene lamps. . . . They had to go out every day in order to light the lights. What they did, they had so many lanterns, and a lot of these lanterns were on top of buoys, you know. They had a little slide to put them in and then put a cotter key in them, or nail, or something to hold them on. Then they had a group of lights. They'd bring back one group, they'd clean them, fill them with kerosene, and then light 'em. Next day, they'd take them out and bring the other group back. They'd clean 'em. Every night they'd have to do the same thing.

QUESTION: So even the buoys that were in the water had lamps on them?

KARNATH: Yeah, some of them did.

QUESTION: So you didn't have any lights on the boat to shine on the buoy?

KARNATH: Well at that time they had lights too, but not the way they have now. They had a light that was absolutely stiff. All you could get was a side motion. . . . Not up and down at all. . . . Then in the early days they had arc lights, just without a reflector behind it or anything, just an arc hanging out on the end of a pole so they could load their supplies, or whatever, at night.

Captain "Shorty" Williams used to know all the old marks, too, and remembers relying on them when lamplighters were negligent.

We used a lot of those things—the tops of trees—and we even had . . . places like Lansing Bend, where there was quite a bit of fog. If there was any fog at all, it'd come out of that creek at Lansing and we could run down through there in fog that you couldn't see the banks, at all, but if you could see the tops of the hills, you could run down through there and make it all right. But, of course, I've forgotten all those marks now. I couldn't do it today, because we have radar, and we don't use 'em. . . . But we did use a lot of those things. And, of course, when I first started, we had mostly kerosene lights—on aids to navigation—those that had lights.

You have lamplighters to watch it, then; of course, he was supposed to check those every day and clean the globes and trim the wicks and fill 'em with kerosene. But in order to conserve on his own energy and time, he would turn the wicks down till they just gave such a dim light that they were lit. . . . But they didn't show you much. And then he'd go every third day, to run his lights. So the old standard method was, that if you could see several lights up there—the one you couldn't see was the government light! The others were houses or something. . . . So that's when you had to use your tall trees.

Stories circulate about old-time pilots who knew where every hog farm and herd of cattle and yelping dog was located along the river. When fog would close in abruptly, as it so often did, and shut them out, these pilots would listen for any kind of familiar sound to give them clues to find the bank safely. Saying that fog stories acounted for much of the river's folklore, Ben Burman recorded one such tale in *Look Down That Winding River*.

"Best fog pilot I heard of was Captain Jack," said Captain Dick whenever this favorite subject of steamboatmen was mentioned. "There was a bad stretch of the river full of dangerous rocks where Captain Jack ran his boat and he had to be awful careful steering along it, even when the weather was fine. What made it worse, most of the time there was a fog thick as a bowl of good Cajun gumbo. You couldn't see your nose in front of you. But Captain Jack managed all right. A farmer there had a dog that was a friend of Captain Jack's and whenever his boat came along in the fog Captain Jack just rang the bell. The dog'd run down to the bank and bark his head off, and Captain Jack'd know where he was to the inch.

"But one night in the worst fog they'd ever had on the river, Captain Jack rang the bell and didn't get any answer. He rang it again and still he didn't hear anything. So he figured he wasn't near the bad place after all and signalled the engineer to get moving fast. Because of the fog they were two hours behind time. A minute later the boat was breaking up on the rocks. The dog had died the night before." [P. 30]

Of course, it was the ordinary pilot's extraordinary knowledge of river marks—of specific humpback and flattop cypress trees—that gave rise to certain "stretchers." Another fog anecdote serves to illustrate:

I heard how Captain Jack, trapped one night in another dense fog, ordered his mate to go ashore and slice off some bark from the shadowy trees to which the boat had drifted.

Captain Jack studied the bark a moment. "I know them trees," he grunted. "Them's the cottonwoods on John Markey's place. The cottonwoods in front of his stable. We're in good shape now. Full speed ahead." [*Winding*, p. 30]

Most veterans with forty-five or fifty years of experience recall a river with sporadically working lights and infrequent buoys to mark the channel. Bob McCann, longtime clerk for Greene Line Steamers, noted the type of buoys first used on the Ohio.

Once upon a time they had what they call spar buoys. They were the first buoys used up in this end of the river. And they were long pieces of timber with an anchor on one end. And they used 'em first to mark the lower entrance to Emsworth Lock when it was first built in 1923. And Ed Simms, I told you he did all sorts of unusual things, he came up with the *Liberty* and ran over one of 'em, punched a hole in her and she had to go to the drydock.

A pilot for the Corps of Engineers, Captain Allen Fiedler of Fountain City, Wisconsin, helped to set another kind of buoy in the upper Mississippi.

The first towboats that the Federal Barge [Line] had, they drew three-and-one-half feet of water. We only drew two-and-one-half feet. So then the

Mark Twain came out, and that drew four-and-one-half feet. Well, at that time the Corps of Engineers was only trying to maintain a six-foot channel. And, of course, there wasn't even six foot on the river. And a lot of places we'd have to go out and sound out a channel and put stakes out and willows out so these barge-line boats could get through. A lot of times there was two, three boats stuck at one time and that was quite common.

The Corps of Engineers at that time maintained all the buoy work and the channel work on the river. So when these barge-line boats would come up, and they couldn't get a crossing, they'd get stuck. We'd have to go down with the *General Allen* and sound out and sound out and sound out, and we'd put—instead of using fifteen, twenty great big buoys, we had willow stakes, you know, and poles, and we'd stick 'em in the sand because you only had three feet of water and you had to jab in there . . . so you could make a snakey channel. So that's how we used to do and stake it out for these boats when they were comin' and couldn't get through.

I always remember one time we were down there at Richmond Island, and we worked for two hours just sounding back and forth, sounding back and forth, and puttin' stakes in, and puttin' stakes in. And then finally the captain went up the river, and the captain looked back and said, "Turn around and go back." I was piloting. Said, "Well, pick 'em all up." So we picked 'em all up and took and went up and got outa there. After working two hours putting stakes in, you know.

QUESTION: Why did you leave?

FIEDLER: Well, I guess he figured that because the barge-line boat was Captain Nyhammer—he was a bullhead. . . . He was comin' up, you know, and we were staking out for a couple hours for him to go through. And instead of him trying to go through where we did, he got bullheaded, he wouldn't believe us, so he went on the other side of the stakes and got stuck. And then the captain—"Go on, pick 'em up."

Even when Captain Arthur McArthur started in the 1930s there were few buoys.

Oh, yeah, they had buoys, but not as many buoys. They just had markings here and there. I 'member times when some of the coal tows'd be comin' down the river, like the old *Charles F. Richardson*, she was a big boat. . . . And I know a lot of times the pilots would take a fuel flat on her head and leave out of Memphis and go on down the river and sound out the river that they had to run over, maybe for one hundred or one hundred fifty miles down the river, and then come back and hook into the tow and go on down over that river.

Buoys were still scarce as late as the 1940s. Captain John Skidmore's story illustrates just how scarce they were:

Like I said, we might put out an old barrel or an old can or something as a buoy to designate the channel. Now this is a true story what I'm gonna tell you. Years ago, like I said, there was no buoys. And the U.S. Corps of Engineers in Vicksburg constructed some buoys, and they took one out and put it up above Greenville somewhere. . . . So a Federal Barge Line boat was comin' down, or goin' up . . . I don't know which, and they saw this thing. It was during the war. And they didn't know *what* it was. So they reported it as a submarine was comin' up the river. Now this is a true story! And so, another boat, they got on the CW, notified the other boat about it, and said they'd passed a submarine comin' up such-and-such a place, be on the lookout for it. So this boat was on the lookout for it . . . they saw it; they located it. They had a high-powered rifle on the boat and they shot the buoy and it sank! [Laughs.] Later, they found out from the Corps of Engineers it was a red buoy. Now, that's just how scarce buoys was back then!

Of course, one wonders how effective a high-powered rifle would have been against a bona fide submarine.

Just as they still relied on hill marks and familiar noises after lights and buoys had been introduced as aids to navigation, pilots continued using the old techniques of sounding the river's depth until the mid-1940s. Every pilot must know how much water his boat draws and discern whether there is enough water in specified spots to carry his boat through. The lead line, more generally used on the lower Mississippi, and the spike pole, popular on the upper Mississippi and Ohio, were two of these old-time ways of sounding. Often, the sound of the leadsman singing the line would carry long distances as the word passed from the head of the tow eventually to the pilothouse. All hands knew that quarterless twain was ten and one-half feet; mark twain was twelve feet; quarter twain, thirteen and one-half feet; mark three (thyree) was eighteen feet; quarter less four, twenty-two and one-half feet; and so forth. The line measured up to mark four, or twenty-four feet, and after that the sweet sound of "NO BOTTOM" greeted a delighted pilot who knew he had entered safe water.

Several pilots admit with a laugh that the soundings passed along in those megaphones were not always empirically tested for accuracy. When reminded of his leadin' days, Captain Rip Ware rared back from the steering levers and bellowed out the old markings. He also confessed:

> See, them old houses on the barges was real high, and when them old pilots would keep us out there (singin' the lead line) so long and we'd be gettin' good water, we'd just stand out there with our hands in our pockets and hollerin' back sumthin'—[Sings.] "Quarter less thyree! NO BOTTOM!" . . . Oh, I'd throw it every once in awhile, but I wouldn't throw it every time I hollered.

When asked if he used to take soundings, Captain Walter Karnath, an upper-Mississippi native, said: "Oh, God, we poked so many holes in the river!" He describes the procedure used by the "Engineer Department" during the days when they had to set the buoys.

> We use to do it with a pole. We had a nineteen-foot pole, measured off in feet, where it was marked with a black, a white, a black, a white, and then a red. The red one was five feet. Then it would continue on—a black, a white, a black, a white, and a red; a black, a white, a black, a white. . . . And you could turn it end for end. It would be the same reading either way. . . . You'd take this thing and stand on the edge of the barge and you'd pull it out, turn it over, and go again.

Captain Harris Underwood's father was a Tennessee River pilot in the late-nineteenth and early twentieth century. Captain Underwood remembers his father's rather curious method of making soundings. "He [father] could get on a boat and then run up on one of these bars. . . . He could just jump out of the pilot's house and go out there and go wading around and find out which was the best channel . . . to try to make it, to get off the bar."

Although the sounding method used by Captain Underwood's father eschewed the lead line or pole for a more "direct" approach, it was apparently not unique, at least not in the folklore. B. A. Botkin found a story in the Concord *Intelligencer* that illustrated the difficulties pilots endured to acquire their knowledge of depths and distances.

> An old pilot on the Arkansas once attracted our attention by pointing out a bed of rock—where we could see nothing. We asked how he had studied the river.

Captain Ed Winford talking on radio to pilot on another boat, 1977

"Why, sir, I waded from the Post to Fort Gibson, three summers, and I guess I took pains to touch bottom."

The distance is near six hundred miles. . . .

His soundings were as follows: "Ankle!—half calf!—whole calf!—half knee!—knee!—half thigh!—thigh!" *Deep thigh* was as deep as he ever wished for the *Trident*; she ran from that depth down to a bare sprinkling on the bars; at a greater depth than "by the deep thigh," the order was usually given, "Head her ashore!"[4]

Technology developed for use in World War II made its way to inland river boats performing necessary home-front functions—transporting submarines, landing crafts, oil, and other commodities. Among those devices was a depth finder that could be attached to the barge itself, thus eventually replacing the old lead line and pole methods. Early fathometers have evolved into sonar depth finders with digital readouts in the pilothouse. Sonar doesn't sing and it never "dry leads" the pilot.

Before the Mississippi and Ohio rivers were canalized, particularly hazardous places required the aid of a special breed of pilots—rapids pilots—who used to navigate the falls of the Ohio and the LeClaire and Des Moines rapids of the upper Mississippi. A pilot license on the upper Mississippi for the stretch from, say, Jefferson Barracks, Missouri, to Fort Snelling, Minnesota, would specifically exclude the LeClaire and Des Moines rapids. Captain Fiedler remembers these daredevils of the river.

We picked up rapids pilots years ago when I was in the steamboats, yeah. . . . We picked up a rapids pilot at LeClaire and he took us down over the rapids, you know. . . . They'd go up there and sit on their fannies until another boat come along and they'd call 'em and, sure—you take that Captain Sutter and his brothers, two brothers, they were crackerjacks, and a fella by the name of Smith was a good rapids pilot, you know. You didn't have many rapids pilots. . . . You had to be nuts . . . That's right. I mean when you see all them there rapids and how the water goes and all, like when you're looking at the Colorado River . . . and there was holes you had to hit in there . . . you didn't have to second-guess. You know, everything had to be—or it was just too bad.

Captain Ray Prichard recalled a story told him by his mentor:

[4] B. A. Botkin, *Treasury of Mississippi River Folklore*, p. 347. His sources for this tale date back to the late 1840s.

Captain Roy Wethern told me one time that he went over the rapids with one of the men that was a posted pilot over the LeClaire rapids with four barges. And this man's name was Captain Harry Lancaster, who was born and raised in that area, whose father before him was an ace pilot. And out in those rapids were piers built of rock similar to a pyramid, only longer. When you go down around the point at LeClaire, that was so swift there that they'd steer right at those things, and the current was so strong that it just set the whole thing right out around it. Captain Wethern said, "I never been so scared in my life." He said, "Harry, you're gonna hit that pier!" Harry says, "You can't hit that pier. Try it." So, Roy said, "All right, I'll try the next one." And Harry told him how to hold on it, and he says, "I thought I was gonna run right over it; we just set right out around it." So it took a different breed of cats—that's the word—to run those rapids.

So the river that now looks so much like a series of lakes was once a treacherous obstacle course requiring special pilots who took even more spectacular chances than those who daily matched their wits against nature's fickle mysteries. And they did it in style. Even with the Chain of Rocks at St. Louis and the rapids upstream, packet pilots and rapids pilots alike made time. "You know, it's incredible to believe that those ace pilots, the Diamond Jo people, the pilots that ran the big sidewheel packets, got from St. Louis to St. Paul in three days. It's unbelievable—you could pret'near water ski behind 'em! They had to be goin'. Look at all the stops they had to make!" (Captain Prichard).

Some of those ace packet pilots were reluctant to use the new aids to navigation—it was a question of honor. Captain Fred Way, Jr., spoke of a very dark night when he snookered his partner.

We had no radar and, of course, we did have government lights. . . . Yes, we had to get along as best we could, all you had was a headlight. Anybody who used a headlight at night to find out where they were was an old woman! So you didn't use it. This was a mark of degradation—anybody who was a headlight pilot. That just meant he's helpless.

In those days, when you were dependent on what you could see, there was no glass in front of the pilothouse. It was open, and that's the reason it was open—you wanted no interference between you and what was out ahead. Another reason was that you were dependent entirely on whistle signals when meeting the boat and you wanted to be sure you could hear what he was trying to tell you when you're up there and make no mistakes. So you

wanted no glass interfering with what you could hear, and you wanted no
lights coming out from cracks and crannies on the boat anyway, it had to be
absolutely dark. Even on the skylights out from there . . . they had cur-
tains over those skylights . . . pulled down tight so there was no light, and
a roof watchman, his job was to sit up and see that there was no light coming
out of anywhere. . . . I've seen a great scene in a pilothouse when somebody's lit a pipe, sitting back on the lazy bench. Just that much light could
interfere with vision. You learn pretty quick that a situation of that kind
that you could see a great deal more than you think that you could see.
Things get lighter, the hills show up, on a moonlight night.

It was glorious. I suppose every pilot back in those days prayed at night
that the Lord would have it to do over again would have two moons instead
of one, to keep moonlight going all the time, instead of half the time. That
was gravy when you had moonlight.

Some of those nights without a moon can get pretty dark. Although I've
only seen it on very rare occasions to be so dark you couldn't see, just not
know where you're going. . . . I remember particularly one night like that.
I got down . . . in farm country, and you wouldn't think that there was no
mist down there or factory smoke or anything, but it was just an absolutely
black night. I was sneaking—I was using a headlight. . . . Be sure about
the points down ahead.

My partner came up to change watch and I had her fixed on a mark by that
time and I was steerin' there as though nothing was the matter. He sat back
there and his was another usual custom—when a man came in the pilothouse he didn't go up to the wheel and say "OK." He sat back on a bench
about five minutes to get his eyesight. Night sight, we called it. So, he
finally come up there and he says, "My God, it's dark! Where are we?" And I
said, "Oh, you'll get your sight." But it wasn't getting any better, and he
thought that he'd gone blind. [Laughs.] I'm happy as a rooster, you know.
Finally I had to laugh and let on. Well he says, "Hold her here a minute. I
got to go downstairs." And he went down and he got back and he had on a
pair of white tennis shoes. He says, "Now at least I'll know where my feet
are!" [Laughs.]

Beginning in the 1930s, the U.S. Army Corps of Engineers shortened the
lower Mississippi from Memphis to New Orleans for the purpose of flood
control. The water would run more quickly to the Gulf if several oxbows and
bends were eliminated by the fifteen manmade cutoffs that eventually resulted

from the program.[5] Of course, the Corps was simply applying its "tools of man's invention" to accomplish a process long associated with the Mississippi's natural inclinations. Mark Twain gave a fanciful accounting of the natural process:

> In the space of one hundred and seventy-six years the Lower Mississippi has shortened itself two hundred and forty-two miles. That is an average of a trifle over one mile and a third per year. Therefore, any calm person, who is not blind or idiotic, can see that in the Old Oölitic Silurian Period, just a million years ago next November, the Lower Mississippi River was upwards of one million three hundred thousand miles long, and stuck out over the Gulf of Mexico like a fishing rod. And by the same token any person can see that seven hundred and forty-two years from now the Lower Mississippi will be only a mile and three quarters long, and Cairo and New Orleans will have joined their streets together, and be plodding comfortably along under a single mayor and a mutual board of aldermen. There is something fascinating about science. One gets such wholesale returns of conjecture out of such a trifling investment of fact. [*Life*, chap. 17]

The artificial cutoffs, however, gave rise to disgruntled complaints from pilots now forced to negotiate such places as the swift Whiskey Chute. Corps pilot Captain Joe Overall was both skeptical and frustrated.

> At first they [fellow pilots] felt about it like I did. They didn't see how it was gonna work. And it didn't work for years and years. The river had to finally quit meanderin' all over creation and go through these cuts after they made 'em. But the river had to widen itself out to a certain point before the boats could get up and down through 'em. . . . It was so swift! But they settled down and quieted down, and they shortened the river 125 miles from here [Memphis] to New Orleans. [Corps Collection]

Only after nature made her alterations, he suggests, did the Corps design become functional for both flood control and navigation. In Burman's *Big River To Cross*, the vitriolic Captain Andy tangled with one of the new cutoffs.

> When you come to the cutoffs the Government people's built so the flood water'll run out faster to the Gulf, you can't go through 'em like any regular

---

[5] Cutoffs between Memphis, Tennessee, and Angola, Louisiana, include Hardin, Jackson, Sunflower, Caulk, Ashbrook, Tarpley, Leland, Worthington, Sarah, Willow, Marshall, Diamond, Yucatan, Rodney, Giles, and Glasscock. Yucatan and Leland were natural cutoffs.

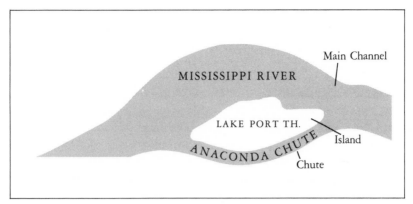

MAIN CHANNEL, ISLAND, CHUTE Pilots occasionally choose to navigate a chute rather than stay in the main channel, either because it is a shorter route or because they can get better water. Sometimes, as in Captain Skidmore's encounter with the bullfrog at Medley Chute, the water is too low and the boat can't get through the chute.

boat. The current's too fast for you and you have to go around.

He chewed his cud of tobacco angrily. "Look at me the last time I tried to get through one of the cutoffs. Didn't have such a big tow. Only eight pieces. And it sure cuts off plenty. Three quarters of a mile instead of twenty-one miles. I started through about breakfast time and then I found out pretty quick I couldn't make it. . . . Mate hadn't fixed the tow up right, or something. I started the long way around the bend, that's twenty-one miles, and going two miles an hour. Couldn't make any more, 'cause the water was running pretty fast. We travelled all day fighting her. I got round to the top of the cutoff about supper time, and looked down and saw the bottom where we were early in the morning, just three quarters of a mile away. "Well," I said to Captain Jack, my partner, who came in to relieve me, "It's something to get here anyway." Just as I said it, the current in the cutoff got the forward end of the barges. And before I could turn the wheel, my whole tow was going down through the cutoff like those streamlined trains go out of St. Louis. And in about a minute we were at the bottom, right where we had started. Then they wonder why steamboat men go to the lunatic asylum." [Pp. 144–45]

Now, according to most pilots, the river is "under control" for navigation—as much as it can be. The permanent concrete dikes are holding, the bank revetment has stopped cave-ins, locks and dams control water levels, and maintenance dredging opens up low-water trouble spots. Buoys are numerous;[6] government lights now reliably blink their presence to mark the bends. The leadsman's song is but a melodic memory and everyone is a "headlight pilot."

As the river would be unrecognizable to Mark Twain and his peers, so, too, would the boats themselves—the equipment, the amenities, the communications, the management. Of course, the old packet boats were wooden vessels, sometimes decorated with ornate gingerbread on the outside and luxury appointments on the inside. They were steam-powered sidewheelers and sternwheelers and carried both freight and passengers. The first wooden-hulled towboats pushed one or two wooden barges, and both boat and barge were vulnerable to snags, rocks, and ice that could puncture or crush them. Now steel, diesel-powered towboats push strings of steel barges that can stretch for hundreds of feet in front of the bow. Though a guest room is provided on most towboats, they are cargo, not passenger, vessels. Smaller, modern triple-screw towboats that can develop 10,500 horsepower dwarf even the most powerful of the older steamers. Captain Prichard described the old wooden barges:

> Now they had wooden barges that they used to bring down coal in from the Ohio River. They called it coal boats. And they were built for just one trip, you know. The barges were loaded with coal and . . . they called them bushels, then, in those days. . . . So many bushels. It was so many tons, it was so many bushels. That was their way of measuring the quantity of cargo. Now there was lots of those barges that never, never got to New Orleans because there would be so many of 'em in a tow, probably fifty or sixty of those small barges in a tow, and they'd just hit bottom and disintegrate. The coal went to the bottom of course.
>
> But those barges were built to make one trip. Those up on the Ohio River made one trip, and then, when they got down here, they'd sell the barges, most of 'em. And people would buy the wood. There was nothing wrong with 'em. And that was another way of getting the lumber down south . . . in the barges. . . . But, of course, those, like I say, were small barges. They were a hundred feet long—a hundred feet long and twenty-five feet wide.

In the opinion of Captain Russell Warner, who started his boating as a coal

---

[6] Though many pilots say they are misplaced since the Coast Guard has taken over these duties from the Corps of Engineers, which handled it in the past. The Corps is still responsible for channel maintenance (dredging, revetment); the Coast Guard is now responsible for aids to navigation and licensing. See Chapter 6 for strong opinions regarding this development.

passer in 1908, "in the 1918 ice, that's what changed the river from wood to steel."

In the wintertime, around the first of December or a little after, all the boats in St. Louis would move to the Tennessee River, and they'd call that their ice harbor. And when 1917 and '18 shows up, the Tennessee River comes out with ice and broke 'em all loose and they come down the river and sunk. . . . Well, all of the wooden boats sunk. The *Jim Lee*—they called her the *DeSoto* when she sunk—and the *Georgia Lee*, the *Fred Harold*. They all belonged to the Lees; they were tied up above the bridge down there and the river was gorged at Richardson—the gorge went from Richardson to Tiptonville, that's a pretty fair gorge—and the water was backed up to where it was runnin' over the banks. . . . Captain Bob Lee asked me . . . , "What do you think about my boats down there?" I said, "You better move 'em while the river's clear." Ice musta been ten, fifteen foot thick, that shore ice; he thought that ice was gonna keep from hurtin' 'em, see. . . . I said, "If I was you, I'd move 'em, but anyhow, if there's anything I can do, let me know." But when the gorge broke, the river rose ten feet an hour.

Yeah, just come up like that, you know, like a big wave. And 'course when it raised that shore ice up, the whole works went with it. No way they could hold it. So they went down and lighted on the head of President's Island and took the *Minnetonka*, that was a big, wooden-hulled government towboat, old ex-coal towboat; they all sunk except the *Fred Harris*, he was steel. The rest of 'em, the *Desoto* and the *Georgia Lee* and the *Minnetonka*, all sunk down there on the head of the island. Well, after that there was no more wooden boats built; they started buildin' steel, and 'course that rejuvenated the river business. A wooden boat just ain't nothin'.

Wood gave way to steel just as ice blocks gave way to refrigerators and browboards gave way to glass windows. Central heating replaced pilothouse stoves, radar took the worry out of being close, and radios supplemented whistles for communicating the pilots' intentions. Veteran pilots remember their days as deckhands carrying one hundred-pound chunks of ice to the cold storage or cutting ash trees to make stove wood. Creature comforts that current rivermen take for granted—like refrigeration, sanitation, air conditioning, treated water, and complete bedding—were not always available. For example:

My first job was to pull that yawl up to this ice plant and get fifty pound of ice for the ice cooler. And then I got back and pulled the yawl across the river. . . . And in the summertime it was hard sleepin', we didn't have all this frigid air then, no air conditioners, nothin' like that. Fact is, the *Charles F. Richardson* was the first boat ever come in to Paducah that had frigeration on it. [Captain Ben Gilbert]

Well, now back in my early days, on those snagboats, if you wanted a drink, you just dipped it out of the river. 'Course, we got real sanitary after that. And each one of us had a tin cup, had a certain peg you'd hang your tin cup on. But, oh, if it was very sandy or bad, we'd let it set. But generally we didn't have time for that—you'd just dip your drink out of the river. I guess they [rivers] were contaminated, but not near as bad, and we didn't think too much about it. In fact, in those days, talk about superstition—I guess that's what you'd call it—the story went out in those days, that water purified itself every sixty feet. . . . Every sixty feet it got pure, just running down the creek. So if you'as ten miles below town, you didn't worry about it. . . . [Laughs.] Oh, we found out later there wasn't anything to that. [Captain Jesse Reed]

Captain Sam Centanni recalls, "Well, I worked on the boat you had to go over the side to go to the bathroom. You washed yourself with a bucket of water." Captain Wallace Grieshaber started his forty-year career with the Corps of Engineers as a gypsy runner ("operates winches and stuff like that") in 1921 on the dredge *Thebes*. When asked about sanitation facilities, such as toilets, he said, "It was open air . . . except the officers. Now the officers had the regular utilities." He also describes the progressive upgrading of bedding on the government dredges. At first each man was issued only one sheet and one blanket, which was "renovated" once, at the end of the season.

Every year we'd go in, they'd take the blankets and send 'em out and get 'em renovated and send 'em back. . . . And then we got two sheets. You think that ain't much? That's a lot. You try to sleep with a darn old blanket on top of you, a dirty blanket. . . . Then later we got mattresses. . . . It was rough. And then in the winter, if they kept ya, if you was an officer, you went on these quarterboats. And they were just bedbug ridden. . . . You couldn't get a night's sleep unless you went out and cut walnut branches and laid [them] under your blankets.

At that time the dredges had mattresses, but the quarterboats didn't. They had a different caliber of men. . . . [The walnut leaves] were to keep the bedbugs off. See, they won't get around walnut leaves. And them old-timers say that if you're gonna get some sleep, you'd better go out and get you some walnut. . . . At first when you went out there and slept on them quarterboats, you'd wake up in the morning and, gol-dog, there was blood all over the place. You thought maybe you cut yourself or something, it was so bad. And them guys'd say, "Heck, no, that's bedbugs!"[7]

Now, according to Captain Grieshaber, a person lives "as good out there . . . as you do in a hotel or in your homes." Captain Allen Fiedler says that the equipment has changed so much that there are problems with comparisons of then and now.

Of course, nowadays you can't compare—compare years ago with navigating today for the simple reason that these towboats got so much more power. They load these barges down to nine, ten feet, and they don't do no sliding, you know what I mean? When they're down on the water there, I mean they aren't going this way and that way. Where you take years ago where you had these—even when the Barge Line started, their horsepower was only about, well, the *Mark Twain* was the biggest one of the boats there and it was 1,000 horsepower, but the other ones . . . were only about 700 horsepower, sternwheelers, and they used to tow these barges. And then they had these big barges that were 2,500-ton barges they classed them, as where all these barges they're towing now are classed as 1,500-ton barges, see. So we used to tow six of them big ones and had 15,000 tons in there. . . . And of course when them barges were light and a lot of wind with that little power, they'd be gone over the river, see?

But it is on the issue of steam power versus diesel power that the closet romantics show their colors and opinionated pragmatists reveal their druthers. The diesel age on the river is itself fifty years old now. The first, or one of the first, twin-screw, tunnel-type diesel-powered towboats, the *Herbert Hoover*, was christened on the lower Mississippi in 1931. Some oldtimers were reluctant to switch from steamboats to diesel. Asked when he had switched, Captain Roy Boyd said, "Well, it wasn't by choice. It was by force . . . the diesel boats took over!"

The steamboats, during their time, was a wonderful thing. But the diesel boats was such an improvement from several ways—economically, have power, and accessibility and adaptability to river, and towin' big tows, couldn't be beat. Now a steamboat couldn't near compare with diesel of the

[7] From U.S. Army Corps of Engineers Collection, interview with Captain Wallace Grieshaber in St. Genevieve, Missouri, August 27, 1980.

same power, because . . . the steamboats all steered from the back end, meaning they're steered from the flow of the propelling power. . . . See, the rudders were back of the sternwheel, and then they had monkey rudders ahead of the sternwheel. Now the monkey rudders was for backing up and flankin' 'round bends. You had a big tow and there was a swift current and a steep curve, you'd back out of it until your tow was just about . . . sittin' still in the water, and you'as steerin' it as the current took your whole thing out—took you and the boat with it. Now a propeller boat, they could do the same thing, and did on occasions. Not so much as a necessity, only as a caution.

But with a diesel boat, you had so much more rudder power and . . . it took in the full flow of the water from the propellers. The rudders were as deep as the propellers and that water comin' back there at probably twice the speed that it was comin' off the paddle wheel, and it'd give you a tremendous force. And the same thing—now you could stop the tow and after you got her stopped, keep one rudder backin' to hold her with the current, and come ahead on the other wheel, and steer around those places.

QUESTION: So it [diesel boat] was easier to maneuver?

BOYD: Yeah. You had it where you could put the power where you wanted it—where it needed to be. And the sternwheel boat was just partial.

Even old die-hard steamboatmen point to the efficiency and maneuverability of twin-screw propeller boats.

Oh, it took me two or three years to give up to it. I preferred the steamboat for quite a long while. . . . I was kinda like the oil company down at Baton Rouge—captain of the port . . . he didn't believe in 'em, either, for two, three, or four years 'fore he'd allow them to go ahead and make a change in their operations. . . . I just was raised on those sternwheel boats and knew how . . . they worked, and so forth and so on. But I finally had to give up to the pushin', the power. That's the main thing is the pushin' power. Takin' the boat, takin' them barges like they have. Oh, some of them, well, like the Federal Barge Line boats, American, and so forth, they carry forty to forty-five barges. . . . Now that'a lot of tonnage! [Captain Harris Underwood]

Captain Russell Warner, who embraced propeller boats early on, considers the biggest difference between piloting a steam and a diesel boat to be the better handling of the latter. Captain John Skidmore didn't regret the passing of steam and the coming of diesel, but he claims steam had the advantage of being more flexible. "I mean, you can get more power when you want it than you can a diesel boat." Captain Ben Gilbert piloted a diesel boat for twenty-nine years; yet he remains partial to steam for very practical reasons.

I still don't like it [diesel]. There's noise on there. You take when a boat's tied up, them generators on there, they make a lot of noise. On a steamboat that steam turbine . . . you can be in the engine room and you can talk just like we're talkin' now and it don't bother you.

QUESTION: How 'bout the handlin'?

GILBERT: Well, a diesel boat is a better steer, steers better, but a steamboat flanks better. . . . They're better I think at handlin' their stern than a diesel boat. You overflank with a diesel boat a little bit and a lot of times they're out of control. But a steamboat, you can flank them around and do a lot more with 'em backin' than you can a diesel boat. So that's what we used to do a lot goin' down on the *Charles F.* We had to flank the biggest part of them bends down there, you know.[8]

Captain Truman Hedrick is unequivocal:

Well it's steam for me. I like the bells — I hear all the bells ring down in the engine room. Quiet — I like the smell of steam cylinders. . . . That's part of the reason I'm hard of hearing today's on account of them diesels. . . . I'd smell the steam-cylinder oil. I smell hot oil, that smell is so good. I've run some darn good boats.[9]

[8] See Glossary for explanation of flanking and steering.

[9] Though whistles are still used to indicate passing arrangements (whether boats will pass port-to-port or starboard-to-starboard), communication is now made by radio and simply confirmed by the traditional whistles. The bells and speaking tubes, however, which used to be the means of communication between the pilothouse and engine room are mechanisms of the past. Captain "Wamp" Poe, who was both a pilot and an engineer, explained the old bell system.

"You could talk through a tube. No, no indicator; no, we had bells. You had a pretty good-size bell, string runnin' to the pilothouse. That was one. And it was a stop-and-come-ahead bell. Then you had a smaller chime bell. It was a backup and a dead-slow bell. Then you had a gong. . . . And that was dead slow and half-head. Now, you see, to be an oiler or striker, you had to know all that. See they rang this big bell. That would mean come ahead. Rang this . . . backup bell — right after you rang the come-ahead bell. That meant come ahead slow. Then if you rang the gong twice, that meant dead slow. If you ring it once, that meant half-head. And if you was gonna back up the same way around, you rang the gong — stop, see, all stop. . . . That's reverse the engine. . . . Then you rang the little bell. . . . If you rang it one time, that was back up. If you rang it twice, that was back up slow. If you rang the gong once, that was half-head. If you rang it twice, that was dead slow. After he got you started, see."

His son, Captain E. A. Poe, suggests the scenario if lawsuits had been as common in those days as they are now. "Can you imagine a lawsuit where this boat hit your boat, and one of these lawyers

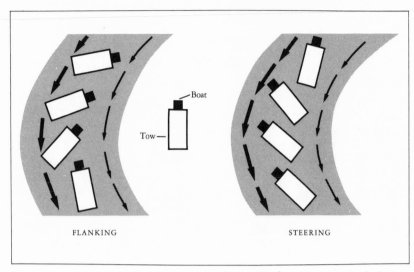

NAVIGATING A BEND
Flanking: The boat is floating with the current and using the pressure of the current against the hull to hold position in the channel.

Steering: The boat is coming ahead, driving hard, and traveling faster than the current. The techniques of flanking and steering are used in several situations, such as navigating a bend, bridge, or a lock approach.

Most pilots weaned on diesel boats can only listen to old-timers' testimonies of the differences in handling, power, crew size, noise, smell, and aura between the vanished steamers and their streamlined descendants. Few pilots today have steered exclusively on steamboats.[10] But take the pulse of one of them, and you'll register the palpitations of Twain-like romance. There is a difference, says Captain Clarke "Doc" Hawley, between steamboat rivermen and diesel-boat rivermen.

And I can't quite explain the chemistry of it. I think steamboat people sort of realize that they are participating in a sort of fine art. . . . Steam, of course, is potentially dangerous and it takes specialized people to contain it and work it. And I think people pick up on that. Even in the pilothouse, where

today would get the engineer or oiler on the witness stand talkin' about these bells? He could confuse a jury, couldn't he? . . . Back then, man, he could have had that jury to where they wouldn't have even probably known what town they was in."

[10] See Chapter 5 for portraits of two river people whose entire experience has been on excursion steamboats.

they don't actually have to work with the steam themselves, but they realize that what they do is all important. Every move counts.

On the excursion steamer *President* in New Orleans shortly before she was to be converted to diesel in 1977, Captain Joseph "T. Joe" Decareaux put things in perspective. He had begun on steamboats in the 1920s, started piloting diesel boats in late 1948, and then had come back to steam when he "retired" fourteen years later.

This will be the second time that I've seen steam go out, incidentally. I saw the biggest steamboat that was ever built, the steamer *Sprague*. Everybody used to call it the "Big Mama" on the river. And I saw the *Sprague* go out. . . . Most everybody likes steamboats, sternwheelers, but they're almost helpless, you know. . . . You can do better work with a screw boat than you can with a propeller boat than you can with a sternwheel.

A practical boatman, Captain T. Joe acknowledges the superior efficiency of diesel screw-boats while simultaneously regretting steam's demise.

Yeah, I kind of regret it. I wish some of it could continue. I hate to see it go out altogether. . . . They still had coal on the river when I started in '26. It was several years after, I saw coal go out. I saw raft boats go out. . . . But I didn't see the raft come back. I saw the steam go out. This'll be the last time I saw steam go out. I don't expect it to come back soon. It might come back if they make some changes.

QUESTION: They'll have to be more powerful.

DECAREAUX: Yeah. One thing about steam, you gotta have more crews. Diesel is like you operate your automobile, or like a truck or tractor. When you take the key, or turn the engine off, everything is dead. You don't have to watch it. Everything is well secured. But a steamboat you gotta have people watch it; watch the water, watch the fire. It takes so many more people to operate steam. But they make pretty boats. You know, they're beautiful. Every steamboat is beautiful, so I hate to see it go.

Captain Ed Winford sees the progress in river transportation mirroring that on land—we've gone from the horse-and-buggy days to the space age. In 1928 it was a novelty to see a boat coming along; it might be "four or five days before we'd see a boat of any kind." Boats had large crews and "things were kind of leisurely back then."

They'd tie up at night quite a bit, and the river wasn't marked like it is now, wasn't developed, banks weren't revetted, . . . some spots the channel might change overnight from one side of the river to the other. . . . And everybody just took their time. . . . Wasn't any big rush then. And these boats would get to town; they'd stop and tie off barges, might stay around town twenty-four or forty-eight hours, just makin' up tow and gettin' on groceries and supplies and things like that.

No hurry. They'd finally get through and take off. But now these storeboats have developed; there's one at Memphis and there's one here at Natchez and one at Baton Rouge, and almost every large town has one, and you radio your grocery order in ahead, or if you need a part for your warshing machine, and they'll have it ready, and a little boat'll run it out to you. The boat doesn't stop; it just stops long enough to put that on and keeps goin' now. It's got so expensive and there's so much money involved now that it's just naturally developed thataway.

The towing industry is big business, and the days of individual owner-captains have given way to multiple-boat fleet companies that are themselves subsidiaries of giant corporations.[11] Traffic (inland river towboats and deep-water ships alike) has become so heavy and congested in the lower Mississippi from Baton Rouge past New Orleans to the mouth that in October 1977 the Coast Guard implemented a controversial computerized communications tracking system (New Orleans Vessel Traffic Service — VTS) for the purpose of improving safety and preventing collisions. Pilots are supposed to radio their positions to a central communications center which then plots the location of all boats in the area, relays information, and alerts pilots to potential hazards. The voluntary VTS system, discontinued, then reinstated in 1980, has not been universally accepted; many operators claim the VTS channel is distracting and the system is unreliable because some pilots either do not report at all or report false positions. Besides, many pilots figure they know more about what is going on in front of them than some "button pusher" in New Orleans harbor. "They're getting the information from us and then reporting it back to us."[12] Mandatory participation may be just around the bend as various agencies and the towing industry try to cope with the ever-increasing number of boats and

[11] For an assessment of the impact on the pilot profession of this kind of management, see Chapter 6.

[12] "New Orleans VTS Reinstated after Strong Show of Support," *Waterways Journal*, July 26, 1980, p. 7.

tonnage now involved in river commerce.

The Coast Guard Lower-Mississippi River Group's sophisticated radio center in Memphis serves as a clearing house for information available to towboat operators and pilots. "If a pilot at New Madrid, Missouri, wants to know the condition of a particular crossing down near Vicksburg, for example, all he has to do is call us and ask. If we don't know, we can call a boat in the Vicksburg area to get an update to pass along to the pilot at New Madrid."[13]

In Clemens's day and later, if a pilot wanted to know the condition of a particular crossing downstream, either he consulted the periodically placed post boxes along the river where pilots left remarks of their last trip, or he sent out a yawl to sound the crossing and reconnoiter firsthand. In Clemens's day and later, if fog came in, a pilot headed for the bank and hoped he got there before he was shut out and lost his bearings. In Clemens's day and later, the pilot used trees and hills and hog farms and "hollers" to mark his specific location. He drank river water, wrapped himself in one blanket on mattressless beds, and looked through glass-free pilothouse windows.[14] Now pilots radio information to each other, consult regular channel reports, receive updates from central communications centers, and look to digital readouts on the pilothouse fathometer. Now a boat can even pass through a bridge in fog using the "eyes" of radar.[15] And now the sanitation and accommodations are "as good as a hotel or your own home" and feature the kinds of comforts possible with smaller crews and larger quarters.

Fifty years from now, the young pilots of today may look back to the "hard times on the river" when the old-time, 10,500-horsepower diesels lumbered their way down the river, primitive radar and sonar gadgets tried to verify

[13] "CG Memphis Center Has Sensitive Ears," *Waterways Journal*, December 15, 1979, pp. 183–87.

[14] Captain Roy Boyd remembered a question on a license exam that referred to old-time packet boats regarding browboards, which had not been used for years. Captain Boyd asked other old-time captains, who also did not know, and then did some investigating himself aboard the old *Coal Bluff*, laid up in the dock. "She had the old-time pilothouse . . . and instead of havin' windows in the front, they had boards, so they could close it up. And it'd close up, all except one would have a half-moon cut out, . . . so if it was rainin', you'd shut those boards and you could still see through there and see the river. And they all folded up and closed tight, except those two holes, they'as one each side of the wheel."

[15] Excursion boats such as the *Delta Queen* and *Mississippi Queen*, though equipped with radar, still tie up in shut-out fog, and many pilots contend—radar or not—that there's no such thing as a fog pilot.

obstructions and depths, and crackerjack towboat operators daily dueled with the wily, unpredictable river. But, like Mark Twain speaking for the 1850s, or Blair for the 1890s, or Way for the 1930s, when asked what makes a good river pilot, they may respond: "Well, I'd say he's got to have a good memory, sound judgment, and plenty of nerve."

You can't make all your money comin' ahead. You got to make some of it backin' up.

Captain Oren Russell

A good mate did not get no work done with his head down and his stern up.

Captain "Rip" Ware

Seems like every time you come on watch, you have a little bit of a close call.

Captain Ted Davisson

One doesn't hit a rock or a solid log raft with a steamboat when he can get excused.

Mark Twain

CHAPTER THREE

Work Life on the Boat

Captain Harry Louden standing watch on *Delta Queen*

Despite Mark Twain's celebrations of the craft, it was not the ambition of every riverman to someday don the pilot's cap. Determined to make a "lightning clerk" out of young Fred Way, the clerk of the *General Pershing* hoped to discourage Way's aspirations by disparaging the pilot profession.

Consider a pilot who has attained success. . . . He draws down the biggest salary on the steamboat and spends all of his wakened hours standing in a glass cage, like a monkey, from which he has no escape, pawing a wheel around one way and the other way; he is limited by law to certain portions of a river, and he is bound to stay within those limits and practice his profession. He does the same things year in and year out, and soon becomes stupid and dull. He cannot carry on a normal conversation; he loses interest in all of the world outside of the two willow shores he watches day and night; he sends his money home for a wife to spend on foolish things; his children grow up and never come to know their own father; his stomach disintegrates from the continual combination of worry and grease; his health fails and the day comes when he is useless. At this time he is sent ashore, where he is an utter stranger, and is allowed to die a lonely and heartbroken man, and somebody has to take up a collection to bury him in a potter's field with no tombstone. [*Pilotin'*, p. 117]

In a moment of frustration even Captain Ebenezer Cline, "a whopping big fellow who could roar like a bull," lectured Way:

"A man is a plain damn fool to work on the river twelve hours a day. . . and tie his stomach up in bow-knots with all this grease and slop they feed you on these boats! He's a lunatic to stand here in a pilothouse in winter and shiver and shake while the wind blows on his face and a red-hot coal stove singes his coat tails. And man . . . I say any man is a plain damn fool and an idiot to learn to be a pilot! No woman ought ever to marry a man that says he's a pilot: there ought to be a law against it! There ought to be a special graveyard to bury such brainless asses upside down in; and a special hell to send them to!"

Eb paced back and forth across the pilothouse while he emphasized these things by pounding his fists on the bench, and on the stove apron. "Do you know what a steamboat pilot turns into when he dies?" he shouted. "He turns into a contrary white mule, and whenever you see a mule on the shore you'll notice he cocks his head and his ears frontward and watches a steamboat until it's out of sight—that's because it's the pilot in him! Get some sense boy, and get away from this business while you are young and have a chance!" [*Pilotin'*, pp. 77–78]

Way saw that, despite all this bluster, Eb Cline "wouldn't have traded places with the King of England." Neither, it turns out, would the future Captain Way. But devotion to one's profession need not blind him to its disadvantages. Work life for rivermen—whether deckhands, cooks, engineers, or pilots—includes a good deal that is simply routine, even dull. The daily regimen is strictly regulated, routine tasks are endlessly repeated, and days off are eagerly anticipated by calendar watchers calculating their time. There are even "routine" hazards, such as drownings, groundings, runaway barges, wind and fog, locks and bridges. And, of course, there is also the exceptional, the traumatic—exploding gas barges, cyclones, fires, and floods.

Still, though the spectacular accidents and ace pieces of piloting are long remembered and easily recalled, the daily life for pilots on board inland river vessels is ordered, segmented into six-hour periods of working, eating, and sleeping. One pilot takes the forward watch (6:00 a.m. to noon, 6:00 p.m. to midnight); the other steers the after watch (midnight to 6:00 a.m.; noon to 6:00 p.m.). At watch-changing time, the relief pilot judges their position, gets his night sight if it is dark, and then merely says, "I got her" to his partner as he takes over between the levers. The pilot going off watch may mention where they are, but it is only a courtesy—they both know exactly where they are. He may talk briefly about notable problems—difficulty at a lock or bridge, fog, low water, or the danged-fool thing another pilot did at Point No Point, but he soon goes below to eat or sleep.

Occasionally, a pilot observes an idiosyncratic ritual when coming on watch. Captain Ray Prichard recollected observing one particular pilot:

He had a thermos thing and he brought his own water to work. . . . He wouldn't drink the water on the boat. He had his own thermos—one of those thermos bottles, and he had a strap around it like a skate strap. He had it around his shoulder like the girls carry. . . . That'd be the first thing he'd take off. Then on the other side he had his binoculars. He'd undress himself that way. Then he'd take the upper coat off—an outer coat. It was quite a sight to see Ernie go on watch. Then before he'd take the handles, you know, he had to put on his mittens or working gloves. Because you see there's microbes on there . . . and they were crawling around. There was millions of 'em on there. He was so sanitary, too.

QUESTION: He brought his own water because he was afraid the water on the boat wasn't sanitary?

PRICHARD: Oh, yeah. That wasn't fit to drink. But everybody else drank it and never died. But he had his own thermos bottle with a spigot on it—er, I guess you pushed it. Paper cups. He had paper cups. Oh, he was so sanitary it was pitiful. Oh, he'll probably die of ptomaine poisoning.

Sometimes there's a deviation from the regular watch routine. On U.S. Corps of Engineers dredge boats, three crews work eight-hour shifts each. This does not, however, include the pilot who moves the boat whenever he is asked. Captain Harry Louden recounted a watch-changing story from his days on the steam dredge *St. Genevieve.*

Captain told him, he said, "Now don't call the midnight crew." They were finishing the cut, you know, and he was gonna change the pump the next day. He wanted all the men he could have, see. "We'll work 'em all day tomorrow, don't call 'em." So, at 11:30, he went around and woke up everybody and tole 'em they didn't have to get up! He'd do some of the damndest things. . . . He never could figure out, you know, who was on what watch. So he'd put little red strings on the springs of the bed that he was supposed to call. Well, then, them boys caught on to that and they'd swap 'em over on somebody else's bed. He called everybody but the right guy.

There is a sameness—about the meals, about the days, about the regimen—that is demoralizing to some crewmen. Captain Oren Russell always felt isolated when he piloted towboats and declared that when he died, he hoped the Good Lord would put him on a passenger boat, not a towboat. He and the first mate compared notes:

RUSSELL: Oh, them things [towboats] never stop. He goes down there and drops that tow and picks up another one and rides back. Does the same thing at the other end.

MATE: Working's the same; don't matter where you are or what day it is. Same thing's gonna happen.

RUSSELL: You know, after you been out there about two months, two-and-a-half months, and you know we had chicken twice a week. You gen'ally had chicken on Wednesday and chicken on Sunday. And you lose the time of the day and days of the week. You'd go down there and see that chicken and say, "What is today, Sunday or Wednesday?"

MATE: You don't really care.

RUSSELL: Don't make no difference if you do. After you found out, it's still the same routine.

Asked if he had a favorite time of day or a favorite season on the river, Captain Arthur Zimmer replied:

No. To anybody on the river, day or night doesn't make any difference and winter or summer doesn't make any difference. . . . Holidays don't make any difference on the river. . . . Now years ago on the river, a lot of these towing companies used to tie up their vessels on holidays such as Christmas anyway. And send the crew home, probably only keep a couple of people on there for watchmen. And send them home for two or three days over Christmas. . . . But they don't do that any more. . . . And in fact, now, they don't tie 'em up for nothing. They don't even stop to take on stores, or fuel, or anything any more. It's go, go, go, all the time.

Though he spent nearly sixty years on the river himself, Captain Brady Smith told his sons never to get on the river.

It's so durn lonesome at times, you know, you just get disgusted. . . . Six hours on, six hours off. By the time you got a change at noon, it'd be 1:30 before you got to bed and then you'd have to get up at five for supper and get ready. . . . There ain't too much sleeping because you just don't have the time to sleep. . . . You just get used to it.

Captain Clarke "Doc" Hawley agrees that one becomes accustomed to such a life. But despite the regimen, he still feels the romance.

It's almost a cliché to say that the river gets in your blood, but I think in a way that if it doesn't get in your blood, it gets in your system. You work on a boat twelve hours a day, sometimes over half a year, twelve hours a day, for several years. And you become sort of acclimated to that regimen, you know. Your system is even tuned in on it.

QUESTION: Would you say it's the river or the routine?

HAWLEY: I think it's the routine. . . . You eat meals regularly, you go to bed regularly, it's strictly a regulated life. . . . And that is a daily regimen, you see. You get up at the same time so you can go relieve your partner and you do six hours work and you get off and you eat your lunch and go back to bed and get a nap, so you can come back on watch fresh at, say six o'clock. After you do this for so long a time, your system actually becomes regulated by your daily activities, and I know people, pilots who are retired, and they still get up at 5:30 in the morning so they can come on watch at six. And they're not goin' on watch at all. . . .

I think there's some romance in about everybody, no matter how hard-bitten an old boatman is. I think he is basically, can see through the fog and see some interesting sights, and I think you're just bound to get caught up in the romance, if that's the right word, the mystique of learning the river and the channels. Then once a person's away from the river for awhile, they want to get back and see what's happened, see what's changed, how's everything comin' along. 'Cause, people just can't stay away.

When most of the veterans began their boating days, they received little or no official time off. They worked the season, often staying away from home for sixty to ninety days at a time, and didn't know the meaning of "vacation time." Certain captains were notorious for tying their boats up in isolated wooded areas away from the towns in order to keep crew members in tow. Such predicaments led to equally notorious schemes to secure a few precious hours in town or a few days off to go home.

Well, back then the Federal Barge Line, it wasn't nothin' for them, them fellas would come down the river from St. Louis and if they wanted to stop over in Cairo for something, they'd just back across a bar and knock a rudder off. Spend several hours hangin' a rudder; that's how they got time off. [Captain Ben Gilbert]

When Captain Wallace Grieshaber first started with the Corps of Engineers in the 1920s, there was no such thing as sick leave or regular leave. He found a way, however, to get some time off:

They wouldn't give it to you. . . . And then it was up to the captain to give you leave. . . . They said, "If you want to get off, just tell him you're gonna get married." I got married three times. . . . That's the only way he'd let you off for a week. I'd say, "Captain Crane," I'd say, "Gonna get married." "OK, how long you want off?" I said, "Oh, a week." "OK."

Next year, he done forget about it, you know what I mean. I'd say, "Gotta get married, captain." He'd say "How much you want?" I'd say, "Oh, about a week." I worked it three times. [Corps Collection]

Gradually, crew members gained progressively more time off—six days for every thirty worked, twelve, fifteen, then eventually the day-for-day time now enjoyed by most towboat pilots. Now they work thirty days, are off thirty days, and are paid for sixty days.

Most rivermen have families on land, and the schedules of their profession dictate the basic aspects of their family life. While the amount of time the family may spend together varies, the division of responsibilities is fairly standard. The husband brings home the money; the wife rears the children. While many pilots regret having spent so much time away and resent having missed out on their children's youth, others see the arrangement from a more positive perspective, preferring to think of the unencumbered quality of their days off which allowed more time, not less, for their children. Some families, of course, measured such things by no other yardstick because they had been river families for generations. Captain Donn Williams, a second-generation pilot, worked elsewhere for eight years before joining his father's Davenport, Iowa, marine service: "Actually, I was probably twenty before I ever thought much about that everybody's dad wasn't a pilot, you know. Mine had been since I could remember. . . . Lot of his social contacts were also pilots. So I didn't think it was at all unusual till I got out into the real world and found out that everybody wasn't a pilot."

Still, many pilots who talk enthusiastically and affectionately of their decades on the river, who made a good living (even during the Depression) and pursued an adventure or two, who came back after retiring because the river was "still in their blood" nevertheless discouraged sons from choosing their profession. Generally, they did so because of the long absences and the daily stresses of the job. Says Captain Ed Winford, "I wouldn't bring my boy out here. . . . I've been away from home more than half my life, and my wife had to raise the children by herself. . . . That's the bad side of the river life, bein' away from your family. . . . It's not the best for married life."

Captain Oren Russell's son wanted to follow his father to the river. "I got him a job one summer on a govament dredge. . . . They kep' him out in the middle of the river the whole three months, just about. And I thought mebbe it'd cure him, you know, and it did." He went on to college and a career in advertising.

"Hell, I didn't want that for him," said Captain Russell. "I was kinda a stranger in my own home. I've never particularly liked the river because I was away from my home. I had to sacrifice my home life for my family's well being. Because pilots back there in 1943, we wudn't makin' but $350 a month, but that was top wages."

Captain "Rip" Ware echoed sentiments about being away from his boys and his desire that they be with their families. "Just look at the hours—twelve hours a day you're not gettin' paid for, but sittin' and can't go nowhere, see what I mean? So look at the hours that's wasted in your life, you might say, just to get to work for your livelihood."

Other pilots look differently at the impact of their profession on their personal lives. Captain Martha Ritchie Dennison, one of the few women pilots on the river, and her brother, Captain Larry Ritchie, shrug off the hardships— after all, that is the way they grew up.

LR: What's the difference of working out there thirty days and then coming home being with your families for twenty-four hours a day for thirty days than it is here in town going to work for eight hours and sleeping for eight or ten hours?

MRD: That's what I like about it because when you're out there, you step in your work on time, and when you come home, you don't have to worry about getting up and going to work every day. You know, your time is your own.

LR: Yeah, I know one man here in Paducah, he's a pilot for Rose Barge Line. His wife cooks out on the boat, and most of the time their days on and off don't correspond to one another. They tried it one time working together, and they said it didn't work out. Too much time together.

Of course, Captain Martha Ritchie Dennison may have an even more difficult family situation should she have children. Traditionally, pilots have been able to leave their children in the care of their wives during long absences. But what if the pilot is also the mother? Just before her marriage (to a riverman who also wants to be a pilot) she skirted this potential problem by deferring childbearing plans to a distant future.

Regardless of his attitude toward the absences from family, a river pilot's family life is inescapably colored by the routines of his professional work. Most feel they have had to sacrifice in some measure a normal family life.

There is, then, a considerable amount of routine regimen, sacrifice, and risk in the working schedules of river pilots who labor twelve hours a day, seven days a week, thirty days at a time, on a constantly moving vessel. An illiterate deckhand character in Richard Bissell's *A Stretch on the River* asks the mate to write a letter home for him. The mate asks him what he wants to say: "Oh," he says, "tell 'em we ben goin' up the river and now we're going down her." The mate and his cronies figured that was a simple but accurate description of steamboating.

In running up and down the river, crew members live with certain risks inherent in their work. In fact, "ordinary" potential hazards are faced on nearly a daily basis—falling off the boat, groundings, weather problems, equipment failure, even gun-happy shantyboaters. One pilot waxed philosophic about that relationship between the routine and the unexpected in his profession. "Well, you have a routine I think in any job. But I would say that in the profession of piloting that the unexpected is always your bedfellow. It gets up with you and comes on watch. And you go down and go to sleep. It may get up out of bed and arouse you" (Knoephle Collection).

Of course, on a boat one of the omnipresent dangers is that of falling overboard. And sometimes the particular needs of one part of the crew contribute to the difficulties experienced by others. The pilot needs absolute darkness; even the tiniest light, even out on the barges, could send an old pilot to cussing. On the old steamboats, they often towed their own fuel flats.

> They had what they call a coal barge, you know. That was their own coal that they used on the boat. They'd have that tied up agin the boat. . . . And then they'd put a plank at night, . . . then they'd put flour on it. And they'd wheel it in. That's the only thing they had to guide 'em was that flour . . . that light line. If you'd miss that, why, sometimes the wheelbarrow would go in and sometimes the wheelbarrow and the guy pushin' it would go in. I never did see any of 'em drown, but they never did get the wheelbarrow anymore. [Knoephle Collection]

Stories of drownings and near drownings are commonplace among rivermen.

> We were coming out of the Ohio River at Uniontown. And I went off watch at midnight and the pilot come up and relieved me. . . . And when he

swung around the sharp curve there on what you call Island Rocks, the mate, Red Coyle, stepped out of the galley door and he slipped on the guards and fell between the chains and fell into the river.

And he kicked off his boots and held onto his flashlight and waved his flashlight, and this other boat stopped and picked him up . . . in the yawl. . . . They come down and woke me up . . . and we put a boat in the water. And I went back over there and we wrapped Red in blankets and he didn't have no shoes and socks. The temperature was 32°.

But it wasn't too far to the bank, but he was lucky that the boat was there to pick him up right away. But anyway, Red got along all right with a lot of hot lemonade and a couple of shots of good whiskey. . . . And we always joked about that. I got the cold by givin' him my socks and shoes. . . . I got the cold and he was all right.

Yeah. And he said . . . he still has that flashlight sitting on the mantel at home. He said, "That's going to stay there as long as I live." [Captain Arthur Zimmer]

In the wintertime we would pull 'em out—and they'd go all the way under the tow and pop out—first thing we do is take 'em back and wrap 'em in blankets and give 'em a little whiskey, you know.

QUESTION: If they fell off the boat and popped around to the back, they didn't get caught in the wheel?

MCARTHUR: No, if you got a tow out there and a fella falls over, if the boat's goin' down, he might come out the side . . . he could pop out. I saw one time on a boat there the man hadn't come out and the engineer just backed her, and he was lucky he wasn't in the wheel. . . . He knew the fella, and when he hadn't come out in a certain amount of time, he just backed her on his own. Actually, he could'a lost his license. But everybody was glad he did do it, later on, because the man did pop out and he was prac'ly drowned. He had a life jacket holdin' him up against the hull of the boat, so he was able to survive all right. [Captain Arthur McArthur]

In his forty years of boating, Captain Bob Richtman lost only one man off a boat he was on, and that man, a young deckhand, drowned.

I think he lost his balance and he went flying over into the water. He was between the piers, you know, and I run out there right away and got a life preserver, and I threw it right over there to him. All he had to do was put his hand on it. But he must have got a swallow of that damn murky water; it started to suffocate his lungs. And he was fighting then, you know. And about that time the guy alongside of me dove in and went for him, and he started to go down. And he . . . brought him out and laid him on there and we called the Coast Guard, it was that close there. They started artificial respiration on him. In those days we didn't have any mouth-to-mouth resuscitation. I don't think he could have saved him, anyway. Good kid, too.

Some mishaps were funny rather than fatal:

I always remember another incident. A coal barge sank up at St. Paul, and I was on the *Fury*. There was about forty ton of coal on it. The government was loading it, and the fella loaded it on one end, and down it went. So we got the towboat alongside of it. We got lines underneath up onto the railroad trestle work there. And we'd get our nigger line in there, steam caps, and then just kinda pull her up a little bit. Then we'd get cables up under the timberhead with these old steamboat ratchets, and we'd bring her up maybe a couple of inches or so, and then we'd have to get in from one end with a wheelbarrow and stand in the water and shovel coal out in the wheelbarrow and wheel it to another barge. So then you'd have to take and try to pull her up again maybe six inches and keep on doing that until you get a lot of coal off of it.

So I can just see to this day, Vince Glumpsky was a deckhand. . . . And he was pulling up on this ratchet here, and the cable broke—down the barge went. And he went in the river, and he had a straw hat on. I can just see that straw hat today. And he went underneath, and he came up, and here there was a great big turd—excuse my language—turd was sittin' right on top of the straw hat. I can just see it as plain as day, you know! This big sewer was right there, you know, and coming out of St. Paul and all that stuff was in there, see. And it came in there—when he went in there, he had it right on top of his hat! [Captain Fiedler]

Even though falling overboard is a risk of working on the river, such events still do not happen frequently, and some pilots have never had a drowning off their boats in more than forty years on the river. But it is unlikely that a pilot can claim he has never gone aground. Captain Donn Williams puts this occurrence in perspective.

Everybody imagines that the runaway barge captured . . . this is real salty. Man, we do that so much! People break up tows and so on—it's not, it's nothing. Just go out and get it and tie up to dock is all.

Buddy Howell is a pilot out here and has been for a long time. He was gonna change jobs, though, from one company to another. So, he contacted the port captain of this other company, and the guy asked him about experience and all that. Buddy said, "Oh, I've been at it for I don't know how many years and size tows and all that stuff." And then he asked, "Well, now, here's another thing, of course, we got to bear in mind. That is, what's your accident record?" And Buddy says, "My accident record is perfect!" The guy says, "Do you mean to tell me that you've been out there for thirty years and you've never had an accident?"

"Oh, no," he said, "I've never made a whole trip without having some kind of minor accident!"

Guy says, "You're hired!"

The Coast Guard now requires pilots to report in every time they go aground. Both Captain Donn Williams and his father, "Shorty," note that this adds to paperwork and ignores what all inland pilots know to be true: "Well, hell, goin' aground is part of the operation!" Of course, nowadays these routine groundings are usually brief (generally a matter of hours), although boats used to be stuck for days or even weeks waiting for a rise in the river or successful dredging to release them. Since groundings are so common, there are stories about the extraordinary cases just as there are about those phenomenal "fog pilots." In *Lore and Lure of the Upper Mississippi*, Captain Frank Fugina offered one such tale.

In time of high water when the river overflows its banks, it is quite easy in the night for a pilot to lose his bearings. A pilot who once grounded his boat on a prairie a long way from the channel sent the following telegram to his employers: "Am out on Lone Tree Prairie. What shall I do?"

They answered, "Go farming, you land-lubber."[1]

Inclement weather conditions—high water, fog, brisk winds—can turn matter-of-fact lockings, or bridge runnings, or landings into adventures.

I had a pretty good record there. I never had a collision or a grounding that lasted more than two to three hours, and I'm not braggin'. I'm one that believes luck enters into a person's life, to a great extent. And especially a river pilot. What I mean by that, I missed the bank many times—and just barely missed the bridge several times—and all that.

[1] Frank Fugina, *Lore and Lure of the Upper Mississippi*, pp. 61–62.

Now I remember one trip I made back to White River, Captain Blank-enship and I, to tow the dredge *Omega* out of there. It was fifty miles up White River and we were gonna tow it with the little *Griffith*. . . . And the *Omega* was really too much for that. But anyway, White River was at flood stage, and instead of goin' around the bend like it would in low water, it went right down through the woods, and that left the bends slack. And we tried to steer a couple of bends and couldn't make it, but we got turned around, headed upstream, some way or other. So Captain Dave, he was out on the dredge and I was at the controls, and he'd motion me when to pull it hard or when to this or that, and we decided after we were turned around anyway, we'd just *back* around that bend. And it worked so good we backed all the way up!

That's the truth! Through the bridges and everything — we just backed through 'em. Worked better than tryin' to steer 'em. We backed fifty miles down that river with that dredge *Omega*. And went back and got the pipeline and backed out with it. We were expert backers by that time! [Laughs.] [Captain Jesse Reed]

Fog, of course, is the stealthy nemesis of the river pilot, who must rely on his other senses once his eyes are rendered useless.

I was on the *St. Louis* as a pilot and I went off watch at eleven o'clock at night. . . . Captain Willie Weaver came on watch to relieve me. . . . And Captain Elmer Good was the master. . . . Went to bed and next mornin' I woke up and we were layin' in the fog.

Just as we [had] started out in the crossin' going across the river, the fog shut down just like that. . . . We didn't have radar in those days. So he [Captain Weaver] set the boat to backin' and called the captain. And Captain Good run up there right quick. . . . He said, "OK, Captain, just let her float." . . . He told the mate, "You get out on the head of the tow with megnaphones [sic], put a man on each corner."

They kep' floatin'. . . . He knew there was a transfer landin' right down below there so he was tootin' his whistle, and he started to hear a bell tappin' — one tap, one tap, one tap. He got out there and he listened a little bit and he said, "Who are you that's tappin' the bell and where are you located?" . . . A roustabout was on there watchin' 'em said, "I'm on the *Pelican*." And the captain said, "Well, where are ya?" he said, "We down just below the Federal Barge Line Terminal into the bank here tied to the bank."

And captain said, "All right. You just keep tappin' that bell a few seconds, just keep tappin' it." Asked him how he was layin' and everything, was there anything right ahead of him, right below him, and so old watchman told the captain the whole situation. And as he was tellin' him all this here, he backed that boat up and backed her right on in listenin' to that bell and backed her right on in by that transfer boat and tied her up there. [Captain McArthur]

Commonplace lockings become potentially dangerous when a strong wind is blowing. Bob McCann told a story of two lockings on the Ohio River when Ralph Emerson, "the showboat man," was captain and Charlie Ellsworth was pilot. The first week at Lock 4 there had been a strong onshore wind, and Ellsworth had hit the lower gate guidewall and "tore eighty-two feet of her [the boat's] outriggers off."

And the next week she came down here when Charlie Ellsworth was pilot and got along up in here, and Emerson came up in the pilothouse and said, "Charlie, do you realize we're gettin' awful close to Lock 4?" And Charlie said, "Yep, I see it down there." He said, "Do you realize the wind's gonna be straight onshore again the same as it was last week?" Charlie said, "Yes, that's the way it look to me."
  "Well," he says, "how do you aim to put her in that lock?" "Well," he said, "I'm gonna drive her full head till the pilothouse gets abreast of the upper gate, then I'm gonna stop her and back her full head." Emerson says, "Oh, Cap, what are you gonna do if she doesn't back?" He says, "Then we'll wreck her on the lower gate instead of the upper gate!" [Laughs.]

Sometimes the danger results from crew error:

The *Delta Queen* was going into Kentucky Lock, going into the lock from the lower end, upstream, the lower gates were open. They were in the lock; the engineer on watch was letting the striker handle, and he got confused, and when he went to back slow, he came ahead slow. Then the pilot made the mistake. Instead of stopping her and chancing that the striker would catch his mistake, he didn't think that he was backin' strong enough. So, he went from slow astern to full astern, and the striker went from slow ahead to full ahead. And the stage was barrelling into that upper gate inside the lock chamber. And then they stopped her—knocked him out of the way. Captain Wagner was on the bridge, yelling, "What are you doin' down there!" And they backed her for all she was worth and she just stopped inches

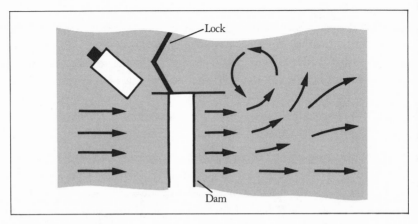

NAVIGATING A LOCK

A pilot must be wary when entering or leaving a lock, always taking into account the current going over the dam and possible eddies at one end. In this figure, he sets the tow toward the dam so that the current going over the dam will push the head of the tow toward the lock. If he sets it toward the lock itself or toward the shore, the current could catch the boat, causing it to spin or run into the lock wall.

from crashing. [Captain Gabriel Chengery]

Sometimes equipment fails. Captain "Doc" Hawley nonchalantly recounts such "adventures" on an excursion steamer.

Oh, yes, we had all kinds of adventures—groundings, and one time up on the Tennessee River the pilot got out of shape because the bridge lights were out on a pier up near Knoxville. knocked both smokestacks down, tore the mast up, gangplank fell off, fell in the river, and we had to put a buoy on it to mark it to go back and get it. . . .

So we turned around and went back into Knoxville again, and they got the smokestacks put back up and all that. . . . Oh, one time we hit a lock up at Pittsburgh. Had 1,180 people on there. part of the ship-up gear didn't work and the boat wouldn't back up, and we hit Emsworth Lock pretty hard. Out of 1,180 people. . . . I think the only claim in all that was a broken lens on a camera. The force of a pretty good-sized boat hittin' the lock gate, you know, with 1,180 people—it's enough to stove her in good, but that was on the *Avalon* and she was an exceptionally well-made boat, still is, the hull is just superb. . . .

Oh, and then we had various things—knocked the *Delta Queen*'s smokestack off on the Keesburg Bridge one time. They didn't raise the bridge up high enough in high water, and we knocked that top part off the stack and it hit the tongue-and-groove roof, and I thought it was gonna go through, but somehow the roof held up. Sure woke everybody in Texas though, I tell you that! They came out of there![2]

And occasionally the "hot rodders" of the pilot set precipitate equipment failure and, hence, collisions. Captain Fontain Johnson told of a dock used by steam tugs just above Algiers Point (New Orleans area) that stuck out into the river.

And those guys would come in there, when they was comin' in, they'd come in all full ahead like hot rodders and . . . ring those two bells—the back-up is what they used on tugs. So Dominick come up one morning about 10:00 a.m.; he was comin' in there full ahead. He rang, stopped, and rang it back up, and the engine hung up. The tug went right up in the office, and the marine superintendent is sittin' in there just at his desk, and he looked right down at him and he just filled out the checkbook just as calmly and wrote his check out and handed it to him.

In the lower Mississippi River, in particular, there was a time when pilots regularly risked being shot at by shantyboaters. While pilots could understand the dismay of disturbed shantyboaters, they naturally enough disliked being shot at. Captain William Tippitt recalled the shantyboaters down at St. James Bayou.

There was always five or six shantyboats in there. So we was comin' down there one trip and it was a pretty fair stage of water, and I decided to steer the darn thing. Well, that first shantyboat I passed—'course that boat runnin', she threw a pretty good swell behind her—that old gal run out on the back end with a shotgun. I know why she done it, 'cause I was really shakin' 'em up. She put two bullet holes through the pilothouse, and we got on farther down, and a man, he come out and he put a couple of bullets through the pilothouse windows. But I done squatted down behind the bulkhead, so it didn't bother me none.

Captain Forrest Harrison of Memphis was foreman on the Corps of Engineers dredge *Omega* up in Wolf River. "There was hundreds of shantyboats in the Wolf River . . . all the way up there. . . . When you got ready to change

---

[2] "Texas" refers to the Texas deck located atop the skylight roof. The Texas deck staterooms served as crew's quarters. On the roof of the Texas deck was the pilothouse.

your swingin' wire ahead, you'd have to move the shantyboat . . . any time of the night. And they're in there sleepin'. You didn't know whether they had a gun on you or not." On one job, he heard an old woman hollering over on the bank. "Tell Uncle Sam . . . your pipeline broke in two up here, and it's warshin' my garden away"; the boat's captain paid her the next day for damages done to her garden. But in another instance, Captain Harrison frustrated the decidedly combustible intentions of a firey shantyboater.

I was over here on the White River with that 2518. And that was a makeshift rig ever there was. But I got orders to go down Poverty Point. . . . They told me to go down there and do a little leadin'. . . . I just ran down there, looked the situation over. Gonna go down there the next mornin'. I had that Johnson 24 horsepower on that skiff. I was really goin'!

And I saw a shantyboat there [layin' against] a sandbar. [If it's] up against the bank, then it's not so bad, but on a sandbar, them waves just keep punchin' him up there to get him high and dry. I saw him, and I knew what was about to happen. I saw him run out on the front end of his shantyboat. I reached back there and I cut her down and she just "chug, chug, chug, chug, chug, chug." And he had his shotgun in his hand. "Chug, chug, chug, chug." I wasn't makin' a ripple. I eased on by him.

When I got down there even with him, I still was just barely "chug, chug, chug, chug." He had that shotgun. He was so mad he didn't get to shoot at me, he turned around and killed his dog right on the sand-bar! . . . I hadn't molested him enough to shoot me. So he just shot his dog! . . . That's the truth ever I told in my life. [Corps Collection]

In the course of his daily work life, then, a river pilot faces the boredom of long, lonely hours in the wheelhouse, the responsibility of lives and cargo, and the frequent hazards that are "part of the operation." If a pilot is "out of shape" in approaching a bridge, that is a tight spot. If an onshore wind comes up at a lock, that is a tight spot. If high water and swift current combine to break up a tow, that is a tight spot. There are countless tight spots, and many pilots develop idiosyncratic, usually nonverbal, mannerisms to help them cope with these tense moments. Frank Fugina described two pilots "known up and down the Mississippi" for their peculiar habits.

"Cherokee Charley," when towing a raft through a drawbridge, used to sit on a chair back of the pilotwheel, steer the raft with the "midship nigger," cross his legs, light his pipe, and then pull small tufts of hair from his head.

He was very calm in other respects and a first class pilot. While running a bridge, another pilot would pull the large pilotwheel to starboard or port, [right or left] with all his strength, and in doing so the rear part of his anatomy protruded through the pilothouse window.[3] [*Lore and Lure*, p. 66]

Captain Oren Russell says that pilots get angry at themselves for getting into the predicament in the first place. He knew one old captain who would always pat the boat and say, "You know my wife wouldn't like it if you'd get in a jam." Another pilot would get so upset, he would "lose his dinner—right overboard."

I worked with a guy on the Mississippi Valley Barge Lines that walked the pilothouse . . . the whole watch. . . . I called him "Prancin' Ed." I said, "Ed, you is the passingest man I ever seen in my life." "Well, I can't stand still." Back'ards and for'ards. Do it for six hours. [Captain Oren Russell]

I've watched 'em do everything. Like one captain, he used to bite his pipe in half, and it would drop over the floor. . . . He'd take that pipe—I don't know how many times it was put back together till it finally got so short, you know. [Captain Arthur McArthur]

Sometimes the action is overt, like "singing at the top of their lungs" or clearing the throat; sometimes it's quiet and unobtrusive.

I used to know one fellow when he was about to gin a lock or something, there was a lot of water running, and it would be critical, or run out a bridge span, and he would—he smoked a pipe—and he would turn around and set the pipe down very deliberately on the stoving. . . . When he put that pipe down, he was going to work. There was nothing said, but you knew when he did that, that was his indication. I asked a pilot one time, I said, "What do I do?" "Oh," he said, "You're easy . . . all you have to do is just watch your Adam's apple." [Captain Fred Way, Jr.]

Captain Lester "Whitey" Schickling carried a small rock in his pocket. Whenever he would get in a spot, he would stick his hand in his pocket and

---

[3] Captain Allen Fiedler explains the term "midship nigger": "A 'nigger' is a steam capstan, and that was out on the forecastle, as a capstan. That used to tighten their lines up, see, and they used to call that the 'nigger' because years ago the niggers used to have poles, and that used to winch and tighten the lines up. . . . And they used to have poles in there, and they used to walk around and tighten these lines up. Then afterwards they got steam. That was called a 'nigger.' So there always had to be one guy to be a nigger runner to turn the valve with steam on and everything."

start working his version of the Greek worry beads. Schickling had worn the rock smooth in his decades of piloting.

Certain pilots performed an unconscious pantomime:

I knew of a pilot that would start takin' his clothes off easily. He'd start takin'—first'd come his tie, then his shirt, then his undershirt, suspenders. I never saw him get down to his unmentionables, but he was gettin' pretty close that way, you know, especially when he was gonna flank a bend or somethin' like that with a towboat.[4]

But a lot of people react in different ways; another pilot sang to hisself. He'd start singin' . . . gettin' in a tight place, runnin' bridges, somethin' like that. Take right there at Louisville, the bridges—three or four bridges in a row—and you have to line up the boat perfectly with those bridges. Sort of have to dot an i. And these fellows would have to start makin' preparation to do that, oh, my, up above Towhead Island, to line up for the Big Four Bridge. [Captain "Doc" Hawley]

Another pilot was less discrete:

Yeah, I worked for one pilot . . . if he ever got in a tight spot, he wore his britches kind of loose anyway, and they'd just keep slidin' down and he would not pull 'em up until he got out of that tight spot, and I've seen 'em pretty near down to his ankles. . . . I think they had thirty barges on the *Frieda Barta*, and he had got so close you could have stepped off the stern of the boat onto the bank, and his britches was way down. He got out to where he wasn't in trouble no more—he pulled 'em back up. [Captain Larry Ritchie]

Captain Francis "Dusty" Walters offered a reenactment of one old pilot's choreography.

This man had been a packet-boat pilot. He always came on watch with those white work gloves. . . . He wouldn't touch one of those levers unless he had his gloves on. I have to demonstrate this. . . . He'd be standing there. . . . He was highly nervous but rather than shaking all over, he just made peculiar movements. He'd be steering down the bend and all of a sudden he'd get down . . . look right over the top of the indicator bar.

Squat down. And then he can't get up and he'd look over sideways and if

---

[4] A similar story appears in William Heckman, *Steamboating, Sixty-Five Years on Missouri Rivers* (Kansas City, 1950), p. 60.

he looked then, he'd think—did he ever see this place before? And he . . . moved the wheel faster. He'd jump up—what did he do that for?—then he'd come down to the bridge and back up again on the bridge. . . . Stop it and back it up and then he'd put her on slow bell. Then he'd get the rudders goin' straight—exactly straight—and then he'd get down at the end of the steering lever. . . . He'd act like that was a telescope almost. Get down just above, look at that bridge. Then he'd move over to his other lever. . . . And he'd make all sorts of peculiar motions.

Captain "Shorty" Williams, too, demonstrated the gymnastics he had observed.

I was with one fella that would, he'd be standin' in between the handles, and as he got closer to trouble, he'd keep spreadin' out till he was almost down on the deck! [Demonstrates the splits.]
    And Captain Hunter used to wheeze—he would wheeze and his knuckles would turn white on the handles, he'd squeeze the handles so hard. And he was not a nervous man.

When one is in a tight spot, it is not a time for conversation—though some captains talk to the boat, take to swearing, or pray for deliverance.

I've seen old Harry get up there: "Come on, baby, come on, baby." And he climbed that wheel till . . . he had the wheel down so hard he couldn't get another inch of slack out of her [Captain William Tippitt]

I remember the time my daddy got off and he got another fella that was a pretty good pilot, considered, but he 'as awful bad 'bout the swearin' and gettin' in a tight place. . . . He'd kick the windows out of the pilothouse. Now that's the truth! 'Course he didn't do that all the time. . . . If we happen to hit a bad shoal or something like that. [Captain Harris Underwood]

I know one fella, Captain Lancaster, Mark Lancaster. He was on the Tri-City boats when I was contact pilot, you know. And he got stuck above 5-A [lock] there, and he said, "The Lord put her on," he said, "the Lord'll take her off!" So he went to bed. [Laughs.] [Captain Allen Fiedler]

I do remember one time that was when I really got excited—more excited that time than I ever remember doin' before. And, 'course, I always had a standby, and when it got so tight, I always had to call on the Lord—and He brought me through every time. And one time, I'as goin' down the river and had a bunch of empty barges. . . . When we got down to the [Fort Madison] bridge, they was no protection at all in a mile space, or maybe more. . . . That shear fence had been taken out to be repaired. Somebody had busted it out and you couldn't run that side a'tal, 'cause nothing but the bare pier to hit.

So I had to run the side that's very seldom used. . . . I went down there, and I'as givin' her all she had. . . . There was two men out on the tow and they seen that one barge was clear over in there—was gettin' down pretty close, and then they both run out on the front end of the barge and grabbed the timberhead and hung on to it. . . . They knew if I hit, they'd be something solid to hold to. And when they did that, I really began to get excited. And I kep' wantin' to pull her over, you know, and something kep' tellin' me, "not yet, not yet—don't pull her over yet!"

Well, I was standing' there between those doggone levers, and my hands got to goin' like this [shaking] and I shoved back, and I says, "Lord, I've got to have some help. Clear my head and steady my hand." As soon as that—just at the snap of a finger—I was calm, everything clear.

QUESTION: You went right through?

BOYD: Yeah. Now, that is one instant answer to a prayer! . . . And finally, the word came, "NOW," just as plain as if it was spoken, and I pulled her hard down. [Captain Roy Boyd]

In high water there are two eddies—point eddy and the bend eddy. And the current streak comes right around like a fish hook. And you either flank that thing or you stay right in that current streak; if you hit either one of those eddies, you will start running into that eddy and turn off. Maybe hit the bank . . . or whatever.

This guy steered around this point. So, roof captain, he's sitting back there on the bench. This guy's from New Orleans and he's always in a hurry to get to the cities. . . . He gets that bend eddy, ya see, and it gets bigger and bigger, see he's slidin'. . . . Well, in a slide like that you get in that bend eddy, you have all that current hittin' down on this side, see. You just go right on to it.

He looks down there at that thing and turns around to old roof captain, says, "Captain, it doesn't look like it is going to make it." The captain looked up—and they didn't like each other—"Nope, it doesn't." See he wants to get the captain involved or try to get him to say one thing to him

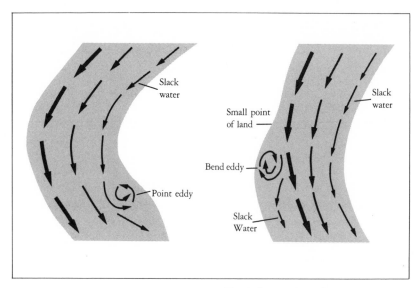

EDDIES
The heavier arrows depict the faster current.

The slack water is good running upstream, but watch out for the place where it ends!

about it so as to say, "Well, it wasn't all my fault. It was his fault too." The captain knew that. I knew it.

The pilot got down there a little closer and he said, "Captain, I just don't know what to do here now; it looks like we're going to hit that bluff. What do you think I should do?" He had to give him an answer then. So the captain got up, and looked up at him, and says, "Well, if I were you, I'd get down on my knees and pray to Jesus Christ to move that bluff back about a half a mile!" [Laughs.] That guy 'bout had a fit!" He knocked the hell out of it! [Captain Francis Walters]

Sometimes these efforts to calm oneself—both conscious and unconscious—don't avert the collision or tow breakup or grounding. The aftermath is also the stuff stories are made of.

Jo [Hawthorne] had not ran Burlington bridge for a long while and they had filled in considerably just above the bridge and as I remember it instead of hugging the Iowa shore the bow of the raft struck out for Illinois and Jo then decided to tow for the outer span but just as he got under good headway the current began to swing the bow back to the Iowa shore and we struck the pier with one corner of the raft and by the time we got the boat loose and the lines quit popping and the windlass poles settled back down, there came that pier out on the opposite corner of the stern just going diagonally through the raft.

As we were all rushing around after brail lines, oars, etc., Jo came walking down to the forecastle with his carpet slippers on and looking as unconcerned as though he was just out of a Pullman diner.

"Well, boys, I give her a good one, didn't I?" and he walked back up in the pilothouse and we went to tying up the fragments. [Burlington *Post*, April 8, 1916]

Well, I heard one story about an old-timer, Captain Billy Mills. And now, he was really an old-timer, 'cause he wasn't here very long after I started. . . . When they first built the Dresback Lock, he was going up there with the Federal Barge Line tow, and he saw that he was in too close, and couldn't steer out, and couldn't get her stopped. But he was backin' her for all he was worth. I believe this was on the *Patrick J. Hurley*. And, just before he hit it, he said, "There goes my reputation for being a fancy pilot!" And it was too. He knocked the whole end of the wall down! [Captain "Shorty" Williams]

THE TRAUMATIC

In the early days of steamboating, the average age of a prime vessel was said to be about five years. Between 1823 and 1863, 360 boats were listed in service on the upper Mississippi. Of those 360, seventy-three were lost by accidents. George Merrick recorded the cause of those losses: thirty-two snagged and sunk, sixteen burned, ten sunk by ice, five stove in by hitting rocks and sunk, three sunk by striking bridges, three sunk by Confederate batteries, two lost from boiler explosions, one torn to pieces by a tornado, and one struck a wreck of another boat and sank on top of the first wreck.[5] Next to snags, fire was the most potent enemy of steamboat property, and the May 17, 1849, fire at the St. Louis wharf was the most disastrous of all such calamities. According to Merrick in *Old Times* (pp. 233–34), it began on the steamer *White Cloud* and spread from boat to boat until the entire shoreline was ablaze; buildings were ignited, and eventually the main business portion of the city was destroyed before the fire could be contained. Damage to marine equipment alone

[5] George Bryan Merrick, *Old Times*, p. 231. Also cited in Herbert Quick and Edward Quick, *Mississippi Steamboatin'*, p. 323.

amounted to $440,000 in cargo and boats—twenty-three steamboats, three barges, one small boat. In *Life on the Mississippi*, (chapter 20), Mark Twain describes firsthand the explosion and burning aftermath of the *Pennsylvania*, on which his brother Henry Clemens was killed. He graphically recreates images of those who died by inhaling the steam, people flung great distances by the force of the explosion, victims suffering the dreadful tortures of scalding, passengers and crewmen trapped until finally "the flames ended [their] miseries."

Even though steel hulls and government improvements have effectively eliminated the danger of snags in the river, major collisions, fires, and explosions can still be the riverman's undoing. And natural disasters still take their toll. Some pilots have worked on the river for forty or fifty years with no major traumatic incidents, but others have survived explosions or weathered nature's most dramatic spectacles. Nearly all have lost some friends to drownings or accidents.

Captain Gale Justice survived at least four river accidents during his long river career, which began when he "jumped away from school" and ran away to the river in 1890.[6] In 1903, Justice ran a little packet called the *Genevieve*.

It was a runner from Matamoras to Sistersville. Five trips a day. Carrying passengers, and one in particular, one trip there was a bunch of WCTU [Women's Christian Temperance Union] women wanted to have a meeting in Sistersville late in the evening, you know. They got me in the notion to take and bring them up to Sistersville and take them back. So I thought it was all right, and I made the trip with them, and come back up in port and tied up and pumped the boat out and went to bed. Went to sleep, and the first thing I knowed, why the river rolled me out of bed. . . . The boat sank, it rolled over and threw me out of bed.

In January 1904, Justice ended up in the water again when he jumped off the *Ruth* onto a cake of ice and it sank with him. In 1902 he was off duty and asleep on the *Belle McGowan* when the boat capsized. He got out just in time to grab hold of a ladder that floated from the roof. A chambermaid also floating in the river grabbed the ladder as well, and both floated down the Ohio until they were rescued by a towboat. Then in 1930 the boiler blew up on the *Martha*, and Justice was severely burned.

Yeah, I was burned all over. And it blowed me in the river. It blowed the

[6] Captain Justice was 102 years old when I talked with him.

clothes off me. Burnt me all over and I had no hair on my head, no eye winkers or anything, and there was ice in the river just about . . . like windy glass. And I had to swim . . . oh, a hunderd yards to break that thin ice and swim to get ashore through that ice.

And I got out of there and went in the hospital on the second day of November . . . and I was in there until the twenty-second day of June. . . . I was the only one who was burnt bad. The pilot got in the pilothouse. He ran back and jumped over the stern end of the boat, over the wheel into the river, and swum ashore. . . . Yeah, and two deckhands they got life floats and swum ashore all on them. . . .

They all claimed I'd never go back to the river. I got burnt there in November and went back to the river in August.

In one river family, history repeated itself. The elder Captain Charles White's father had a dry wit and a narrow escape. Mrs. Leona White remembers her father-in-law's story:

He was telling about one time when he was out . . . and they were layin' at Muscatine, Iowa. Their boat was tied up there, and it caught on fire! In the middle of the night! And the engineer rousted him out of bed, and of course, they didn't have any lights, it was all lamps, and I guess he couldn't find his clothes. So the engineer give him a pair of his trousers. . . . And there was a lot of people on the bank, you know. They were watching the fire, the smoke comin' out. . . . Everybody was out, but the captain. And they said, "Oh, the captain is the last one to leave the boat." Grandpa says, "Just because I couldn't find my pants!"

Years later, Captain White had two dramatic experiences himself, though he did at least salvage his own trousers. One time, he was asleep when the boat hit a bridge pier and everyone had to scramble onto the bank. In retrospect, however, he considered the burning of the *Weathers* in 1970 to be the only bad accident he was involved in.

We were southbound. We just left the Keokuk Lock . . . just before midnight. And the pilot was up already, some of the deckhands had called him to go on watch at midnight. He hollered up the stairway, "The engine room's on fire!" So I rang the emergency alarm, but everybody was up— they'd called already, the watches. Everybody was up but the cook. She didn't have to get up until 4:30 or 5:00 o'clock.

So there wasn't a thing they could do down there. The flames were so bad you couldn't get anywheres near 'em. So I set the boat backing full astern, and stopped the headway, and we got everybody out on the barges. I lost all my clothes—my watch, my binoculars, oh, practically everything but what I had on. And the boat and tow floated over on the Warsaw side and hit the bank and laid there, but she was full, just blazing. Just nothing but fire all over, and so we had one barge, right next to the boat, loaded with linseed oil, and I was afraid that load would catch fire. The wind happened to be blowin' down river; I had the crew get the fire axes and chop the boat loose. But in the meantime, there was a little dredging outfit waiting for me to come out of the lock up there at Keokuk, and they had two tugs pushing that little dredge, and they had radios on there and they heard me call for help.

They come on down there, and when he chopped the boat loose from the barges, we got ahold of the back end, threw a line or a wire, caught one of the cavels, and pulled the boat out in the middle of the river and turned her loose and let her float. Because right there where she was layin', there was grain elevators, big oil-storage tank. . . . And I'as afraid that would catch fire. . . . And it floated on down behind an island and finished burning there.

Empty barges, particularly gas barges, are more dangerous than loaded ones. Captain "Rip" Ware has a healthy respect for "empties." One trip he had four empties and a 1,200-horsepower boat.

The wind was blowin' so hard, the water was so high and so swift that I aimed at one side of that bridge and went down the other side, and when I got through with it, I had two Camel cigarettes burnin' down and I was lightin' the third.

QUESTION: Have you ever been hurt in a boat accident?

WARE: Just been scared a lot. I've seen a time when the pain would start right there at the end of my tailbone and nearly knock the top of my head off. Now you know that was a pain, wasn't it? That was a strain. . . . Look, when you foolin' with them gasoline barges, you jest foolin' with you might say atomic bombs. Empty, you know. I wasn't near as scared when they were loaded as I was when they was empty. 'Cause a loaded barge'll burn and an empty barge blows.

QUESTION: You said you saw an ether barge blow up once.

WARE: I was about ten miles away from it, across the corn. Actually, around the river where . . . I couldn't see it, but I heard it and saw the glare. I was

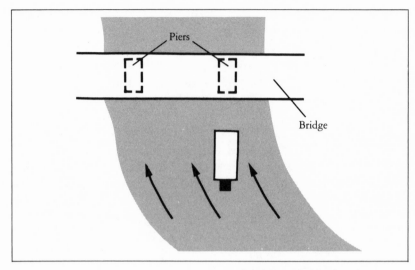

NAVIGATING A BRIDGE
Depending on the set of the current, the boat is pointed away from the current to differing degrees, keeping the boat to the right of the channel as far as possible. To the uninitiated, it looks as if the boat will run directly into the pier, but the current then pushes against the load and the boat goes between the piers. Knowing where to point the boat, how swift the current is running, and how much clearance one needs—that's where the piloting comes in.

that far ahead of it. And it lit up the sky so right there above Caruthersville, where I sit, that I could read a newspaper in the pilothouse.

Certain bridges are recurrent trouble spots because of the width of spans, the difficulty of lining up to run it, or the current. One of the worst bridge accidents occurred on March 4, 1948, when the *Natchez* hit the Greenville, Mississippi, bridge. Fourteen crewmen were rescued, twelve drowned.

I lost a lot of good friends there on that boat. See, I'd worked with a lot of those people. I had a friend in the barge line who was on leave of absence actually . . . What happened was, above the bridge the reeds moved in and a big eddy formed up there, so when she went up there that eddy caught her and slung her into the bank. He had a bunch of gas barges. So she hit the bank and it broke the tow up. So the barges topped on around and he [captain] was lookin' for the barges and he was broadside comin' down on the bridge. . . . They hit the bridge pier broadside and she flipped over. Well, some of the messboys and things on there, I think, one of them dove into the river and he dove right into the pier and broke his dern neck. [Captain Arthur McArthur]

The Vicksburg bridge has also taken its toll in damages and lives since it was built in 1927.

Well, it's just the way the current is. Pilots years ago fought to not have them put this bridge here; they wanted it put on down the river further . . . up in the turn here where there'd be a straightaway where they could come. . . . But they didn't listen to the pilots, you know, and so they went on anyhow and they usually—lot of times, they go on and have these hearings and it's useless sometimes when they make up their minds where they're gonna put a bridge. See, if they had a put it down here, there'd a been more of a straightaway comin' around that point up there in the delta. . . .

It's hard, kinda, to flank, too; they have the eddies and things up in there that work. . . . So it's been hit by most all the pilots there years ago; they'd hit that sucker. You heard about one pilot, he was comin' down the river with his tow, and he come around there and he hit the bridge and he scattered the barges and sank one of 'em. He worked for the Federal Barge Line. They fired him. When he got to New Orleans, he told his wife he didn't have any job, he got fired, and she said, "Why?" He said, "Well, just get in the car and I'll show you."

So . . . he drove on up to Vicksburg here and he got up on top of the hill and he said, "You see that pier there?" She said, "Yeah." And he said, "You see that pier out there?" And she said, "Yeah." He said, "Well, I hit that pier out there; I was supposed to go between those two piers." And she said, "Well, anybody'd miss a hole that big, they oughta fire him." [Captain McArthur]

The vertical height of a bridge may also create problems for the pilot. If bridges are too low to permit boat passage, usually they are equipped either with swing bridges or hydraulic lifts operated by attendants who monitor boat traffic (and often rail traffic). Or the pilothouse of some boats can be lowered to allow clearance. Captain Ed Winford vividly recalls his encounter with a bridge on the Illinois River.

Well, I was workin' for Captain Bill Ripley on the *Martin*. The *Martin* was a little single-screw boat, 1,200 horsepower, nice little boat. Had two-piece unit tow, each two hundred and forty feet long, and they had a small refinery. . . . We went up through the island and loaded out two loads and laid up. About midnight I came on watch leavin' out, and the *Martin* had an up-and-down pilothouse, a greaserack pilothouse—just like a grease rack in a service station, same thing—sits on a big cylinder about a foot in diameter and maybe eighteen inches, this thing's bolted on. There's a lot of electrical wires danglin' underneath the stack where they go up and down with the pilothouse. And we started out, and there were some low bridges about a mile below the refinery. And I wasn't going too fast; I had about half a head. I got pretty close to the bridge—now, the pilothouse was about halfway down, and I figured that would clear the bridge 'cause the pilothouse on this boat, it was slow operation lettin' it up and lettin' it down. (A lot of 'em you just hit that lever and the pilot house just drops, zip, or comes right on up.) The *Martin* didn't do that. . . . Well, it's like on the expressway, you come to one of those overpasses and think, "Well, I've got plenty of clearance." Well, I got within about a hundred feet of it and it didn't look right. "Oh, oh, I better let this thing down." I reached over and hit that little knob; somethin' happened, it didn't start down like it should. And this thing went on just like a truck hittin' one of these overpasses and not makin' it. . . . We had two levers and I was sittin' between 'em in a chair—that pilothouse just laid back on top of the roof of the boat and you could hear those bolts just like all hell breakin' loose down there.

And electric wires were lettin' go and fire was flashin' and I didn't have time to get scared. I just think about the next stage; that pilothouse could roll off into the canal and drown me or I could'a been injured for life. And the radio sittin' in the corner, they were lettin' go and rollin' all around. Here I was—when it wound up, I was layin' flat on my back on that back part of the pilothouse . . . still holdin' those levers. . . .

I hollered down to a deckhand to go tell the engineer to stop the engine and wake the captain up—that was the first thing you do, wake the captain up when something like that happens. Hell, he's probably had experience before in things like that. Now that happens every year up there, some pilothouse mechanism fails to operate or the fella forgets. . . . But they'd been talkin' about gettin' a new pilothouse ever since I'd been on that boat. So I got 'em a new pilothouse!

Many years after the event, Captain Winford chuckled as he told that story, just as Captain McArthur did when he told a story he had heard from an old packet-boat man, Captain Elmer Good, who had worked in the days when snags were the prime culprits.

He was pilot on a boat . . . and they hit a snag up there at Cottonwood Point, Missouri, and the boat started sinkin'. They had a load of cotton on her, and it was on the way down the river to New Orleans. . . . They didn't have time to get her to the bank. And he said he and Captain Al Smith — Al Smith was mate on her — went out on a bale of cotton and they had 'em a fifth of whiskey. Said they made sure they got that fifth of whiskey, you know, off of her before she sank so it could keep 'em warm. The river was up pretty good, so the boat sank. Cotton was all over the river and bales of cotton floatin'. It finally got logged and went on down. He said that's what they went out on — a bale of cotton and a fifth of whiskey!

Occasionally, a single trip will be plagued with multiple difficulties that leave a pilot shaking his head in wonderment. Captain Harris Underwood recounted one such mobile disaster that started on the *James N. Triggs* in March of 1922. It was his brother Paul's first trip as captain, and they were going down to a place called Bobo's Incline on Sand Mountain. Captain Harris Underwood was pilot; when they neared Gondola, Alabama, "it set into raining." He fought the rain, wind, thunder, and lightning until watch at midnight and then, unable to sleep because of the excitement, heard the commotion in the predawn hours. The wind caught the boat "in the mid-ship and just blowed that thing all the way around."

It did finally get her turned around and it had a barge on the side, and rode around to the . . . righthand bank goin' down, and just picked 'er up, all at once, and knocked 'er right into the bank, and the hull, of course, hit the bank first! And when it did that . . . it 'as such a heavy wind — why she hit that bank, the hull of 'er just stopped, just like that [bangs hand down], and the top of 'er . . . the pilothouse and the cabin there on the top deck just fell right down in the middle. It happened to be, we only had about four passengers on there and they 'as in their room, but they got up pretty quick, as well as I did.

Didn't hit anybody. . . . Just lucky that they 'as sittin' on the back. And I had my pilot license — I had just had 'em sent to get renewed some week or two before that — and I had 'em up on the wall, where they 'as supposed to be. . . . Next morning when it got daylight, and all, I looked around there and I couldn't see 'em nowhere. They 'as just — wondering what I'd done with 'em. I didn't have no idee. But, anyhow, the wind had calmed down enough to where everybody could kinda get out on the bank if they wanted to and look around, 'cause they'd blowed a lot of stuff like that off in the bank — the eatin' tools, forks and knives and things like that.

I got out there, myself, lookin' around after a period of time, and I saw them things. Now, they hadn't even got stretched out after they'd sent 'em to me from Nashville. They hadn't gotten really stretched out—they'd come in an envelope, and I found those things . . . and there's my license out there, and the frames was still in the cabin deck!

The wind-wrecked *Triggs* was, however, only the first problem on this memorable trip. The Captains Underwood went on to Chattanooga, secured another boat, loaded up at Joe Wheeler Dam, and came back up on a rising river.

We had another pilot down there, and he'as running up close to the bank, and you see the smoke comin' out of that cornfield down there and knew pretty well what it was. So they slowed down little bit and got I don't know how many gallons of liquor down there. . . . So we come on up to Decatur again. We stopped there, and one of the niggers on the boat, he'd been up town, hisself, and got a few drinks, and he come back down there and he started raisin' a racket, little bit. He jumped on Paul out there, and I just happened to be comin' by when they started right close to where they were, and I reached down and got that shovel and hit him across the head and knocked him down. He liked to never got up.

Well, then after we got up to Decatur, somebody'd reported Paul in for lettin' them get that whiskey down there. . . . Well, before daylight, why they'd come down there and got him out of bed and told him he'as under arrest.

After a friend posted bond for him, Paul was released and they went about their business—which included salvaging the disabled *Triggs*. Still on the second boat, they took the *Triggs* in tow by putting her on the side and using the engines of the healthy boat to push them both. They navigated both boats through Hillsborough Lock and were running along fine—until, that is, they hit that island and sank the lumber barge ahead of them. "But we brought the other boats on in, and he [Paul] had an awful lot of that, being his first trip on there as a captain. It was quite a trip!"

Besides accidents resulting from explosions, bridge collisions, fire, equipment failure, hard groundings, and the like, a pilot's log records numerous instances of natural disasters as well—cyclones, storms, blizzards, and floods. One of the most familiar old-time cyclone stories involved the *Alexander Mitchell*. She was already an unlucky boat—"If there was anything in the river or over the river to hit, she hit it. When there were no snags, she would bump an island or climb a tree" (Burlington *Post*, October 18, 1913). The pious owner, Commodore William Davidson, allowed no gambling, dancing, or other diversions not sanctioned by the Methodists aboard his boats—especially on Sunday. However, against the rules of God and Commodore Davidson, the boat's captain, William Laughton, finally yielded to the persistent requests of the passengers and allowed dancing on Sunday, May 7, 1872. Even before the *Alexander Mitchell* had taken the two hundred excursionists aboard at LaCrosse, Wisconsin, she had run into weather trouble; in trying to run the Hastings bridge she had been struck by a squall and thrown against the bridge abutment, tearing off a portion of the starboard guard. The unrestrained passengers danced all the way to Lansing and then chartered the boat for a run back to Victory—dancing all the way. Captain Fisher, pilot on the *Mitchell* and a very religious man himself, finished the tale:

> Leaving them at Victory we proceeded on our way down the river. When about twelve miles above Dubuque, a little below Wells' Landing, at three o'clock Monday morning, we were struck by a cyclone. We lost both chimneys, the pilothouse was unroofed, and part of the hurricane deck on the port side was blown off. Mr. Trudell, the mate, was on watch, and standing on the roof by the big bell. He was blown off, and landed on shore a quarter of a mile away, but sustained no serious injuries. The port lifeboat was blown a mile and a half into the country. Following so soon after the Sunday dancing, I have always felt that there was some connection between the two.[7]

The Commodore is said to have been even more emphatic when he heard the news: "You see, that's what comes of dancing!"

Storms can come up quickly and strand a boat in midstream—vulnerable to the lashings of nature's blustery fury. Captain McArthur described the scene of one such storm.

> We were goin' down river one afternoon with all this bunch out of the commission office on a low-water inspection trip. It was in July. . . . 'Course, hot and muggy it was. . . . But I looked out across, the sky was all pink. And I said, "Man, I tell ya one thing, I don't like the way that sky looks down there." John [his partner] said, "Naw, it don't look good." Little while, the wind come up. I said, "What was that went across the head of the boat? Was that some corn shucks?" "No, that was a fish!" He got up and he took off, see. I said, "Call Captain [Skinny] Lindsey and tell him I

[7] Merrick, *Old Times*, pp. 122–23. Accounts of this *Alexander Mitchell* tale can also be found in the Burlington *Post*, October 18, 1913; Quick and Quick, *Mississippi Steamboatin'*, pp. 126–27; and Mildred L. Hartsough, *From Canoe to Steel Barge*, p. 138.

think we'd better get into the bank awhile. It looks like we're gonna be hit by a heck of a storm." Kind of black and pink, you know, that sky.

So Skinny come on up. I said, "Captain, I think we'd better pull into the bank. It looks like we're gonna have a heck of a storm comin' up." "Ah, it ain't gonna be nothin' but a little rain! Keep on goin'." I said, "I don't know, I think we oughta get landed." "Ah, keep on goin'." So he's standin' around up there, and 'fore a little bit, why she started blowin' some more, and I said, "Still think we oughta go in and land." "Ah, not gonna be nothin' but a little rain."

So they started shuttin' all the glasses up, and that thing started hittin' us, and you couldn't see nothin', and that wind was a blowin' and a carryin' on and all I could see was the flag out there, you know. And I put the rudder over hard tryin' to hold her hard to the wind, see. I couldn't see nothin' else and the radar was blacked out—you know what happens in a rainstorm. And Skinny said, "Head her to the wind! Head her to the wind!" I said, "Head her to the wind? What you think I'm doin' with this rudder now? I can't catch up with her!"

That glass was on the side loose and they were all standin' there, about twelve of 'em, tryin' to hold it in. So Frank Fir grabbed life preservers and started a givin' 'em around. . . . Yeah, I said, "Open that door back there." And the captain kep' sayin', "Head her to the wind! Head her to the wind!" I said, "Open that back door!" And . . . I said, "Here, hold her." I told the captain, I said, "You head her to the wind!" And I kicked that back door open and about that time, the aftermast left her, and that lifeboat was just pickin' up and down, slammin' herself, and I looked out—we were in a trough, in the eye of that thing. I told the captain, I said, "You know we're in the eye of a storm? We're in a gully and we're spinnin'." . . . Yeah, we were spinnin' just like that [illustrates a whirlpool].

When the storm had passed over, they checked the damages and accounted for all crew members. One in particular, Frenchy, had held on for the duration. "He was wrapped around that timberhead on the head of the boat and it took us thirty minutes to massage him loose. He got froze around it!"

Those surprised by the Armistice Day blizzard in the upper Mississippi could enjoy no ribald ribbing when it had passed. November 11, 1940, started out to be an unusually mild day in the northland, with a warm sun sending temperatures into the sixties and even seventies in some areas. About twenty-eight people died in the Minnesota-Iowa region and scores of others suffered from frostbite and exposure when the temperatures plummeted and the blizzard raged. Duck hunters in light clothing were caught in their blinds unable to make their way back to solid shore. At least two of them froze to death, literally standing in their tracks. "They froze right quick — they froze so fast they couldn't fall over." Captain Joe Toomey of Brownsville, Minnesota, paddled across the river in his boat the next morning searching for a missing LaCrosse man. The man had survived by lying under his overturned boat with his dog. Captain Allen Fiedler had been duck hunting himself but made it home and then got orders to go out on rescue duty. Two other pilots were on boats in the river when the blizzard hit. Captain Roy Boyd remembers getting as far up as the Burlington Lock. They could only open one lock gate because all the launches were in the lock and the storm, calmed for a while, had come up again.

And it was blowin' right straight up the river into the lock, and they couldn't open that gate because it had sunk all those launches and stuff they had in there. So we had to break up our two and slip 'em in one at a time to get 'em in there. . . . 'Course we were all wore out — the terrible storm. But it turned cold so quick, it didn't make any ice in the river. . . . The river was warm. See, it was 65° in the morning that storm hit.

Captain "Shorty" Williams was on a brand-new boat named *Tri-Cities*.

Armistice Day we were goin' up the river below Lansing. Above Gutten-berg, in that area, and it was a real nice warm day. . . . But there was a pretty strong wind, and kind of from the east, as I remember. And long about four o'clock or so in the afternoon, we'as just coming out of Crooked Slough up there. . . . And that flag just hung right straight down for a little ways and all of a sudden just picked up a-goin' just the opposite way! Really kickin' it. And it was blowin' a gale in just a little while and started to snow.

And I wandered around goin' up the river, 'till I got to just below Lansing, and I tried to push up a little slough there, and . . . the boys got there with a lantern and got off and got two big stumps — put a line around each one — tyin' it off, and all this time, I'm bolted up as hard as I can with the engine. And as soon as I slacked off one of those engines, up came the stumps. So we moved back along side of that Lafayette Slough pier and they got about four or five cables with wires tied around the big concrete pier and there we held till . . . about eleven o'clock and broke loose. And we had quite a time finding it again.

Boy, it was snowin' and blowin', and those guys — there was ice clear over the header lines of an oil tow . . . and they had to chop out to tie onto the timberheads—chop out with an ax; it was freezin' that snow and water. And got down to five below zero that night.

The Armistice Day blizzard remains one of nature's bizarre anomalies, but floods are the periodic companions of river pilots. And for twentieth-century veterans, the granddaddies of the floods were in 1927 and 1937. Though, of course, these floods cost countless lives, caused millions of dollars in damages, and involved many pilots in long stints of dangerous relief and rescue duty, some of the experiences, at least in retrospect, illustrated either novel opportunities or occasions for whimsy. In the 1927 flood Captain William Tippitt nearly had a chance to perform services generally reserved for taxi drivers.

She [*Kankakee*] worked the Mississippi River from Cairo to what we call Dog Tooth Bend [about twenty miles below Cairo]. . . . And they hired me to be the pilot to go down. The flood was moving south then bad, so we went by Columbus, and the water was right to the top of the levee, just about a half inch sticking out. So we went by on the other side of the river so there would be no swell. We went on down to Hickman, and then they expected the levee to break someplace between Columbus and the bend at Island 8. And I went down at what we call St. James Bayou, and we tied up there that evening.

About eight o'clock the next morning, a man came riding down the levee and he just hightailed it on a mule, hollering they wanted us up at Dorena, the levee broke. . . . So we went on back up just above Hickman there. . . . I went up on the Kentucky side because I was afraid of the draw. I guess it breaks in with about nine hundred feet wide, and that water is like you see it on the ocean, you know, swells. That's the way it was rollin' through. There's a big batch of timber about a half a mile back. You could see it bowling, you know, bending it over. So I went about a mile above there, went across the river, and landed at the levee. Now there was people all on the levee, cattle and stuff; they was drivin' the cattle up to the levee. People was going to be takin' off. So we done got over and got landed. That crevasse had already increased to three quarters of a mile, and while we was over in that deep, I can look back and see that levee crumbling there and see the river going through there.

See it went through there and come at New Madrid—St. James Bayou is where it came out at. So we took those people over to Hickman on the high bluffs and unloaded them, and then we had orders to go to New Madrid.

They were evacuating New Madrid, so we went on down to New Madrid that night and tied up right there at the foot of the main street. . . . They all knew the water was comin'. . . . So about nine o'clock the next morning, why the water started rolling down that main street. And we was loadin' people—drizzly, rainy, cold. The captain said, we're only supposed to carry three hundred and there was six hundred or seven hundred on the levee then. I said, "You're goin' to have to take all them people . . . ten o'clock, and I told him, "You want to get to Hickman, we'd better get started." We had about, oh, about eleven hundred people already on that boat. The cabin was full.

This wasn't time for comfort. They was stacked in the engine room, boiler room, down in the hull—wherever we could get 'em. We had four [*sic*] women on there about to have babies. So we backed out and started up the river. . . . The river coming out of St. James Bayou was a torrent. You could see barns and houses and outhouses and things just come out there in this great big eddy out in the river. They went in that eddy and they disappeared and never come up. So I had to drop down about a half a mile, go across the river, and went around them on the Missouri shore.

Well, we got on the way good—there was no way in the world to feed them people or anything on there. And they were all in our rooms . . . you know, just put as many as they could in there. Old man came up, said, "Well, you're going to have to be a midwife on here. Got three women down there just about to have babies." I said, "Oh, wait a minute . . . you're captain on the boat." "Oh," [he] says, "you have to make the delivery. By God, I don't know nothing about it." I said, "What the hell do you think I know about it? I ain't had none yet!" We got into an argument pretty hot and heavy up there—four or five people up there, too. I said, "You go downstairs, take some of these people with you." I said, "Now doctors are not plentiful down there. You can go down there and you can find three or four women who are good midwives who would do that all the time."

So they went down and found 'em and cleared the place out in the dining room there so in case it did happen, got to have everything ready. . . . But the old man went down and that boat ran faster than she ever ran, and I got over against . . . wherever I could find some slack water. So we done telegraphed Hickman to have the ambulances down there while it was about to happen. I had asked the mate if we get there about 4:00 or 4:30, you know. . . . Well, we made it 4:15 and we landed there and of course the ambulances were sitting there and they rushed on there and got the women. They just got them to the hospital and three babies was born. And it was luck! [Laughs.][8]

Captain John Skidmore did rescue work in both the '27 and '37 floods.

I was on the *Minnesota*—that was the 1927 flood—I was still steersman. I think I'd had a pilot's assignment, and they took me off of it and put me back steerin'. But anyway, I never shall forget it, I was comin' on duty at twelve midnight right above Greenville, up at Mounds. And the pilot instructed me to go out and change the carbon in the searchlight; it burnt out. He said there's something wrong. He was backing the boat full astern. When I got the searchlight on and got it burning again, and he turned it over on the levee, you could see the levees just crumblin', goin' in the river and broken. We almost went through it. But anyway, we went on down to Greenville and tied off our tow down below Greenville and took a barge, which was three hundred feet long by forty-eight feet wide, we went up to Greenville.

We picked up about sixteen hundred flood refugees, people just lined up on the bank . . . some of 'em had their belongin's, maybe a dog or a cat, some of 'em. They were colored people and white people—it was pitiful. . . . We brought 'em down here to Vicksburg and put 'em off right down here at the old depot. And they took care of 'em out in the park; they put 'em in tents. This whole area was covered; that was the '27 flood.

In the '37 flood Skidmore met one reluctant refugee.

We went on up to right below Caruthersville, Island 18, and we went out to a house there—it was a two-story house, old farmhouse. And we went all around it in the motorboat, couldn't find anybody. We hollered. I think somebody said, "Hello." He was an old man upstairs; he was in the upper story. Now the water was up to the first story. But anyway, we asked him if he wanted anything. He said, "No." And we told him the river was gonna get to a certain stage and probably he couldn't get out. He said, "I been here a long, long time and these floods don't bother me at all." He said, "You boys wanta come on up?"

He had a ladder on the outside of the house and we went up there, and he

---

[8] For other eyewitness accounts of the flood of 1927, see Pete Daniel, *Deep'n As It Come: The 1927 Mississippi River Flood* (New York: Oxford University Press, 1977).

had a beard down to here, down to his stomach [laughs]. And I never shall forget it, he had a coupla dogs and a cat and two or three chickens in there. It was the most terrible lookin' thing you ever seen [laughs]. And we told him, we said, "It's gonna get high and how you gonna get out of here?" He said, "Well, I got a boat; I can get out." I said, "Where you gonna get any food?" He said, "I got plenty of food." And we fooled around there a little bit, saw he was all right, and told him we'd bring him some food. "No," he said, "I've seen these floods ever since I was a little boy, come up and go down, and never have got me yet." But he was a character. . . . He just stayed there.

And he had a little whiskey along, a little ole demijohn. He gave us all a good drink of whiskey, but only one. That's all we could have, one drink of whiskey. [Laughs.]

Captain Skidmore also remembers a grateful father.

We was doin' refugee work up at Tomato Landing, that's about half way between Memphis and Cairo. Yeah, I think it was in March. Well, anyway, the pilot and I went out in a motorboat to rescue people out of houses or maybe trees, somethin' like that. But we went to one house that the water hadn't got up in the house yet. We knocked on the door, and the man come to the door, and we told him who we were and that we had quarters for 'em about a mile away and asked him if he and his family would like to get out because the river was gonna continue to rise. And he said, "Yes."

Well, he came out, and his wife was carrying a little baby, and he was carryin' one. And we took 'em and put 'em aboard the quarterboats. Well, they was only just a few days old. Two boys, and they was nice-lookin' boys. I never shall forget 'em, they was big, husky kids. But anyway, about four or five months later—I forget the people's names—they wrote to the captain, the master of the *Minnesota*, I believe it was, and tole him that they'd named these two boys. One of 'em was Noah and one of 'em was Ark! That was for the flood of '37. [Laughs.]

Both regulated, orderly routines and unexpected, sometimes traumatic disruptions are the river pilot's daily partners as he works at his profession. He knows periods of isolation, tranquility, even monotony; he knows moments of intense excitement. The pressure of guiding large tows over long stretches of the inland waterways has caused many a pilot to suffer an early death by heart attack; the dangers have sent many others to watery graves. A pilot dares not grow complacent after a few uneventful trips; the next trip may present him with high water and swift current, or low water and probable groundings, or equipment failure that causes collision, or fires and explosions that threaten the lives of his crew. Yet, despite the long hours, critical responsibilities, and potential dangers, most pilots have loved their profession and thrived on the very challenges they face and the skills required. Their work still sets them apart from "the common herd."

River's so low I seen a catfish swimming upstream had a bull-frog going ahead of him taking soundings.

Ben Burman, *Look Down That Winding River*

Going to Minneapolis they put old dead crayfish, dead mice, and cockleburrs in my bed. That'd get you up in a hurry!

Captain Truman Hedrick

CHAPTER FOUR

Social Life on the Boat

Fred "Pinky" Hill (left) and John Skidmore, 1940

Among river people it is axiomatic that when a riverman is home, all he talks about is the river; when he is on the river, all he talks about is home. Because of the extended periods of time crew members spend together on the boat, and because many stay on the same boat for several months or years, it is not unusual for them to speak affectionately of "their" boat as if it were a second home. The crew can become a surrogate family — only in this family members are confined to a prescribed space with infrequent access to terra firma.[1] Working companions are also social companions. Although at least twelve hours of every twenty-four are devoted to working one's watches, and it can seem that working, eating, and sleeping take all of one's time, crew members do have chances to interact on a social, casual basis. When boats tied up more often, crew members entertained themselves by hunting or fishing. Though television viewing now dominates the activity in a towboat lounge, crewmen have traditionally played cards, shot craps, played dominoes, read, or listened to radio for relaxation. The more social aspects of life on the river can be seen in the interaction between boat people and bank people, the camaraderie between crews of two or more boats as heard via radio communications and revealed in the traditional impromptu races, and the relationship among crew members as they pass time by playing practical jokes, trying to keep pets, and telling endless stories of extraordinary boats, unusual animals, and colorful people.

In the packet boat days, there was significant social interaction between boat people and land people. Boats ran regular trips and answered hails from remote clearings along the bank. Fondly remembering his days as owner, captain, and

[1] This varies, of course, depending on what time period we mean. In the twenties and thirties, men might ride three months without a day off, but the boat would tie up more often — for fog, for loading and unloading, for fueling. Later, when days off became more regularized, the men had more time away, but now the boat almost never stops moving except to wait for lock passage.

pilot of the *Betsy Ann*, Captain Fred Way, Jr., emphasizes the difference between this social, friendly feeling of paddlewheel days and the isolation of the towboat era.

> When I started in we ran a regular trade, like Pittsburgh to Cincinnati, on a schedule, and when we were wakened up on Tuesday morning, you knew you were going to be in Cincinnati, and every town had its wharf boats and you got so that you knew all of the people and you were always landing in different places, going out and shaking somebody's hand.
>
> We often landed at farms and got to be so that you knew the neighbors around the towns, but you knew everybody in the houses up and down the river on both shores. It was a continual whistle fest because you couldn't pass these people without giving a wave. In order to attract attention, why you blew the whistle, and at nighttime you could go along three o'clock in the morning and there would be a light in the window, and you would be wondering who was sick, and how they're getting along, and so on. You miss this.
>
> So many people were involved, you know. I think I always liked people just as much as I liked boats. On a towboat you're isolated from all that. You just sit up there in the pilothouse and a couple of West Virginia guys sitting behind you, and if they don't have a guitar, why they want to turn on the radio and play and listen to hillbilly music. There's a big difference.

Two particular incidents illustrate what Captain Way means by personal involvement with people on the bank.

> We had a man who was paralyzed from the waist down, otherwise okay, and he wanted to go to a landing along the river bank. No civilization close by. We got there at some odd hour; well, he was adamant about getting off there. He said, "Don't worry, my folks know I'm comin'." We'd blown a big long whistle, but there was nobody there. So we left; we took a chair out of the cabin, took it down there, and left him sitting in that chair. Well, I never went off from anything in my life feeling more uncomfortable about it than that, but when we got back down there, why there was a kid standing there alongside the chair. We made a landing and got the chair back and forth and everything had gone okay. . . . That was probably a dollar-and-a-half deal for the whole thing—the fare and whatnot. But, on the other hand, why people would name kids for the boats. . . . I know about a half dozen Betsy Anns.

On another trip, this time on the *Crowder* as it hustled toward Cincinnati with a crew eager to have a night in town, a man hailed the boat at Ellison's Run Landing and the crew anticipated just a short stop to pick up this "walking freight." As it turned out, it was not the man but his sick wife who was the passenger, and she was not at the landing but "ovah the hill yonder." Over the hill turned out to be a considerable trek in early March snow, as crew members mentally calculated the time lost from their night in Cincinnati town. Suffering from acute appendicitis, the woman had to reach a hospital and be operated on within twenty-four hours. Because of the delay, the *Crowder* did not reach Cincinnati until 11:05 p.m., the woman was transferred to an ambulance, and nobody saw the show in town. In June, the *Crowder* was hailed at Ellison's Landing by a big man in blue overalls announcing he had a bunch of flowers for the crew.

> The captain came out on the guard to see what was going on. He recognized, as the boat neared the shore, the husband of that frail lady who had gone to the hospital early that spring. "How are you?" he called, waving a friendly hand.
>
> "How's the Missus?" called the Captain.
>
> "She never came back," the big man said simply. "Last thing she asked wuz that you get this bunch of posies. They're fur you fellers on the boat. She tol' me particular to pick 'em outta her own little patch back by th' house."
>
> The flowers were fixed in a big glass vase and placed on the officer's table. . . . The second mate slung his cap on the table, bottom side up. Then he tossed a fifty-cent piece in it. The rest of the boys said nothing, but added their contributions. The clerk gathered the money. It was an unspoken service; a tribute to a frail lady's gallantry.
>
> The money bought a wreath for a small grave out back of Ellison's Run Landing. [*Pilotin'*, pp. 203–4]

Although contemporary towboat crews seldom stop, and they have little contact with people on the bank (except perhaps at locks where people sometimes gather to watch the boats), in earlier towboat days along the Illinois River, they often depended on a woman known as Steamboat Elsie. Captain Art Zimmer remembered her and said that even for years after her death her house was known among pilots as Steamboat Elsie Light and was saluted by passing boats.

> She run a beauty shop in that place and her husband a barber shop. And they

erected sort of a small lighthouse out in front of their house. . . . But, before the days of radio, these barge lines used to telephone her, call her long distance, and relay the orders to the boats through her, to the captain of the boat. In a lot of cases, why she'd take a rowboat and go out and deliver these orders. . . . Of course, she had trophies or knick-knacks galore from these different companies for her services. And she was known to even take sick people off of the towboats on the Illinois River and bring 'em into her home and get 'em medical attention, and also, knowing the people back in those days, they wasn't too many boats running like they are today. And she was known to know everybody. She knowed most of the crew members and knowing when they had a birthday and such, why she always baked a birthday cake and sent it out to 'em. And also, . . . if ice prevented her from going out in the rowboat to the boat, why she'd cross this bridge and leave messages and cake, or whatever it was, down on a rope in a bucket to the bridge. . . . I know she was doing this up until—oh, I'm going to say to about 1945.

After she died, Illinois River pilots tried to raise enough money to buy that property and preserve it as Steamboat Elsie's Lighthouse, but they were unsuccessful. In 1977, Captain Zimmer noted that "the last time I was up there, the lighthouse was still standing there, but of course, big old Elsie isn't there anymore."

Perhaps the most bizarre incident regarding the boat-land people connection is told in Burman's *Look Down That Winding River*. Captain Bill Menke of the *Goldenrod* showboat told the tale.

Queer thing happened once with a calliope. We were playing for a couple of weeks in a town on Bayou Teche, not far from New Orleans. A woman was in jail there waiting to be hanged—the only woman, so I heard, ever to be sentenced to execution in Louisiana. Every afternoon we played the calliope, and the second afternoon the condemned woman sent word to me how much she enjoyed the playing, and please would I have the calliope play something while she was being hung. I did what she asked, and we played, "Nearer, My God, to Thee!" Human beings are hard to figure. [Pp. 115–16]

Pilots used to leave notes they had made about river conditions in boxes placed at intervals along the bank. Since the advent of voice-radio communications, they've arranged passing signals, discussed the current at such-and-such bend, and inquired of one another's families via channel seventeen or nine or six. Whether near Stumpy Point, Arkansas; or Scrubgrass Bend, Mississippi; Davenport, Iowa; or Gallipolis, Ohio, the radio communications between boats are generally characterized by a "down home" quality of camaraderie and friendliness between pilots who may have talked to one another for thirty years without having met in person. When inquiring about one another's well-being, or signing off until the next time, they commonly say, "mighty fine, cap'n, gotcha fine." Captain Ted Dean sounds a familiar tune when he says: "I never met him personally, but my gosh, I talked to him on the radio for years. Of course out here on the riverboats, you say, 'Do you know Jocko?' 'Oh, sure, I know him real well.' Sure, I've been talking to him for fifteen years, but I never met the man."

While most conversations are between pilots on two boats in the same area, others tuned to the same channel can listen in. Captain Ray Prichard recalled a time when the crews of four or five boats tied up at St. Paul had returned from a night on the town. One of the fellows, inebriated after his time-off adventures, tripped into a fuel-drip tank. Several crewmates retrieved him with no problem, but one of the boat captains saw the incident, called the dispatcher, and essentially "snitched" on the drunken deckhand. A pilot on another boat, who had orders to leave at midnight, "backed his boat away from the docks. He sat out there about five minutes, brought his boat back in, climbed off, climbed on this other boat, walked to his [the snitching captain's] cabin room, and beat him up"—just on general principles—because he'd tattled. The zealous upholder of principles was forced by his company to "apologize publicly on the radio to the opposing fraternity." It was to be put out as a general broadcast at noon the next Tuesday. The taleteller had been a thorn in everybody's side, and the two men had not been friendly even before this incident. "And so everybody had their radios tuned in, of course, waiting for this big apology." With the river fraternity listening in, the "offender" apologized. According to Captain Prichard, it went something like this: " 'I guess I was a little hasty clippin' Cap'n ———,' " and so and so forth. And he said, 'I will make it up to him. . . . I'm going to take him down to Prescott and go fishin' with him next Sunday, 'cause I know where there's a lot of deep holes.' " Asked if such an apology had been accepted, Prichard laughed— 'Yeh, that was because [he] didn't know any better than that I guess. [He] wasn't what you'd call bright and brilliant, about certain things."

A less direct form of interaction between crews on different boats, unacknowledged impromptu races, spice the riverboat tradition from Mark Twain's times to the diesel days. Perhaps the most famous of all steamboat races was the one between the *Natchez* and the *Rob't. E. Lee* in 1870. Both captains published cards in the New Orleans *Daily Picayune* denying there was to be a race, both captains made special arrangements regarding cargo or fueling, both boats left New Orleans wharf at five o'clock in the afternoon of June 30, and both boats steamed full ahead toward St. Louis with millions of dollars of bets from here and abroad resting on the outcome of the nonrace. It was not a close contest, however, and the "Hoppin' Bob" beat "Big Injin" by nearly six and a half hours. The legendary ovation the *Lee* received at St. Louis wharf, the song that keeps waiting for the *Rob't. E. Lee*, the Currier & Ives lithograph showing the boats bow to stern in smoke-belching concert, and the amount of money that changed hands make this the most famous of all palatial packet contests on record. [2]

Most extemporaneous racing received considerably less fanfare than the well-orchestrated *Natchez-Lee* extravaganza. They were sometimes spur-of-the-moment contests between rival boats of the same company with crews eager to have a little sport and prove themselves the pride of the fleet. Reasons for such sport ranged from intangibles such as pride, excitement, and notoriety to more practical concerns. George Merrick of *Old Times on the Upper Mississippi* corrects the popular perception of racing.

> It is popularly supposed that there was a great deal of racing on Western rivers in the olden time — in fact, that it was the main business of steamboat captains and owners, and that the more prosaic object, that of earning dividends, was secondary. There is a deal of error in such a supposition. . . . It is true, however, that whenever two boats happened to come together, going in the same direction, there was always a spurt that developed the best speed of both boats, with the result that the speediest boat quickly passed her slower rival, and outfooted her so rapidly as soon to leave her out of sight behind some point, not to be seen again, unless a long delay at some landing or woodyard enabled her to catch up. These little spurts were in most cases a business venture, rather than a sporting event, as the first boat at a landing usually following so soon after, would find nothing to add to the profits of the voyage. [P. 142]

At one time, the first boat to reach St. Paul in the spring was awarded the season's mail contract between St. Paul and St. Louis or free wharfage for that

---

[2] Actually, the two steamboats never ran as close together as the Currier-and-Ives print indicated. See Ray Samuel, Leonard Huber, and Warren Ogden, *Tales of the Mississippi*, pp. 95–101, for a detailed account of the famous race.

season. In later days, boats could save hours of time if they were first to arrive at a lock or at loading facilities. Despite these practical reasons, though, there was undeniably the occasional pilot or captain who went for the gusto of a good race. According to William Petersen, the intrepid Captain Daniel Smith Harris was one of them.

> Harris showed a mania for racing and his boats were usually the swiftest on the river. His most brilliant exploit was achieved in 1857 when, in a race against time, he carried from Dunleith to St. Paul a copy of Queen Victoria's message to President Buchanan, congratulating him on the successful laying of the Atlantic cable. At this time the telegraph lines extended only to Dunleith and Prairie du Chien [Wisconsin]. Captain David Whitten of the steamboat *Itasca* left the latter place at the same time that Harris left Dunleith with the *Grey Eagle*, having a lead of sixty-two miles over a course of two-hundred and seventy-five miles. Harris sighted the *Itasca* a short distance above Hastings and although Captain Whitten put on a full head of steam, the two boats came snorting into port at the same time. While the *Itasca* was putting out its stage, Captain Harris attached the message to a piece of coal and tossed it to his agent who stood waiting on the bank, thereby outwitting Captain Whitten and winning the race.[3]

Though races between packet boats have long captured the popular fancy, these "loose-headed ladies" (boats without tows) cornered no market on the venture. Stories survive of races between raft boats, and tales can even be heard of diesel towboats with fifteen-barge loads trying to outsmart one another to the appointed finish line. In the September 21, 1918, issue of the Burlington *Saturday Evening Post*, C. N. Edwards wrote of his experience with raft racing on the *Louisville* in 1883.

> I have been in many steamboat races during my fifteen years of river life, but this summer was the first time to engage in racing with a raft.
> These two boats with fourteen strings of lumber each left Reads the 14th of May for St. Louis. Seven hundred miles and we raced all the way. With ten bridges to get thru and two sets of rapids each twelve miles long to cross it took lots of nerve and good management to make time. Both boats had nearly the same power the *Louisville* a trifle the best boat.

[3] William Petersen, "Captains of the Early Mississippi Steamboats," *Wisconsin Magazine of History* 13, no. 3 (March 1930), p. 3. Petersen based his account on the Merrick river columns in the Burlington *Saturday Evening Post*.

With strong electric lights for night work we both reached the end of the run together the 22nd of May. Eight days run from Reads with rafts that contained over two million feet of lumber each over 500 feet long and more than 200 feet wide.

This was apparently no singular occurrence. Captain Walter Blair described an 1878 race between the *LeClaire Belle* and the *J. W. Van Sant*, each with fourteen strings of lumber and each trying to reach the LeClaire rapids first in order to engage the aid of the one rapids boat, the *Prescott*. The second arrival would then have a long delay before the *Prescott* could return to help her. Blair's boat lost, but it was a gentlemanly contest.

> Both boats were doing their best and so were their pilots, but there was no swearing or calling of ugly names—it was all as quiet and orderly as a well conducted funeral. That stretch of river then was wide enough for two full rafts to run abreast all the way to LeClaire. Neither crowded the other on shore or out on a bar; it was a fair test in every way and we were loser. [*Raft Pilot's Log*, pp. 117–18]

An animated Captain Loren "Shorty" Williams became absolutely apoplectic when recounting with sweeping gestures and sparkling eyes the modern-day diesel towboat equivalent of the unacknowledged river boat race. In about 1950 or '60, he is not exactly sure, his fifteen-barge tow was making up at Peabody, opposite St. Louis, for the first trip going north in the spring. The *Prairie State* passed them with fifteen barges, heading north, and were about two and a half hours ahead of Williams's boat by the time they left Peabody.

> Of course, we knew they were going to St. Paul and they knew we were goin' to St. Paul and it was kind of a race. There were several other boats—oil tows that were coming up part way—as far as Bettendorf. But we were the only ones going to St. Paul. So . . . we got up the line and we of course talked back and forth—makin' about the same speed, and they'd be just maybe gone up on the lock and out before we got there, and so forth. So we stayed right about so far behind them. Well, it's always a great effort to be the first ones into St. Paul, for several reasons, the one of which I'll explain here a little later.

DONN WILLIAMS [SON]: Most important of which, though, is the notoriety that one gains.

SHORTY: Publicity! Yeah, that's the most important to us. The most important to the company was—we were both towing to the same place, Northern States, and whoever got there first wouldn't have to wait until the others were unloaded because we wanted to bring . . . six barges back. So we'd have to wait for them. In other words, we'd have to wait up there until they unloaded their tow, and then they'd unload six of ours before we could start back. Take several days of delay, which is costly. So we got up the line to Quincy, and the water was so high they wouldn't pull our first cut out—they made us double-trip. [See glossary.] So *Prairie State*, he tied off his tow down, oh, four or five miles below the lock, and we're double-tripping. Well, we got there with our second half about the time they were leaving the lock. And, then, they double-tripped up to Lone Tree, which is about five miles above the lock, or six. And we just went through the lock, and at the first dock, we tied off, went back, and got our second part. So we passed them! Through a little skulduggery!

We weren't suppose to tie off to the docks, but . . . nobody would notice it—maybe! We weren't gonna be there long anyway. So we got by . . . ahead of them there. Well, we went on up to Canton, and the Des Moines River had run out a lot of ice and trash, which was in the forebay, the whole place above there was *full* of trash. So we had to move some of their drift to get out, which we did. And that made it, of course, easier for the other boat, but we got out first and got on up through Keokuk, and when we got to Lock 18 at Burlington—just before we got there, there was an ice gorge had turned loose at Oquawka and come down in there, and ice was piled ten feet high in that place above the lock. Well, there was an oil tow, settin' there waitin', and 'course, we would have been behind it, but we shoved up to the lower end of the wall and I got off and went up. . . . We got there about three or four o'clock in the morning, and they waited, and then, after breakfast, I went up and they were telling us, "Well, they got a rig coming down from Rock Island to bail that ice out of the forebay, so that they can get the gates open and get our boat through." And they said it would probably take a week or ten days.

Well, I looked the situation over and I said, "Now, listen, if you can get those gates just a crack, I think we can break that ice loose and get it out of there." So they said, "Well, sure like to have you try it." . . . We got all that ice out of there in about seven or eight hours. And then, of course, we had the advantage. They made that boat that was waitin' there, that oil tow, made him back out and let me through first. . . . Yeah, they [*Prairie State*] had to wait for that other tow, too, then, see. That put 'em a little bit farther behind us. And then we went on up the river, all the time talking back and forth, you know. No race ever mentioned. But you know everybody was gettin' just every inch they could. We knew they were and they knew we were. . . .

Anyhow, we got on up the river and stayin' about the same. When we got to Lansing, they dropped off three or four barges . . . then they started gainin' on us, you see. . . . Well, we got up to Lake Pepin; we were not very far ahead of them. And I knew he had some more to drop at Red Wing, which would make him a single locking—those he was gonna take on to St. Paul, say six. . . . Yeah, we were taking all fifteen into St. Paul. So we just knew we'd have to wait for those other six up there. Unless we did something. Well, he said, —that ice on Lake Pepin is about eighteen inches thick—and he says, "I'll help you up through there if you want." And I said, "Sure." So he tied his tow off at the foot of the lake, and came up with his light boat and helped us push up through there, which we could have done, but it would have taken a long time . . . but this way we were able to push 'em all through. We run out of ice about four or five miles down in the lake, below Red Wing, and of course, he just helped us up to there. And then, of course, it was my obligation to say, "Here, I'll help you." And he knew that, see. He knew I'd have to offer, and he knew that I knew that he didn't need it, because he already had the hole through. But, soon as we got up into the lake, I says, "Captain, do you want me to come back and help you push yours up through there?" "Oh, yeah, that'll be fine, that'll be fine."

So, of course, we tied our tow up, soon as we got up into the little river above the lake. We tied our tow up, but we knocked the coupling off so that we'd only have six [barges]. All we did was just leave two lines, hangin' with those six. Well, I went back. We helped him up through there, and as soon as we got into clear water, of course, I took off with the boat. . . . My obligation was over then. And I went up and hooked on to these six and took off. Left the other nine there. . . . And that gave us a single, too, see. So when—the pilots were on watch when they got up there, and their pilot said . . . he was comin' around the corner and he knew we wouldn't have time to be gone with our fifteen yet. He says, "I'll take it easy goin' by you, there, so as not to shake you up any." And my partner . . . he says, "I'm already gone!" And the pilot on the *Prairie State* says, "You're what?!" He said, "I'm already gone—I only got six; I left nine of 'em back down there." Well, then they knew they were stuck!

And so we went on in to St. Paul . . . beat 'em in there. 'Course they met us at Red Wing with television cameras and all that stuff. . . . Yeah.

We got up there and spotted our six barges — Northern States — took off and went back down and got our nine and came up. And by the time we got up there, they had just finished our six, so we could hook into them and went. So we didn't lose a bit of time, you see. We'd'a had to wait that long, anyway, and longer, for him. And well, they would have been starting our six when we got through with this up there. If we hadn't done that.

QUESTION: Did you have occasion to talk to them on the radio after this?

SHORTY: Oh, yeah. But nothing was ever said about us racin'. . . . No needling, at all. Nobody ever mentioned that we were racin' to be first into St. Paul, but everybody *knew* it. . . . Saved hundreds of dollars by that little maneuver.

Captain Williams's race story illustrates two of the unwritten codes followed by rivermen — the obligation to assist one another in difficult situations and the tacit understanding that races go unacknowledged because the potential dangers could affect insurance and jobs, and because obvious gloating is bad form.[4]

Other rules of behavior among members of the crew were often prescribed by general river superstitions. Though most pilots now claim to disregard such "hokum" and attribute superstitions to the olden days, some omens of bad luck have traditionally affected the operation and naming of boats. It is unlucky to name a boat with a word starting with the letter *M* (thirteenth letter of the alphabet).

Any boat that had a name commencing with *M* was doomed from the beginning. . . . That superstition goes way back. With some justification. Now I'm getting up a directory of all the passenger steamboats in the river, and the *M* listings are short; there aren't as many *M*s as you would think there would be. The percentage of the ones that are *M* that ended disasterously are appalling. . . . Oh, yes, [more] than any other letter, no doubt about it. . . . Now you can figure that one out for yourself. [Captain Fred Way, Jr.]

Another popular superstition transferred to a river situation involved Friday, though not exclusively Friday the thirteenth. To start a season on a Friday

---

[4] The obligation to assist other boats is changing somewhat. Boats still come to each other's aid quickly when there has been an accident or explosion. Regular groundings or difficulties perceived by fellow pilots to originate with a pilot's carelessness or ineptitude do not necessarily elicit aid.

meant bad luck for the entire season. It was also ill-advised to carry a white (or grey) mule and a preacher aboard the boat at the same time, to sweep anything across the bow of the boat, to bring peanuts aboard, to allow blue paint in the engine room, or to whistle. There are ghost stories about crews and boats plunged into the icy depths in a long-ago time. Periodically, subsequent crews navigating that chute or that bend or that reach, always at night, see the outline of that boat. But the phantom boat fades from sight just as they are ready to blow the passing signal. In *Mississippi Steamboatin'*, Quick and Quick recount the ghost story with a twist.

> A story is told of a pilot aboard the *St. Louis* who, having to share his place with a corpse which had been put there to keep cool, kept up his nerve by drinks every half hour which were brought him from the bar-room. As he stood there in the impenetrable gloom by the wheel, steering by the dimly seen marks along the shadowy banks, glancing now and then at the forbidding square of black by the window, he looked over his shoulder and saw a human figure in spectral white. He did not wait for another look, but went over the wheel in one jump, clear to the hurricane deck twenty feet below. As he painfully got to his feet for another leap, he saw over the wheel which he had just left the head and arm of the specter. "Hey," it yelled, "where the hell are you goin? Here's the key to the bar. Come and get it before I take my death of cold. I forgot about it till after I was in bed, and I tell you it's chilly up here with nothing but my underclothes on." [Pp. 233–34]

Some animals brought good luck and others signalled doom. Rats were a bad sign. "The alighting of a crow on a raft or two meant a smash-up of the fleet. Conversely, when a pigeon took a steamboat ride it meant good luck" (*Lore and Lure*, p. 78). Cranes are old steamboatmen reincarnated to bring pilots and vessels safely into harbor. Even bullfrogs can be significant navigators. Captain John Skidmore, who often punctuates his reminiscences with a softly emphatic, "I never *shall* forget it," acknowledged his idiosyncratic superstition.

> Well, I'm kind of a superstitious sort of person, in a way. . . . Shortly after I got married, we was coming up the river below Cairo. And I come on watch at midnight and I knew if we got in there before six o'clock in the morning, that they wouldn't start working our barges. [He and his bride lived in Cairo, so he would be able to see her.] It was a pretty good stage of

water, and I decided I'd go up through a chute . . . Medley Chute. I looked at my book and thought perhaps I'd have maybe ten or eleven feet, just enough to go through the chute, which would save about an hour and a half's time. . . . So I started up through the chute; it was a beautiful moonlight night. I got up about—in the spring of the year—got up halfway through the chute and I heard an old bullfrog: "You better go 'round, you better go 'round" [uses deep voice]. You know how they are. I didn't pay no attention to it. And I went on up, the boat begin to act like they got on shoal water. . . . I blew the lead on, the leadsman. I think the first cast I got twelve feet, then I got ten and a half feet, nine feet, and I stopped. And backed the boat. And there wasn't enough water to go through there; there was only about eight feet. So I was backin' down through the chute and I heard this old bullfrog: "I told you so; I told you so." [Deep voice, laughs]

Of course, not all creatures were signs of good or bad luck—some were carried as cargo or harbored as pets. In the packet boat days, animals—cattle, hogs, chickens, turkeys—were frequently shipped as freight. Occasionally, a less common sight greeted the levee loungers. In St. Louis in 1831 they could have seen a gigantic elephant amble off the boat. The wharf boat in Dubuque served to display one of Barnum's "rare Specimens," a gorilla; and in 1861, "the genial clerk of the Minnesota Packet Company found Dan Rice's rhinoceros making heroic efforts to extricate himself from the buoy chain of the wharf boat."[5] In 1853 the Territory of Minnesota sent a splendid buffalo to the Crystal Palace Exhibition in New York:

The patience of this rather surly beast was not improved by the irritating prods of the roustabouts on the *Ben Franklin*. After being roughly pushed from boat to boat, led through the streets of Cincinnati, and finally shipped by train to New York, the distracted beast gave vent to his feelings when the committee appeared to pass on his fitness as an exhibit. A furious charge sent the committee scurrying for safety as they formulated their verdict. He was not accepted.[6]

Then there is the story about the steamboat carrying a circus. It sank up near Memphis "and a big lion swam onto a island where some Holy Rollers was

[5] Petersen, "Captains of Early Mississippi Steamboats," p. 233.

[6] Ibid.

having a revival. When that lion dripping wet stood roaring beside the preacher they says more people got religion from them two than Billy Sunday and all them other shouting sky pilots put together."[7]

Though most rivermen will instantly proclaim "Pshaw, a boat's no place for a pet," there have been varied menageries aboard riverboats: dogs, cats, goats, chickens, squirrels, pigs, raccoons, and even a monkey. Captain Gale Justice had a pet hog back in about 1914 or '15. He got him when he was "just a little feller" and "fed him up until he weighed 350 pounds. I sold him to the wharfmaster—yeah, sold that hog for ten cents a pound." Captain Justice had made a place for him back under the kitchen and made the deckhands clean it out every day. In warm weather, they'd hose it and the hog down. Asked if the hog had a name, Captain Justice replied, "I called him Peggy. . . . And he knowed—you get a bunch of hogs out on the shore and take Peggy out and get him in the bunch, you know, and let him run around there for a minute and holler, 'Come on, Peggy,'—Peggy'd start and come in on the boat and the rest of the hogs would foller. . . . Peggy was quite a package, yes, Peggy was some hog."

Captain Ben Gilbert remembers a trip on the *Husky I* when the engineer kept a pig in the engine room.

> Oh, he'd fall off in the grease, you know; we'd have to take him and warsh him up, you know. And finally he got pretty big, and they put him out on the barge. And you know that thing was smart. At dinner time, he'd come back there and he'd go from one side to the other side, and if he didn't see nobody, over he'd go down there and turn over the garbage can and everything. Well, that pig, he kep' growin' and he got bi-ig. I was out there; I'd take out coal, you know, I'd take him out milk and brown sugar, you know, stir it up there and make him a hot toddie like.

Not all pets rated a hand-carried hot toddie; in fact, some are fabled to have done the work of exterminators or deckhands. Captain Way claims "a hog is death on rats." Dogs were interlopers on a number of boats.

> Yeah, they used to have a dog on the *Chris Greene* and they had him trained so that he didn't like gas boats. Gas boats were beneath the dignity of steamboaters and he'd be lyin' there by the cabin in the sun curled up, and all you had to do was to say "Gas boat, Rags," and he'd just tear out the front door there and down the steps and be barking on the front end of that boat

---

[7] Ben Lucien Burman, *Look Down That Winding River*, p. 66.

there at that gas boat. . . . I know I've seen a dog that they trained, when they threw the line out, the dog would grab the line and go up the hill with it. They get pretty knowledgeable. [Captain Way]

The engineer on Captain Charles White, Sr.'s boat brought a goat on one time and they painted it—hoofs were red, horns were green, and the whiskers a different color—just to be ornery, apparently. The tame goat followed deckhands up the steps, out on the barges, all over the boat. But "they had to watch him—they'd bend over to work on a ratchet or something, that goat would . . . liable to boot 'em in the river." Another pet goat took a particular dislike to the boat's captain. Captain Arthur McArthur peppers his account with hearty laughs.

There was a goat back years ago and it was on the *Baton Rouge*. Captain Charlie Moore was captain on there. And Captain Charlie was always raisin' hell thisaway, that way, you know. And so this goat took a dislikin' to the captain. Every time Captain Charlie Moore'd come down and get ready to go to dinner or supper or somethin', that old goat was out there on the boiler deck, and soon as the captain would come up the steps headin' for his room, that damn old goat'd throw his head down—billy goat—and run like hell and butt the livin' hell out of the captain and knock him down. And the captain would get up and run. And the goat would get ready to make another attack. So it got so bad that the captain was peepin' out the door and the old goat was a peepin' around corners lookin' for the captain. He didn't take it out on nobody but the captain of the boat. So the captain finally made 'em get rid of it.

Some pets capture the crew's fancy (and good will) more than others. Captain "Rip" Ware differentiates between an old hen and a nasty raccoon.

He'd [captain] buy chickens from old fishermen, anywhere, and we'd keep 'em back there in a coop. One time down there in Louisiana one of them old hens—we'd turn 'em out you know and let 'em go around and eat the bugs around on the barge and all—one of them old hens fell in the river and I know we was two hours tryin' to change and get her. 'Fore we got there, she drownded. If that company knew we was chasin' that hen. . . . You know, a chicken can't swim; they sink. We killed 'em down to one little ole chicken, one little ole hen. And that thing stayed on there. . . . When we got to them locks on Ouachita River, we'd throw it out on the wall and let it get out there and get in that sand and dust itself. When they blowed that whistle or turned them lines loose, he'd come on back and get on the boat. And he got stole down there in New Orleans. And that old captain got so mad.

Damndest thing we had, was the old captain had an old coon on there. And there ain't nothin' as nasty as a coon. That coon come up missin' and don't nobody know where that coon is 'cept me and the second engineer. But we started combin' the river, and we didn't make no attempt to git him. [Laughs.]

Jocko the monkey, though beloved by the captain, did not endear himself to the entire crew. It proved his undoing.

Jocko kept running up and getting up—see we had the old type aerials, you know. Had four wires off across it. Jocko would skin up the jackstaff there and he'd get on them wires. The old man told the operator—never to send unless he went out and seen Jocko wasn't on there. Well, Jocko was messing with everything, and everybody hated Jocko. So he was watching one day when he knew the old man was sleeping. Old Jocko got up on that wire and that guy turned the juice up and hit that key and Jocko went overboard. . . . We never did see Jocko no more. [Captain Wm. Tippitt]

Now, in the age of 10,500-horsepower diesel towboats with spare crews (generally eleven to thirteen people) and more compact units, one hears fewer stories of pets. Captain E. A. "Li'l Wamp" Poe of Nilo Barge Line does admit, however, that one of their towboats, the *City of St. Louis*, harbors a lizard. "It's been up there I guess over a year. They got it last spring. . . . What do you call them things that change colors: . . . chameleon. He's just loose in the pilothouse." In the air-conditioned wheelhouse, the chameleon seeks warmth by climbing into envelopes: "They've come very near mailing him to the office several times."

Still, the varied cargoes no longer include turkeys, or buffalo, or bulls, or circuses, and the pilots on at least one modern towboat, the *Ann King*, claim that pranks and practical jokes are stories from the past. Noting that the chief engineer has "all the time in the world" to think of crazy pranks—and does—master-pilot Captain Gordon Nelson compartmentalizes his work and his fun. "I never had time for pranks on here. . . . No, I'm not a prankster. I never did believe in horseplay. . . . We pilots got to dedicate our whole watch and concentrate on our work. That's why we don't have time to dream up nothing." When asked if he played any pranks, Nelson's partner, Captain Ted

Dean, agreed. "Not any more—they used to. Not any more. They don't have time for stuff like that. . . . A guy gets off watch, he's so darn tired he goes to bed. Back in those days, hell, they had crews on these boats. I know whenever I was shipping a coal boat, we had three deckhands and a mate, four in the engine room, two in the galley, had a sailor man . . . kept the inside clean."

Besides the smaller crews, the constant movement of diesel towboats also leaves less tie-up time when leisure could provide the catalyst for such practical jokes among the crew. If what Nelson and Dean describe is more generally true on the river today,[8] there is, nevertheless, a rich tradition of pranks played by old-timers in an era when boats tied up more frequently and crews remained confined together for longer stretches of time. B. A. Botkin relates a mid-nineteenth-century story about two rival pilots on the *Uncle Sam*. Calling the pilots Smith and Brown, the teller acknowledged that a bitter feeling of long standing existed between these pilots, and each had enlisted the sympathies and aid of one of the engineers—the first engineer sided with Smith, the second with Brown. One day Brown was steering as they left Natchez and wanted to pass the town under a full head of steam.

Just as he was abreast of it, the first engineer, who was working the boat, shut the steam nearly off; nor would he put it on again until they finally and very slowly passed the town.

Brown saw the finger of Smith in this maneuver, and determined to be revenged in kind. He was. On the next down trip a heavy fog arose at sunset, and Smith, who at that time abandoned the wheel to Brown, ordered him to run the boat until nine o'clock and then to tie her up; to have steam kept up all night; and, if the fog should lift, to call him.

"Tie the boat up!" exclaimed Brown. "I can run her in any such fog as there is tonight. I'll run her till twelve, and then tie up, as you are afraid."

"I can run her any night, and anywhere that you can," replied Smith; "and if you *do* move her till twelve, call me then, that's all."

Brown kept on for a time, but the fog came on heavier and heavier, and having made sure that his coadjutor was fast asleep, he rounded the boat to a woodyard and tied up. His friend, the second engineer, was on duty, and according to Brown's directions, the wheel was unshipped and the steam kept up. At twelve, Brown went to the wheel again, and sent a waiter to call Smith, who soon made his appearance, rubbing his eyes and anything but

[8] My sample is too limited to say for certain that it is.

pleased at the prospect before him — although, strictly speaking, prospect there was none, for he could not fairly discern the top of his nose for the fog.

"Hallo!" said Brown, "are you there? I've called you according to your orders, and now I think you'd better tie up and turn in again, or you'll make a smash-up before morning."

Smith growled out that he was able to steer any boat in any fog, and took the wheel. Brown went below.

The boat was fast to the bank, but neither bank nor anything else could poor Smith see. The wheel, which was ungeared, turned around and round with the swift current, and the splashes reached his ear; the hissing of the steam in her low pressure boilers sounded all right to him; so cursing his bad luck, Brown's obstinacy, and his own stupidity in accepting the banter, he turned his wheel now this way and now that, expecting every moment to hear and feel the boat crash against something. A thousand times, during his dreary watch, did he determine to give up his desperate undertaking, and as often did pride step in and prevent him; and so, finally, having made up his mind to let the worst come, he gave a tubular order to the engineer to work her very slow, and keep on — as he supposed.

About sunrise, Brown, accompanied by the captain and other officers, ascended the hurricane deck.

"Hallo! Smith," said Brown, "is that you?"

"Yes, it is," replied Smith, crossly enough.

"You haven't been running all night, I reckon?" continued Brown.

"Can't you see I have?" answered Smith. "Don't you know where you are? If you don't, you better get your eyes scrubbed out."

"No," returned Brown, "I can't say I do. Where are we?"

"Just above Natchez," was the reply.

"There's matey," said Brown. "You *have* done it this time, and I wouldn't be in your boots for a hogshead of niggers."

"What have I done, and what do you mean?" demanded Smith, ferociously.

"Done! Done enough!" roared Brown. "I left the boat tied up to old Jones's plantation, and if you have gone and towed *that* down to Natchez, they'll have you up for abduction, and sea-duction, and nigger stealing, and putting obstructions in the channel of the river, and the Law a marcy on ye."

A very moist ray of the sun peeping through the mist, at this moment, partially disclosed the situation of the boat and shore to the astonished and discomfited Smith, and darting below, he remained there until the boat *did* reach Natchez. And from that time ever after, neither the *Uncle Sam* nor the Mississippi River knew him more.[9]

Some pranks hinge for their success on the superstitions or greed or opposite watch rivalry of certain crew members. Captain Ben Gilbert remembered a deckhand on one boat who believed in "spooks and things."

So he was up in the pilothouse one night . . . I think it was on a wood boat. And you could throw a rudder hard down and the pilothouse door would come open a little. You know, the way the boat leaned. So this old boy was up there one night in the pilothouse, and the pilot he throwed her hard down, the door opened, and he said, "Come in, Cap, come in and set down. This is deckhand so-and-so. Set down there, and let's talk awhile." So the boy moved over a little bit, you know. Went on there for awhile, and then he throwed her hard down, and he said, "Come in, why here's so-and-so," says, "Come in and have a seat. Move over, boy, and let Captain so-and-so sit down." Fourth time he throwed the boat, throwed her hard down again, the door flew open and the old boy didn't wait for Captain so-and-so to come in; he just up and got out of there!

In some cases both the greedy and the prankster become wiser indeed.

I was deckin' on a boat and we were double-trippin' . . . above Helena, Arkansas. So we got up to Swopes, that's approximately thirty-some-odd miles below Memphis, we tied off the first barge of tows. So the mate tells the barge watchman, he says, "I want you to know if you go huntin', bring us back somethin' so we'll have it for coffee time." Every afternoon we had coffee time. . . . So we went on down the river and left this barge watchman on the barges; we got back the next afternoon and this mate was standin' up on the barge and he said, "What didja get?" He said, "I got a squirrel and a rabbit and a duck." He said, "I'll tell y'all one thing, y'all can have that darn squirrel and that rabbit, but that damned duck's mine." That's the words he [the mate] used. He said, "I don't want none of you gettin' it either." So we were on out there and we was makin' it up and so it was clean, you know, the old duck—'sposed to be a duck—was clean. More I looked at it, I said, "Hell, that ain't a duck; that's an owl!" I told this boy, "You not gonna give him that for a duck; that's an owl. That's liable to

[9] B. A. Botkin, *A Treasury of Mississippi River Folklore*, pp. 80–81. His source for the story was *A Stray Yankee in Texas* by Philip Paxton (1853).

make him sick." And he said, put his fingers up to his lips, said, "Don't say nothin'."

This man [the mate] was a good friend of mine, and I was scared he was gonna get sick or somethin', and I said, "This is an owl that he's tryin' to put off on you." He said, "You just want that damn duck yourself, you chintzy sucker!" [Laughs.]

And so he told everybody again that that duck was his, you know, and he asked the barge watchman again, "That is a duck, isn't it?" "Oh, yeah." The mate said, "I want you [cook] tomorrow afternoon to cook that rabbit and that squirrel up and cook that duck up for me. Now don't let nobody else have that duck. And he [cook] looked at it and he said, "Did you say duck?" He said, "Yeah, that duck! I want that duck for myself!" So, he said, "OK" — he didn't want to cross him, a Negro you know. He didn't want to cross him.

So we went in the next afternoon at coffee time, and he had that squirrel cooked up and that rabbit and that good gravy; they'd made us biscuits. Myself and these friends — 'course we'd worked together and all that on the boat there — and here he comes in; he plops down and he has this ole owl in front of him, all cooked out there. I said, "Y'ought not to eat that. Now, look, that's a darned owl." He said, "I'll tell ya one thing again, you better shut up, I know you want this duck. And you ain't gonna get this duck." So everybody set around there and kep' quiet. He ate that old duck, you know, and little ole bones — you know, an owl's got little small bones to it — finally he cleaned it up and they was just as shiny when he got through.

So he went on out of the mess hall and around through the galley and there was a partition between the crew's mess and the cook's quarters back there. He goes around and that's the way he used to listen in on our conversations, what'd we be talkin' about, if we was talkin' about him or anything. . . . And I said to this barge watchman, I said, "God, I hope he don't get sick from you lettin' him eat that owl." He said, "Oh, heck, if he hadn't been so greedy about jumpin' up there wantin' that darn owl for a duck, I'd'a told him different. But the way he was hollerin' to give all the rest of us, to have that squirrel and everything, I just decided to let him go. It won't hurt him. If it makes him sick, it won't be anything bad anyhow. But he won't get sick over it."

And, man, that fella come back around there and, God, he was mad! That door's open and he sent us to the tunnels — that's down where the shafts of the boat goes through and they had the tiller arms. Back there you

Captain Arthur MacArthur (left) and Captain John Skidmore, 1977

had about this much room between [gestures about two feet], and he told us to get all the mud and the sand out. So we had to crawl on our stomachs, and every time the pilots would move the rudders, we had to get down or it'd clip our heads off. And I tell you, when we got through, there wasn't a grain of sand or mud in that tunnel. He sent us down there every day. [Captain McArthur]

And, of course, practical jokes allowed behavior across the ranks that normally would be neither considered nor tolerated.

Captain Charlie was another thing; he had Ben Walker and Dee Reeves, they were two real fine pilots on the river. And they had a fella named Garvey, he was a second mate on there; Whiskey Carter was the mate. Old Captain Charlie sent up to the pilothouse early in the mornin'—on the *Baton Rouge*, she had a long bench across the back of her there; you had a step you come up and a little trap door. It was kinda hard to see out of the back of her. . . . So the mate always stood the after watch. Captain stood the fo'ard. The captain was up for some reason or other, and he stretched out on the bench up there and was sleepin'. So about quarter to six, it was dark, and so Garvey came up in the pilothouse and said, "Ben, Captain Ben, did you see Whiskey anywhere?" He wanted to relieve Whiskey 'cause Whiskey Carter was the mate. He said, "Yeah, the damn sucker's layin' back there on the bench and been sleepin' the whole damn watch. Can't get nothin' out of him. Here, take this damn board and bust him across the rear with it." And the old man was layin' partly over on his side, 'nough where, Garvey hadn't got his eyes good, so he grabbed this board and whooped the hell out of the captain! And old man Charlie come up. . . . And when he woke up, Ben said, "What the hell you doin' to the captain, you tryin' to kill the captain!" [Captain McArthur]

Other antics likewise led to physical or psychological discomfort or even temporary trauma. Captain Lester "Whitey" Shickling, one of five brothers who were river pilots, proclaimed his eldest brother, "Wimpy," to be the "one with the pranks." Some of the crew had been giving him a rough time, so Wimpy "put a bunch of Epsom salts in the chili," which he, of course, passed up. "Then he locked the bathroom doors and crawled out the window. . . . That caused quite a stir for about two days. They actually had to break the doors down."

Another time that he got in the locks, he had it all made up with his deckhand . . . they didn't like the lock master or the operators anyhow. The deckhand was down there and Wimpy was hollering at him and got to cussing at him and "Do what I tell you to do," and the deckhand told him he'd do what he wanted to do. Wimpy run out there with a shotgun—he had blanks in it—and shot at the deckhand and the deckhand jumped down on an empty barge. The lock man went and called the sheriff. That was something. I heard that all up and down the river. . . . They had it timed. Called the sheriff and this sheriff came out and talked to the lock man and explained what happened and he asked the deckhand, "Did he hit you?!" He said, "No." And then he left.

One of the crueler pranks involved a crewman who wore glasses, even while he slept. A couple of cronies sneaked into his room and rubbed oil on his glasses. Then they blew the distress signal. The rudely awakened crew member sat straight up in bed yelling, "I'm blind! I'm blind!"[10] Though deckhand dogs and acrobatic monkeys seem to have disappeared from riverboats, and though pranks may be out of favor, at least one form of social entertainment—story telling—is alive, lively, and well among pilots. Some tales grow taller than others. Some are "the God's honest truth, now." Others are embellished a bit here and there. There are straightforward accounts of past experiences jogged from memories by a certain cutoff or town or submerged wreck—and generally recounted in similar terms each time that place on the river is passed. Some are not firsthand experiences but stories told this pilot by the man who "learned him," an old-time packet boat man, you see, who had forgotten more about the river than we will ever know. Talk passes the time, and there is a lot of time to pass standing two six-hour watches every day. Besides hearing talk about families, the welfare system, the Coast Guard, crime, or education, a bench sitter in the pilothouse becomes privy to tales about extraordinary boats, remarkable animals, and colorful people.

When Samuel Clemens returned to the river in 1882, he contrived to observe his beloved pilothouse incognito. The pilot loaded up the supposed greenhorn passenger with one false "fact" after another, warming to his subject and outdoing himself with his account of the alligator boats. An alligator boat was used to dredge alligators with. The government keeps them down now, but they used to be pesky devils, congregating as they did in alligator beds. Why, hardly a trip passed when they didn't go aground on alligators. In fact,

<hr />

[10] From the U.S. Army Corps of Engineers collection of oral interviews for the history of dredging. This story was told by Captain John Homer Bird.

alligators were such a problem that certain pilots were eulogized for their ability to navigate alligator water. These top-notch alligator pilots could read wind reefs, sand reefs, and, most difficult of all, alligator reefs. They had a natural talent for it and were paid handsomely in return.

It is at this point that Clemens realizes the hyperbolic pilot, now mustached and stately, had been a "slim cub" in Clemens's time. Clemens goads him on by puzzling over the efficiency of dredging alligators who would seem likely to simply come right back. The pilot rounds out, finishes up, and polishes off the alligator business in grand liar's style: "You dredge an alligator once and he's *convinced.*" Besides, alligators belong to the government; they are scooped aboard and made into soldier's shoes.

But the knowing Clemens, succeeding in tripping up his willing informant on a later story, is himself the sucker. Caught in an obvious lie by the bemused Clemens, the perspiring pilot stepped back from the wheel and declared to his curious visitor:

> "Here!" (calling me by name), "*you* take her and lie a while — you're handier at at than I am. Trying to play yourself for a stranger and an innocent! Why, I knew you before you had spoken seven words; and I made up my mind to find out what was your little game. It was to *draw me out.* Well, I let you, didn't I? Now take the wheel and finish the watch; and next time play fair, and you won't have to work for passage." [*Life*, chap. 24]

"Alligator boats" were not the only extraordinary vessels plying the rivers. Mark Twain himself exaggerated the speed deficiencies of the *John J. Roe.* She was so dismally slow that "ferry-boats used to lose valuable trips because their passengers grew old and died, waiting for us to get by." Captain William Heckman remembered Captain Ben Jewel's stories about the *Jim Johnson*, which are much like Captain Dayton Randolph's tales of the prodigious *Hurronico.*[11] The *Big Jim*, as she was called, was so large . . .

> The big pistons, went out every morning and came back in them engine rooms the next morning. And what a whistle we had on that old craft! But we only blowed it once. We were laying in at New Orleans one bright moonlight night. Both the moon and our pilot was full. And he wanted to try out our new whistle. The pilot, Joe Ulman, put his fancy foot down on the pedal and gave it one long toot. It was up so high and so much steam

[11] See Introduction.

came out that it blowed a piece out of the moon, which accounts for the moon being out of shape ever since. [12]

Such obvious tall tales as those of the *Big Jim* and *Hurronico* are offset by stories whose basic outline can be confirmed by other witnesses, though specifics of the contours may be flexible. While kibitzing in the pilothouse with his partner and guests, Captain Ray Prichard described, complete with sound effects and animation, a memorable exercise on the Tennessee River years before. The story begins with the lockmaster at Old Lock 1 on the Tennessee.

The lockmaster there, I can't think of his name, used to have a little black dog, 'bout the size of a beagle. Smart little dude. . . . That lockmaster also had some of these musk-. . . . muskegum?—what do you call those ducks, those white ducks, big, big, ducks? Muscovits? Muscovis? That's pret'near right. . . . Now then. The dam at Lock 1 was about six feet; there was no gates, just spillway. When the water would come out of the old Wilson lock, why it would spill over . . . and those ducks—there musta been a couple or three dozen of 'em, I don't know—big, big white ducks, they'd keep lookin' down there and they'd get into that draft and over they'd go.

One'd go thump, tump, tump, tump, and they'd all go, see. There'd be a leader, you know. The little dog, he saw those ducks goin' over; he'd go across the gate and down the wall and he'd look over at his master—I forgot the dog's name. "Go get 'em." He'd jump off the lock wall; they'd open the gate, he'd round up those ducks, they put 'em in the lock, they'd lock them up, all together, see. And I've got a movin' picture to prove it! [13]

Naturally, one expects rivermen to tell fish stories. Captain Roy Boyd's fish story is reminiscent of Davy Crockett-type tales where the prize is displayed in a local drinking establishment in order to lure curious customers. When he was about fifteen, Boyd saw the biggest alligator gar fish ever taken in those parts [Louisiana, Missouri]. [14] And it was caught by a "one-legged fisherman, in the wintertime."

[12] William L. Heckman, *Steamboating: Sixty-Five Years on Missouri Rivers*, p. 50.

[13] Captain Ted Dean confirmed the story about the ducks being locked up in the chamber, though he did not remember the black dog.

[14] He is not certain of dates, but he was still in school, about fifteen years old. That would place this story circa 1908. Two weeks before I talked with Captain Boyd, a representative of the Illinois Historical Society had come to see him specifically about this fish. They were trying to talk with any surviving people who could have seen that particular catch.

He had an old crutch like John Silver had . . . and he could handle that thing; you know, he'd just stand on one leg and could use that crutch and he could "whoop" a dozen men! A-standin' on one leg. . . .

Anyway, it was the fall of the year; in fact . . . the ground was frozen and the shore ice was frozen, and he was huntin' turtles. Them big snappin' turtles, you know. They bury in the mud . . . along beside an old log, or something like that. . . . And he'd feel along right under that log . . . with a steel rod with a hook on it. And he could hook that under the shell . . . and he could pull him out of the mud. Well, he seen this big log, what he thought was a log — it was only about two feet of water there, or maybe a little more, and he noticed that he touched that thing and that it had sidled away. Just keeps getting away from his hook. Kinda roused his curiosity, and the water wasn't quite clear enough that he could see distinctly, but he could see the shadow of this thing under the water and he thought it was a rock. So he got to payin' close attention and was lookin' as close as he could, and finally he seen it — fin move. . . . Stirred up the mud. And he decided it was a fish of some kind! And he had a two-horse wagon — to put his turtles in — and had a long chain that he carried with the wagon all the time — and very carefully, he punched holes around there and he got that chain . . . around there and got it hooked, and backed the machine up close . . . so he could get the chains hooked to the wagon, and pull it out on the shore. How he got it in the wagon, I don't know, but he must have got help, because — well, a fish that big would weigh a ton, or more.

It come out of the Mississippi. And it was alligator gar. . . . It was in a trap and the water turned cold . . . and it began to freeze and then the water fell real fast and caught this fish in there. . . . Well, anyway, he got it out and he got it uptown, and it was such a curiosity. I don't know what the deal was, but anyhow the saloon keeper there got him to hang it in his saloon.

I can remember it just as plain as anything . . . they got that fish hanging up — and I don't know how high the ceiling was — but his bill was tilted . . . under the ceiling, and his tail was layin' flat on the floor. Now, that's how long he was. . . . I figured he'd be about two feet in diameter. And I thought, "Well, that would be a excellent display for Smithsonian Institute."

We got to talkin' about it, and somebody wrote in, and they sent a couple of guys supposed to prepare it to stuff. And them coupla guys come, and they worked on that fish. They got him . . . outside, backyard of the saloon, when they skinned it, there, and the skin was so tough that they split him down the middle and they did it with an ax. The scales was about that [two inches] thick and just like flint. And everytime they'd hit that, the fire would fly, just like you'as hittin' a flint stone.

I didn't see the finish of it. I didn't know how all the rest of it went, but . . . years afterward, I was in Washington and I thought I'd go in and inquire and see if that fish really got there. Well, I went to the office and told him what I wanted to find out, and I said, "Have you any record of that fish?" And he got all excited right away, and went to the file . . . where they keep all that stuff and there was no record of it, whatsoever. And I figured these guys got that fish, . . . kep' it themselves, and made a sideshow out of it.

Besides stories of boats and animals, pilots hand down tales of unusual happenings among the colorful human figures in the river scenario. Captain Charles Fehlig's grandfather was "a very distinguished old gentleman. And he was a pilot out here back in those days. Leading citizen in the community. They were respected as such in those days—silk shirt, gold-dipped cane, always." These were the days, he says, when pilots made $600 to $700 a month and bank presidents made $75 to $100. Though his grandfather, Frank King, died when Fehlig was only eight, he remembers one story King swore to be true. Listeners often took it for a yarn, which angered King mightily and resulted in their quick departure from his home or pilothouse. In the pilot-house of the *Delta Queen*, fifty years after his grandfather's death in 1927, Captain Fehlig held his listeners entranced as he repeated King's story.

The packet boats, the pilothouse was back in mid-ship, you know. And they had the hurricane roof up there. They had left St. Louis on the old *Spread Eagle*, one of the Eagle Packet Company boats. Of course, those packet companies had their agents in various towns along the upper river here. Dubuque was their main passenger and freight stop. They had left St. Louis, oh, eight or nine o'clock at night. Got well above Alton. And grandfather was on watch by himself up there in the pilothouse—beautiful moonlight night. And all at once a well-dressed gentleman—he could see, of course, out on the roof there—walked up on the roof a little while. Finally found his way back to the pilothouse. Came up the three steps and came in the pilothouse. Well, grandfather recognized him . . . they talked and greeted each other. And he stayed in the pilothouse roughly ten to fifteen minutes. Then he left. Said he was goin' below.

Well, after he had left, grandfather called down and summoned the watchman up. . . . He didn't know that Mr. So-and-So was on board. The watchman said, "Well I don't think anyone is aboard other than the crew." "Well," he says, "he definitely is. He's on this boat." Well, with that, they summoned the clerk. The clerk said, "No, he definitely isn't on this boat. There's no one on here but the crew." Grandfather said, "I beg your pardon, but that man was just up in the pilothouse talking with me."

They landed . . . and they searched the boat. Couldn't find hide nor hair of him. They landed at Hannibal the next day. And they had learned that this man was murdered in his office in Dubuque at the time that he was in the pilothouse.

Heroics, even when accompanied by a generous dash of the illogical, memorialize certain pilots. When the steamship *Mayflower*, the only steamship launched on the Fox River to carry freight and passengers, slid down the ways at Aurora in 1876, it was cause for celebration. The launching has indeed become celebrated, but not for its clockwork smoothness. When the boat reached mid-stream, Captain Octave Landry noticed it was going downstream instead of up. Because he saw that the power of the engines was not great enough to work against the swift current, Captain Landry rushed to the lower deck and shouted to his mate: "Throw the yank [anchor], throw the yank."

"Aye, aye, captain. I can't throw de yank, got no rope." "Well, throw the yank, anyhow, might do some good," Landry cried, and the dutiful mate obeyed, his anchor going over. Captain Landry then jumped into the water and put his shoulder to the stern of the boat to hold it from floating over the dam. He stood heroically in this position for almost an hour when he learned the craft had grounded. [Burlington *Post*, December 26, 1914]

Pilots and engineers have traditionally had their differences, and in the days when the pilot rang bells that were answered from the engine room, more than a few tempers could flare. A classic story of this situation has made the rounds for years.

Tyler Rowe, the old engineer of the *Menomonie* [*sic*], was a humorous old grease-back. He got his leg into the dynamo and smashed it all to pieces. . . . but he bore it like a man. There was a story current on the river involving Tyler Rowe and Captain Stephen Withrow. Captain Steve was a very active and perhaps nervous commander, and at times he rang bells fast and furious. The story is that in making a particularly rough landing he rang a great many bells—more than usual. When the boat was made fast, fore and aft, and the "all done" whistle blown, Rowe began to open her up, ahead and astern, fast and slow. . . . Captain Steve . . . shouted down the tube: "What in h——ll are you doing, Tyler?" "Oh, nothing, Captain, just catching up with your bells." [Burlington *Post*, May 19, 1917]

Then, of course, there's the one about the pilot who was very handy with the bottle, and one particular night he was a little too handy. Thought he was going upstream. He had topped around and was going down river at about twenty miles an hour.

Telling stories passes the time among crewmates and continues the proud tradition of "loading up the confiding stranger" with picturesque, if not always accurate, verbal souvenirs of a trip on the river.

Pilots often share similar professional experiences that allow us to generalize about them and their work, but of course they are distinct individuals, different from one another in personality, style, idiosyncracies, age, and experience. These portraits of five pilots—a long-dead crackerjack whose reputation in the lower Mississippi links him to other "legendary" rivermen; a "crusty old salt" from Hernando, Mississippi; a steamboat captain reminiscent of nineteenth-century masters; and two youngsters whose careers have just begun—explore those distinctions.

CHAPTER FIVE

Individual Portraits

Captain Harris Underwood

THE LEGENDARY

Mike Fink, the legendary Indian fighter, keelboatman, and trapper, who died in 1822, was known for his unmatched marksmanship, his brawling strength, his blustering braggadocio, his crude pranks, and his adherence to the unique code of honor followed by those river rowdies of newly independent America. These ring-tailed roarers of the river proved friendship by shooting cups from atop each other's heads; Fink added gruesome antics like shooting the scalp lock from an unsuspecting Indian and the heel from a Negro's foot. This keelboat king, cut from the half-horse, half-alligator frontier mold, never shirked a good fight nor whimpered over the wounds such eye-gouging, nose-biting, fist-crunching contests incurred. Though the scope of the real Mike Fink's exploits is unknown, the legendary Fink was credited with all manner of boating skills and derring-do. According to one story, he outshot Davy Crockett when he challenged Crockett to shoot at Mike's wife's hair comb to win. Crockett declined to shoot at a "shemale" and gracefully conceded. Another time, when the crew's food supplies ran low, Fink duped a farmer with a tale about the "black murain" disease that seemed to be affecting some of the farmer's sheep. The "affected" sheep had, it seems, been given a dose of snuff by Mike's companions, and when Mike allowed as how this disease was infecting many of the flocks along the river and that it had no cure and that all the sheep would die if nothing were done, the farmer persuaded the well-known Fink to cull the diseased sheep from his flock. Pleading that he was no expert on the "black murain," Fink remained reluctant until the farmer pledged a barrel of whiskey to the crew if Fink would help him out of his predicament. Fink consented to do the neighborly thing. The relieved farmer returned to his house while Mike's crew slaughtered the "diseased" sheep and sank their carcasses in the shore-water, where they were retrieved after dark, dressed for the cooking, and added to a menu that now included generous portions of whiskey as well.

Fink's stubbornness and pride as a boatman were illustrated when he challenged the mighty steamboat that made the keelboat obsolete. The story is told of his orders not to yield the river channel to an oncoming steamboat. A determined Fink bragged to the steamboat: "I'm King of the Keelboatmen, King of the Rivers! I'm a ring-tailed screamer from the old Mississippi! I can out-run, out-shoot, out-brag, and out-fight any man on the rivers! WHOOP! I've got the best crew and the fastest boat on all the rivers, and my muscles are as rusty as an old hinge. WHOOP! So come and see what you can do about it! Cock-a-doodle-do!" Neither boat gave way and both were smashed in the collision.

So, one of the earliest "heroes" of the river was admired for his skill, his antics, and his stubborn pride—all of which led him to mischievous, if not downright illegal, deeds. Perhaps the next and best articulated hero of the river was Mark Twain's steamboat pilot. Like those who passed on the feats of Mike Fink, Twain told a tall tale or two along the way and made legendary the exploits of certain remarkable boatmen like Mr. X, the crackerjack pilot and somnambulist. [1] Also singled out by Twain was a certain Stephen W., "a gifted pilot, a good fellow, a tireless talker" and a man with both wit and humor in him. The easygoing Stephen cherished a "most irreverent independence," and though he always had work, he never saved money, was a persuasive borrower, and was "in debt to every pilot on the river, and to the majority of captains." An admiring Twain described his talents: "He could throw a sort of splendor around a bit of harum-scarum, devil-may-care piloting, that made it almost fascinating—but not to everybody." Among the unimpressed was Captain Y, who relieved Stephen from duty and shuddered at the mere mention of his name.

"Why bless me! I wouldn't have such a wild creature on my boat for the world—not for the whole world! He swears, he sings, he whistles, he yells—I never saw such an Injun to yell. All times of the night—it never made any difference to him. He would just yell that way, not for anything in particular, but merely on account of a kind of devilish comfort he got out of it. I never could get into a sound sleep but he would fetch me out of bed, all in a cold sweat, with one of those dreadful war-whoops. A queer being—very queer being; no respect for anything or anybody. Sometimes he called me 'Johnny.' He kept a fiddle and a cat. He played execrably. This seemed to distress the cat, and so the cat would howl. Nobody could sleep where that man—and his family—was. And reckless? There never was anything like

[1] See Introduction.

it. Now you may believe it or not, but as sure as I am sitting here, he brought my boat a-tilting down through those awful snags at Chicot under a rattling head of steam, and the wind a-blowing like the very nation, at that! My officers will tell you so. They saw it. And, sir, while he was a-tearing down through those snags, and I a-shaking in my shoes and praying, I wish I may never speak agin if he didn't pucker up his mouth and go to *whistling*! Yes, sir; whistling 'Buffalo gals, can't you come out to-night, can't you come out to-night, can't you come out to-night;' and doing it as calmly as if we were attending a funeral and weren't related to the corpse. And when I remonstrated with him about it, he smiled down on me as if I was his child, and told me to run in the house and try to be good, and not be meddling with my superiors!"[2]

When one captain persuaded the financially strapped Stephen to hire on for half wages and then bragged to the boat's officers of his conquest, Stephen winced at the humiliation but outwardly attended to business with his customary whistling. Stephen kept the boat out in the middle of the river on a high stage of water instead of steering in the easier water toward shore. The puzzled captain chafed at Stephen's choice, knowing that, at such a pace, he might well die of old age before his boat reached St. Louis. Next day Stephen likewise stayed in the middle of the river, "whistling the same placid tune," and watched as a much slower boat clipped along in the easy water, gaining steadily, and making for an island chute. Finally, the captain could endure it no longer and asked whether that chute didn't cut off a good bit of distance. Stephen answered tersely, "I think it does, but I don't know." Excited and perplexed, the captain inquired whether there was enough water in the chute to go through. "I expect there is, but I am not certain." The exasperated captain confronted Stephen, "Do you mean to say that you don't know as much as they do?"

"*They*! Why, *they* are two hundred-and-fifty dollar pilots. But don't you be uneasy; I know as much as any man can afford to know for a hundred and twenty-five!"

The captain surrendered.

Five minutes later Stephen was bowling through the chute and showing the rival boat a two-hundred-and-fifty-dollar pair of heels. [*Life*, chap. 14]

[2] "Considering a captain's ostentatious but hollow chieftanship, and a pilot's real authority, there was something impudently apt and happy about that way of phrasing it" (Twain's note, chap. 14, *Life*).

In the oral narratives of modern-day river pilots, there are likewise heroes whose feats outlive them. Captain Pat Wilson was neither the nationally known legendary figure Fink's anonymous songsters perpetuated (and Walt Disney popularized) nor the object of such eloquently articulated praise as Twain reserved for his somnambulist wizard of the wheel and the good-natured dare-devil Stephen W. But, though he died over forty years ago, the mention of Pat's name to many lower-Mississippi River pilots will elicit both respect and a new tale or an alternate version of an oft-told antic.[3] A light named for him on the lower Mississippi River proclaims his prowess, and all rivermen who knew him or have heard the tales about him describe four memorable characteristics: Pat was a crackerjack pilot, an unrelenting prankster, a superstitious riverman, and a creative kleptomaniac. Like Mike Fink, who had been an Indian fighter before running the river, Pat had another career before turning to the river — he was a policeman in Memphis, a cop whose reputation earned him the nickname "Iron Jaw" among segments of the city's population. When he later became a pilot on the steamer *Herbert Hoover*, Pat would greet the city by blowing the whistle long and loud before bringing her into the wharf — a greeting which prompted onlookers to announce the imminent arrival of "Iron Jaw and the Hard Times." Police work was not an ideal career, however, for one afflicted with the disease of kleptomania, especially when he sometimes "borrowed" from those he was charged to protect.

However, it is as a river pilot that Pat is best remembered, and reputedly there was no better, natural-born, clever crackerjack than Pat Wilson. Of course, his unorthodox behavior also fostered the reputation of being a mite troublesome. Says one fellow pilot: "Well, Pat was a crackerjack pilot, now there's no need of people sayin' he wasn't. 'Cause he was good, you know. And you got to hand it to him — he was good on sternwheel boats and he was good on screw-type boats. I guess . . . when he wanted to have fun, he decided to have his fun his own way" (Captain Arthur McArthur). For example:

I was on the *Iowa* steering. Simmons was captain. Silvernagle and Peoria Johnny Brown were the pilots and . . . it was rough down on that bridge . . . Silver was on watch. He come on down there — put a little short flank in her and straightened her up. We had six heavy-loaded barges and went on through there and went over there to the Arkansas side and tied off and brought a barge over. We all walked up on the hill there — up the incline, you know, where Patton's office [terminal superintendent] was. We was

[3] In keeping with the wishes of my informants, I have used a fictitious name for this pilot.

standin' . . . there talkin'—here come Pat down, on the *Minnesota*. He had one more barge than we did, and Patton said, "Look at that crazy son of a bitch. Hot-damn, he's going to steer that bridge!" And he started jumping up and down. And he says, "He knows better than that. He shouldn't do a crazy thing like that!" And old Pat come on down there and never rang a bell, and he steered that bridge and he shaved the whiskers off that lower pier, you know, on the Harrahan as he went by, but he made it. He just barely did make it. We all just stood out there, and Patton was as mad and his face was as red as a beet.

So, here comes old Pat up the hill all dressed up. Patton got on him . . . about that. "Aw," he says, "Captain, I had plenty of room." He says, "You could stick your hand between that barge and the pier. . . . You didn't need no more room 'n that." [Captain William Tippitt][4]

Wilson obviously bedeviled his superintendent on more occasions than this one. Once, when Pat had got aground at Helena, Arkansas, Patton wired him, asking how they were getting along. Wilson wired back: "We're doin' really fine; we're gettin' whiskey for fifty cents a gallon" (Captain Charles White, Sr.).

In the early years of this century, crews didn't get the day-for-day time off that is common now. In fact, they seldom got any time off at all until the season was over. Not one to let mere policy stand in his way, Pat (and other pilots as well) occasionally assured himself at least overnight respite from the daily rigors of piloting. "If he decided he wanted a little time in town, he'd come down and flank the boat right on in and whack the bank and maybe knock a wheel or rudder off." And he took chances that probably caused apoplexy in more than one roof captain.

Oh, they used to call him a "bar pilot." Yep. Instead of goin' down the bend, runnin' the bend, ole Pat threw her way out on the bar and drove her hard down. 'Course that's okay comin' up, you ain't likely to get in no trouble, but doin' it goin' down you're takin' an awful chance . . . I don't know; he was just naturally a good pilot and he was very jealous of what the other fellas's doin'. He tried to outdo 'em. [Captain Tippitt]

Still, he was so skilled at his craft that his services were in demand. One fellow pilot eulogized Pat's skill:

[4] This story was recorded by Captain Tippitt in 1976 for the Mississippi Valley Collection at Memphis State University.

I remember when I first started with the Federal Barge Line. I can remember them makin' up those tows at St. Louis at North Market Street there and they'd make 'em up five wide and then three or four long, and old Pat, he'd get in that pilot chair. I seen him do that at night, day, or anytime. And he'd top that thing out of there [turn tow around so it was heading in opposite direction] . . . and go on down through those bridges. Nobody else would do it. But he could do it. He was a crackerjack. Just a world of judgment. Old man Jim Simmons was captain on the *Iowa* and Pat was on there, piloting. . . . He said, "You know, old Pat, he's hard to get along with, . . . but I have to have him." And he said you can't find any better. He's just, just one damn good pilot. . . . He was a young fella when he learned the trade from those old fellas on that big boat. And he was a crackerjack. He picked it up real quick. . . . There was probably no better that ever lived than Pat Wilson. [Captain Ray Prichard]

Probably because he was such an ace pilot, Pat could commit with impunity pranks that might well have been disastrous for a less-talented man. One of his former partners recalls the time he went to the pilothouse at watch change only to find "there wasn't a darn soul" there. "Pat was up on the after jackstaff on the rear end of the boat fixing the antenna for his radio. Now that's the God's truth, so help me. Boat right in the middle of the river going on up." Such habits, as one can well imagine, were not condoned by the various captains he served. One pilot who served as steersman for Pat declared him to be "one of the best nighttime towboat pilots I ever saw in my life." However, he did have a habit of letting just anybody steer the boat.

He knew it was good river, see, but they wouldn't know it. They'd be going up the river. And . . . captain gave orders, absolutely, through the mate and the whole crew—"Don't steer that boat for Pat." And the Captain thought he really had him fixed this time. He walked up to the pilothouse one time, and there's this . . . maid, she's up there steering the boat. Captain said . . . "Jesus Christ, what're you doing up here? Where's Captain Wilson?" She said, "I don't know where Captain went, I don't know where. He just said come up here and grab hold of this thing. That's all I'm doin'." Old Man said, "Do you know where you're going?" She said, "I don't know nothing about it!" . . . He was . . . down in the galley playing around with something. . . . And the captain come busting down there yelling at Pat, and Pat takin' [took] off right quick. [Captain Francis "Dusty" Walters]

Though he knew it was "good river," this behavior was, of course, irresponsible and potentially dangerous. Other pranks, however, illustrate that playfully mischievous side of Pat that pilots remember. Frequently testing his piloting skills against others in impromptu races and casual bets about making a bend, Pat seemed to thrive on the thrills inherent in taking calculated risks. And so, even his pranks hinged on his ability for possible rescue.

Well, Captain Rogers, an old captain, was on the *Herbert Hoover*. Pat'd be comin' down the river and be goin' into a bend . . . the captain was up in the pilothouse with the pilot. Pat'd go down there and go on in and have the searchlights on headin' into the bank and lookin' at buoys . . . and get her just about right and set the *Herbert Hoover* to backin'. When she was backin' up, he would listen then for the water to start . . . catchin' up out there and take a look at that buoy, and then he'd turn the searchlights out and turn the light on in the pilothouse and get down on the floor on his hands and knees. And the old man started gettin' nervous, said, "My God, Patty, what are you doin'?" And Pat'd say, "I dropped a dime down here somewhere, Captain, I'm tryin' to find it." He'd be down on his hands and knees crawlin' and there the boat was backin' and the old man was worried and he said, "My God, Pat, git up there and turn the light off and I'll give you a dime!" [Says this very excitedly, laughs.] And he worked that on him all the time, you know. [Captain Arthur McArthur]

When one roof captain refused to buy a fan to alleviate what Pat considered to be stifling heat in the pilothouse, Pat arrived at his own unique solution. Of course, it was one that didn't "set well" with the captain and encouraged him to furnish the fan.

They had spike poles and they're about twenty feet long and . . . they're made with a spike down on the end of a hook. . . . Use 'em a lot of times to fish things out of the river, or push a piece of drift away from the side of the boat, or get it out from back there around the paddlewheel, or anything like that. . . . But he'd get one of those up here and then tie it on to the steerin' levers . . . and then, he'd get out on the bridge and steer the boat out there, you know, and guide her up the river. That'd aggravate the captain a lot of the times on the boat. . . . They figured he really wasn't watchin'—he was a good pilot, old Pat was. [Captain McArthur]

Practical jokes often relieved the tedious routine for rivermen confined to the boat for weeks or months at a time. When both pilots were known pranksters, it paid to be alert. Sometimes pranks backfired—literally.

Well, Pat Wilson and Captain Fred ["Pinky"] Hill were pilots on the boat, . . . so Pinky was always tryin' to pull jokes and things like that. So he knew old Pat was scared of snakes. . . . He went down and bought him one of these real long ole black-lookin' snakes, you know, and put it in Pat's bed. And he had his room next to him [Pat] . . . there was just plaster-board in between the rooms; the bulkheads was actually thin. So old Pat walked into the room and turned the light on, pulled the covers back . . . and there was that snake, and it scared the livin' heck out of him. It looked like a real snake, and he reached over there and grabbed his shotgun and "Whoom!" shot right through the mattress and the bed and all! And old Pinky was over there next to it and he come sailin' out of there in his shorts, sayin' [laughing almost uncontrollably], "Oh, Lord, Pat, don't shoot no more, don't shoot no more! That wasn't nothin' but a toy snake!" [Captain McArthur]

This crackerjack pilot with a "fun-loving" disposition was also superstitious. Pat was particularly frightened of ghosts and the bad luck associated with being in rooms where someone had died.

Old Pat was very, very superstitious. And Cutting told me that they were together—Cutting was captain—and as soon as he got that boat [Herbert Hoover], he got Pat Wilson over there with him, because he was such a good pilot. . . . He and Pat Wilson went on it and they put it down in the lower river. Well, Cutting said that he never knew why, but . . . the port door to the pilothouse, every once in a while, it was the vibration, and the door would swing open and then in a minute or two it'd go shut. It was the vibration and probably a little breeze.

And another thing that use to happen to it—now they use to have buttons to turn the searchlights on on the floor—floor buttons, in those days. And every once in a while the starboard light would come on all by itself. It was the vibration of the diesel engines would make the lights go on. Well, Cutting said, "I'd been on the boat for about a month before Pat got there, and I was use to all that stuff." Well, the first captain on that boat was called . . . Moore, and he died in the pilothouse, on the boat. As captain. And he didn't stand a watch; he had two pilots.

But they changed their modus operandi and had the captain stand a watch. . . . So Pat was on there the first night, and he got on the boat at Baton Rouge. And they changed watches at midnight, and Cutting said he was . . . over in the corner marking down the midnight miles at a little desk there—and the door come open and Pat says, "What'd you open that door for, Carl?" "Well, I didn't open it." "Well," he says, "it came open, then it went shut." "Yeah," he says, "that's old man Moore's ghost." Pat said, "Don't you leave this pilothouse unless there's somebody up here!" And he wouldn't—he wouldn't stay there alone. He was scared to death.

And he no sooner got that out when this starboard light came on. He says, "That's the end. I'm goin' to get off this thing." And he did. He wouldn't stay on that boat. He was superstitious. 'Cause Cutting said that was old man Moore that turned that light on, you know. And he was just kiddin' him [Captain Ray Prichard]

Says another former crewmate:

So old Pat and Skid were the two pilots that come over [to the *Minnesota*]. Pat always wanted to get the best of everything . . . and they'd just worked the pilots' rooms over and one room was really nicer and bigger. It was on the stern of the boat. So Pat said, "I'll take that room." So he put Skid in the forward room.

While we were layin' there, Pat was wanderin' around the boat and somebody just happened to mention to Pat about an electrician'd died in that room in New Orleans while they were puttin' in the wiring . . . so Pat checked around to see if that was true. He ran in and he told Skid, "You got to change rooms with me; I'm not gonna stay in that room." And Skid said, "Why?" And he told him, "A man died in there and I'm not gonna sleep in that room. You get up and get your clothes and move 'em all in there."

Well Skid was a little bit superstitious too, and Skid wouldn't move. So Pat went to the captain and the captain said, "No, you picked the room, Pat, so you get in there and stay in that room." So he got mad and run in there and pushed Skid over on the side and crawled in bed with him and slept, see. Finally, old Skid the next day . . . moved over there in that room. Let Pat have the other one. [Captain McArthur]

And, of course, there was the kleptomania. Current tale tellers implore the listener to understand that Pat couldn't help himself, that it was a disease, that they liked him (ornery as he was) in spite of their need to guard their possessions when on a boat with him. "He didn't steal to be mean. It was a sickness. He couldn't help it. He'd steal anything . . . like a crow, you know, anything that was shiny, he'd take it home with him." His larcenies ranged from appropriating all of the cook's preserves and jellies to "borrowing" a car belonging to his lady friend's husband. Whenever he went into a department store, he'd come out with something he'd snitched—fountain pens, floor lamps, watches, typewriters, or clothes. And, of course, a kleptomaniac doesn't necessarily take items that have practical value.

> He would steal anything. . . . They picked up a German cook down in New Orleans that jumped ship, that could get by with a small amount of English, and Cutting [the captain] said he was an excellent cook. And one day his false teeth showed up missing. And Cutting said to him, "August, where's your teeth?" He said they turned up missing. And Captain Cutting could understand a little bit of German. And he said, "I think I probably know where they are." And he went up, and of course he had a master key to every bedroom, you know. He went upstairs [to Pat's room] and here was the cook's teeth on the dresser! He couldn't stand it. He had to steal those teeth because they were made in Germany and they were . . . a pretty expensive set of dentures. [Captain Prichard]

Pat got away with stealing the preserves, the pens, the thermos jugs and overcoats, and even the cook's teeth. However, as one story goes, what put him in the workhouse for a stretch was his theft of the diamond ring, the Maxwell touring car, and the commodore's watch. He persuaded a woman of his acquaintance to let him wear one of her big diamond rings and to drive her automobile when he was around. Both were presents to her from her husband. Then Pat, who had been running packet boats into St. Louis before being laid off, paid a call on the commodore of the packet line, and "when he walked out of Commodore Lehye's office, Commodore Leyhe's watch went with him." While Pat's wife and kids were in St. Louis, Pat was living it up in Memphis on the money he got from selling the watch, the ring, and the car. The outraged commodore and Pat's wife conspired to snare him. Thinking the commodore wanted to talk to him about the river-season opening, Pat took a train to St. Louis, where two detectives grabbed him as he prepared to greet his wife at the station.

The career of this superstitious, prank-playing, kleptomaniac crackerjack ended on the river—he died on the same boat, at the same spot where several years before he had refused to sleep in the room where the electrician had died because it would bring bad luck. While no one claims that he could take his boat over a low crossing at Helena in his sleep, his skill was rated as "gold-leaf, kid-glove pilotin'." His antics could be entertaining, irritating, illegal, and even hazardous, not unlike the antics of Stephen W. or Mike Fink. Perhaps the river of American myth is the natural spawning pool for legendary American characters. At any rate, the stories about Pat Wilson, though fewer and more local than those of the nineteenth-century Fink, nevertheless live on among rivermen who cannot disguise a gleam in their eyes when they hear his name.

Captain William Tippitt at home

I wanted to be a towboat pilot.
I wanted to be among the big men.

OLE CRUSTY

Born June 8, 1900, in Cairo, Illinois, Captain William Tippitt is the image of the crusty old salt of the river. He wouldn't be offended by this characterization; in fact, he nurtures it. When he steams into a story about his river-piloting days, the listener is treated to a dramatization performed by a slightly built man propelled by remembered excitement. He may unexpectedly lay his pipe on the table, catapult from his seat, and dance around the floor demonstrating with gestures and words just how that boat negotiated the Vicksburg Bridge or how one pilot outsmarted another in an impromptu race. The study in his Hernando, Mississippi, home is packed with steamboat pictures, projects, boat models, file cabinets of old river news columns and other steamboat memorabilia, and his own writings. Always interested in history, Captain Tippitt has accumulated drawers and drawers of materials, has written a collection called *Steamboat Stories*, a history of the Anchor Line and Lee Line, and works periodically on a history of the Federal Barge Line.

Captain Tippitt is an independent, plain-speaking, proud, knowledgeable boatman whose gusto, mischievousness, and cantankerousness probably elicited few lukewarm reactions from colleagues. One suspects he has been either well regarded or roundly dismissed in the affections of fellow rivermen. At the age of seventy-eight, a cancer-stricken Tippitt drove himself the forty miles each way for his treatments, continued working as a Hernando city inspector, and still traveled with river-buff cronies to ferret out new information or attend meetings in distant places. He is accustomed to such battles; in the 1918 flu epidemic, young William Tippitt, U.S. Army, helped nurse victims and never had a bit of flu. "I took quinine and whiskey and I didn't have no flu. Maybe I was just too ornery." After his five months of duty in World War I, he finished high school in Cairo and then persuaded his railroader father to supply him

161

with passes on the Illinois Central, Southern Pacific, and Union Pacific so he could travel alone south to Mexico and west to California and Oregon for some postsecondary adventure. In fact, though he had passes, he figured out ways to stump the railroad bulls and "hoboed" part of the route, because it was a challenge and because he "just took a notion" to try it.

Back in Cairo after three months or so on the road, Tippitt worked in turn on the river, the railroad, and the newspaper for awhile before turning to the river for good. As a river reporter on the Cairo *Citizen*, he wrote the "Snag Town River Ripples" under the pen name "Huck Finn." Characterizing his reports as a "regular Walter Winchell column," Tippitt noted boat arrivals and departures, chitchat, scandals, and rumors. In 1922 he went back on the river; then he quit to go back on the railroad; then quit the railroad to go back to the paper. But though he liked to write, he never considered newspaper work as a career. "I had no intention of being anything but a steamboat pilot . . . I just couldn't get the river out of my blood. I could stay away for so long, and then I'd throw everything up and back on the river I'd go until I got fed up with it."

As a youngster in 1915, Tippitt had worked the summer for the Barrett Fleet, and in '16, '17, and '18 he had steered for Old Man Hacker on his ferryboat. In 1924, he got first-class pilot's license. In his subsequent career, which ended with retirement in 1966, Tippitt piloted towboats, dredges, inspection vessels and showboats.

Beginnings

Bill Tippitt grew up in a river town where most all the young boys could tell you the name of every packet boat that landed at Cairo by the time they were five years old.[5] Every kid in town knew Old Man John Hacker, captain of the ferryboat, and several of the pilots lived in the neighborhood. "So us boys knew all the steamboat men." The steamboat men appeared rich and classy as they walked down the street "all duded up." "And every kid wanted to be a steamboat man." The Cairo kids practically lived on the river, swimming endlessly and taking the summer shade provided by cottonwood trees outside the levee. By the time he was about eight years old, Tippitt had decided to be a steamboat man. He had even met Mark Twain's mentor, Horace Bixby, though at least in retrospective hindsight, he was hardly awed by him.

Oh, yes, all them fellas around here knew Bixby. I met him when I was a

[5] See Chapter 1 for Tippitt's recollection of boyhood ambition.

kid, but he was a pompous jackass. Oh, he was respected, highly respected, a great man. See, 'course his day was gone, you know. Back then, he was almost blind; they just give him a job. There was no pensions, you know. And the old man had been a big shot in the old Anchor Line for years. Then of course he had his reputation from Mark Twain.

Tippitt's Fourth-Street neighborhood in Cairo was half Irish and half German.

It's really down in the old part of the city that was first settled, and steamboat families predominated down there among the most influential people in the neighborhood. . . . Now you see, the people we admire, us boys, back there in those days, was the railroad engineer and the railroad conductor, engineer preceded over conductor. Now the pilot, he was the big man, so we all knew that the pilot was bigger than the captain. Now the captain might be in command of the boat, but when the pilot stepped up there and took charge, he was the man responsible for navigation. We all knew that.

I wanted to be pilot. I never did want to be a captain. I'll be frank with you, I never wanted to worry. . . . When that boat hit town, I wanted to put my duds on and go to town. I'd rather be a first-class pilot than anything because a first-class pilot always has a job.

Tippitt learned to steer on Old Man Hacker's ferryboat running local trips. His first long-distance on-river experience came during a summer vacation as quartermaster on the lighthouse boat *Oleander* and turned out to be more strenuous than he had expected.[6] He had hoped to "be riding the pilothouse, but [he] found out different" when he learned the nature of his duties: filling lanterns, shining brass, grinding pump valves during repair layup, toting five-gallon oil cans, and replenishing light poles. His first job began at 4:30 a.m. when he filled about twenty lanterns.

Well, then breakfast was about 6:30. Before breakfast I had to have all the brass shined. . . . Now there was two flights of steps from the main deck up to the boiler deck and from the boiler deck up to the hurricane roof. Now those steps had big brass plates on them and they had a brass kickplate below 'em. Now they had to be shined every morning and they had brass handrails on each side. They had to be shined all the way up. And then on the roof

[6] Lighthouse boats tended the buoys and lights and furnished navigation and channel reports. These functions have since been taken over by the Coast Guard.

there's a search light up there. I don't know where it ever came from. It was about the biggest one I have ever seen. . . . The barrel of it was about three feet in diameter, and it was about four and a half feet long. It was solid brass. Now you had to have it polished and the bell was brass. Great big bell, steamboat bell, it had to be polished. Well, then by the time you got that all done you were supposed to be ready for breakfast. So you had to go down and clean up and come to the table with your coat on.

We got off the way right after breakfast and they said in the summertime we run from can to can't. We got out with the sun . . . and we run until about 7:00 that night before we'd tie up.

When they landed in St. Louis for repairs, Tippitt spent thirty days grinding ninety valves in a pump "and getting them polished up like that engineer wanted them." When they left St. Louis, the "old man worked the daylights" out of Tippitt, who had to carry five gallon oil cans to light tenders.

Had a house maybe back on the high bank. . . . Well, we landed on a sandbar that was a mile and a half, maybe a mile back there. Well, you had to tote them five-gallon oil cans back . . . to the lightkeeper's house. Maybe got twenty of 'em or twenty-five of 'em, enough until we come back again. . . . Boy, in August you trudge across the Mississippi River sandbar toting something like that, and I mean we all done it. I mean the old man stood up there in the pilothouse and made us all work except the engine-room crew. Of course, that wasn't under his jurisdiction.

But the mates, the clerks, that was us two boys, and all the deckhands used to see us going across toting them cans; and maybe he wanted some new light poles. Well, them poles were about sixteen-to-eighteen feet-long 4 x 4s, you know, and they're pretty darn heavy. Maybe I'd have to tote a half dozen or a dozen of them over there for him to replace the lights and things. Then as we went down the river, we'd stop at every light. If there was any brush around it, we had to go up—of course, the deckhands done most of that—he had me doing too many other things. I couldn't get around to that brush cuttin'. I was writing channel reports and doing various other things that he wanted done. Maybe polishing up all that brass, and that pilothouse was loaded with brass. It took me half a day to polish all that brass in the pilothouse. So I didn't have much time for that, but I would have to get out and help tote them cans.

One night after finishing his duties, for which he was paid a dollar a day plus board, Tippitt and the captain's two sons left the boat without permission, walked the three miles to town, drank a few beers, and walked back. When the captain found out about it, he "raised the devil" with them, chewed them out, and henceforth laid up "out in the woods where there was no getting off. We just had to go to bed after we got done working, that's all there was to it."

Well, I done learned enough. I didn't want no more of the *Oleander*, I'll tell you that now. So I went back to riding with Captain Hacker on the ferryboat. So after I rode the ferryboat then—of course I knew everybody down at the ferry line, you know, I was just like homefolks down there. I was down there every day in the world all over there, and I knew everybody, so I got to ridin' in the Barrett boats. I was right there and I learned to pilot a towboat there. I knew all them fellas, they'd let me steer, see?

Well, of course, going up the river, why the pilot he's sitting back there and reading the newspaper, and then he'd cast a wary eye out every now and then to see that I was in the channel, and he'd let me do his, stand in his watch, so I stood many a watch on the Ohio and Mississippi that a'way, learning. And of course coming down now, he never let steersmen have it coming down. Only going up. That's what he had to learn on his own when he started out. . . . That's a trick of the trade, you know.

After graduating from high school, Tippitt had signed on the *Choctaw*, a Corps of Engineers sternwheel towboat, as a cabin boy. "That's when I made my first trip to New Orleans, and I had great expectations. I didn't fare too well, though. I got off on the way back at Memphis. The old man threw me off." That trip yielded no piloting experience at all, but it was indeed a memorable venture.

All I got on it was experience as a scrub brush because I caught the old man in bed with the cook. So that ended my happy days. She was a female, naturally, and her husband was a steward and he was a no-account, absolutely no-account. So, to get back at me they put me to scrubbing all the gingerbread work coming up the river in the main cabin. . . . I've always admired gingerbread work, but I'm going to tell you, before we got to Memphis I was sick of it! You get up on top of the stepladder and get all them doodads and them little curlicues and warsh them off with soap and water there and then rinse them off and then dry them. The old man would come in there now and then: "There's a spot on that, get back there and get it." They was a little rough on me.

Still, he remembers it was a good trip because they lost Jocko the monkey and dispatched the captain's two kittens.[7] "He had two daggone kittens he got down there at New Orleans. And you know there was only one place they could do their business—that's in the pilot's toilet. Then I'd have to run and get the dang mop and clean it up again. Well, we fixed the cats!" On a "yawl call" at Natchez to take the mail off, Tippitt and his buddy pitched the cats on shore and "lit out" to the boat. "Well, that old man had a hemorrhage after that. . . . He figured I done it. I got the blame for it. He really was on my duster from then on, and I got off at Memphis."

In the late 1920s, "If you made ten dollars a day, you was on top of the world. . . . The average pay was around three or four dollars, that is if you was a college man, or somethin' like that. Common labor was a dollar. . . . Deckhands got $37.50 a month." Tippitt did not spend a lot of time decking.

I never did really deck any; I did a little playin' like I was deckin'. I had to have a little experience there to get my license. . . . I was already a good steersman, see, 'cause I steered on that ferryboat. The old man'd go on there; soon as we got away from town, why he'd just turn it over to me and go on downstairs to his room. He'd come up for the landing and then back her out because we never knew when the inspectors would be on the bank, see. So when we were out in the river—"Here, take her"—and he was gone.

Oh, I had a lot of teachers—Haptonstall, the two Conner boys, and a number of 'em. The worst thing I ever did, I was with old man Charlie O'Neal. He was a crack towboat man; he was in the old Valley Lines. I was steerin' for him one night, and they wanted you to steer steady, they didn't want you a wobblin'. When they said, "Hold her on that tree," they meant hold her on that tree. You get to wobblin' and he'd get on you. So, he give me all the lights in that damn crossing and how we was to run 'em. Well, you know, it's hard to memorize all that stuff if a man just tell ya, you know. Then after we got up top of that next bend, he'd say, "Hey, that ain't how I told you to run it." And he just chewed me out goin' and comin'.

Them little lighthouse books—well, I didn't know there was such a thing. They wouldn't let me see it. But I'd see 'em reach down there in their pocket and look at somethin, you know, and I wondered about that. And him callin' off them names, and that's the way you learnt the river, they told ya. 'Course all that stopped after the barge line [Federal Barge] got in, 'cause they needed men; they didn't have time to fool with that old-fashioned way

[7] See Chapter 4 for story of Jocko the monkey.

of learning it. They just needed you and . . . they gave you the mapbook. And I didn't even know anything about a navigation mapbook. They all kept them down in their rooms, see.

Tippitt's first stretch of pilot's license covered Cairo to St. Louis. Then he extended from Cairo to Memphis, and later from Greenville to New Orleans. For awhile his license had a noticeable gap—Memphis to Greenville— because he "wasn't ready to face old John B. Wykoff," the Memphis examiner yet. When asked how long it took him to become familiar with stretches of the river, Tippitt gave the only response a seasoned pilot would utter: "It all depends."

Well, the whole thing is this, it depended upon how often you get over it. Now if you get over it fairly often, it don't take you long. . . . Now let me make this clear, you might learn it at low-water stage, see, and about six or eight trips over you'd learn it in low-water stage, and then when you've got a high-water stage, you're lost because everything looks different. So you've got another picture you've got to get in your mind. So really it takes a couple of years for a man to really learn the river because he's got to learn it at all the different stages, and he's got to learn the shorelines, and he's got to keep up with all that and the height of the barge and everything. It's always fluctuatin'.

So, after you get your primary knowledge of the river, then you've got to take your secondary, and then your postgraduate course. The postgraduate course is when you get behind a big tow, and the little boat ain't got enough power to handle the tow, and you've got to take it down the river and deliver it safely. That's your postgraduate course.

I'll tell you this much. Wherever I had a stretch of license, I could run, I knew the river. I wouldn't go up for a stretch of license if I didn't know the river. . . . Some of them has. Some of them have skipped in there, a lot of people, you know, would get these maps, memorize the map. We had a boy over there at the Army Engineers, drew as pretty a map as you ever laid eyes on. Perfect. He was a very competent, skilled, and mechanical engineer. He got it in his head he was going to be a pilot. He come down and asked me about it. I told him in three years he could be a pilot. I said, "You just have to start at the ground like the rest of us did." He said, "I don't have to start no place. I got all this education." I said, "All right. You got your education." He got on the boat . . . had enough experience there where he could creep under the regulations—you had to have so many months experience on deck and so forth. Well, he had that covered . . . he got his license.

Well, the *Chiska* wasn't no great big boat, but she was a pretty good-sized boat. He was on there with Lee Campbell, and I was on there. We started down the river with a light boat, we was going down, the water was high up, right up to the top of the bank. You could run almost any place. We was going down the river, and I was on watch, at suppertime. . . . Him and Old Man Campbell come up, right after supper, dark wintertime, and it's kind of misting rain, and it was black. You know, nothing can get as black as it can out there on that river there. Especially in high water when you've got no shadow or nothing—that timber seems to blend in, you know— and I was just letting her go. I paddled her down that river there about ten or eleven miles an hour, and them notches was going by out there, look and see, watching the timber just going by. He come on . . . "You got her partner." I went down. I had no more than sit down at the table there and I heard every bell on her ring. I didn't get up and go up there. I heard him and the old man a'hooping and a'hollering up there. It done got turned around. He didn't know which way they was going—whether she was going up or down. The old man couldn't see very good anyhow, but he was just on to kind of cover, to help 'em with the boy. He got nervous. So finally they sent for me to come up, and I went up there, I got them straightened out and showed them down there, and the old man said, "Bill," he says, — we was only about two hours out of Helena—"you mind staying up here until we get down to Helena and we just tie up for the rest of the night?" Well, I knew I was going to have to come back on at midnight, see. I said, "Well, seeing as I'm up here, I might as well do it." I said, "You want me to hold her while you go get your cup of coffee?"—to this fella. He says, "Yes." He went downstairs and got his cup of coffee and he never did come back. He done went right then.

Now he was good in daylight, he was just fine in daylight, but he didn't know what to do with a tow. You put five or six barges on him, and he didn't know what to do with them. Light boat, he could take it any place. And daytime, he'd go any place. When that sun went down, it got black and misty. You've got to know that river where you can run it as black as the ace of spades as well as you do in daylight. And it's altogether different looking.

With justifiable pride in having accomplished the difficult task of obtaining first-class pilot's license, even a neophyte pilot refused to sign on in any other capacity. "Oh, once you had the license, you never would be nothing but a pilot. That's below your dignity! That's below your professional standards!" The new Captain Tippitt had taken notice of the "old heads" and respected their style and abilities.

Haptonstall, he was one of the best. He was up to Henry Nye, "Quaker Oats," or any of the rest of 'em. . . . I knew all them old-timers. . . . Henry and I had the largest collection of diamonds of any pilot on the river. . . . Oh, yes, that's how you always invested your money. When I was a young man comin' up, the first money you got when you was a pilot, you bought yourself a diamond ring. Yeah, that's so you could hock it whenever you got broke. [Laughs.] In fact, I was out with Denny Lucas; we pawned his ring so many times down there on St. Charles Street, we just walked in the door and Denny laid it up on the counter; the man would write out a ticket and hand out $150.

He'd take the $100 and I'd get the $50. He'd go out to the race track, and I'd go to town. Then we'd meet when it was time for the boats to go back out; we'd both be broke. Next time we come in—we generally got a check always at New Orleans, you know—well, we'd go 'round and redeem the diamond ring, see. . . . All them old pilots, they all done it. That's one of the things they taught us. You had a gold-headed umbrella or a gold-headed cane, or you had diamonds. Gold-headed umbrella or a cane always worth ten dollars, see. Any pawn shop.

The diamond studs, cufflinks, and tiepins were not laid away in some secret cache, either. They wore them.

Oh, when they come on watch at night time—now you take Haptonstall was one of 'em—you take them old-timers, when they come on watch at night, they'd have on a clean white shirt. Every time they come on watch, they'd be dressed up. Even ole "collars and cuffs," this Harry Nichols, the Crown Prince. . . . Well, see he had a white shirt, but they used to sell only collars and cuffs; he had on clean cuffs and a clean collar every time he come on watch, no matter how often he came on watch. . . . Night or day, and he always wore a suit. He didn't go around in slacks and blue jeans like we do. He always had a suit, shoes polished, and everything. All them old-time packet boat pilots did. . . . Most of 'em didn't have any money. Few of 'em, like Haptonstall had money because they made big money. Them towboat pilots was the ones that made the money.

Tippitt's admiration for Captain Haptonstall's abilities is apparent when he talks of the latter's last trip around 1934.

That old *Harris*, no one could do anything with her; I seen him bring her through [Island] 35 when she was very worst, and the only bells he ever rang was stoppin' bell, full astern and come ahead on her, and we had six barges, and he made her go down there and make all them twists and turns, and there's no one under God's green earth that could do it but that man. . . . He just knew. He just had the feeling. Some people got a natural knack to it. And timing. Timing is the most important thing.

Well, old man Haptonstall set up on that stool there and took that boat through there, and I'd a bet a million dollars—'cause I done been on her three years and I knew her, you learn a boat in three years . . . I'd been in all kinds of scrapes with her. I'd hit the bank so many times I didn't count 'em and hit sandbars and everything else, and I jist been through there the day before. I told the old man when he got on there, he just laughed. "Oh, Bill," he said, "let the old master have her." And I was settin' on the stool and he just took that big—that hand of his reached down and grabbed me right here [seat of pants] and lifted me up out of the seat and set me back on the bench, that was how strong he was.

He got up there and he took her and went on down as unconcerned as you please. . . . It was just a question of timing, now, he just had it, that's all. He was a marvelous pilot.

Makin' It

Tippitt served first as steersman, then as trip pilot, with the Federal Barge Line through 1926. But he and Superintendent Patton "couldn't get along."

He got mad at me. I'd been married and had been three months in Cairo and St. Louis trade. We'd always lay up in the woods; we never laid up in Cairo. We'd go into Cairo and run over and drop a tow on the east side, come over on the west side and pick our barges up, and there was the mail and groceries, and we'd go right back out, and then we'd lay up in the woods where there was no way in God's green earth to get off. So I told him, "I been on here three months; I wanta go home." And he said, "By God, you work fifty-two weeks, and I might give you two weeks off if you're a good boy." Uh, uh, he ain't gonna give me two weeks. Bye. And I grabbed my suitcase and got off and walked on home. That's the way it was, you see. They had you over a barrel.

Still, one of Tippitt's most effervescent tales comes from his barge-line days. It was one of those infamous, impromptu races, you understand.

I was on one of the damndest races ever run on the Mississippi River. I was on the *Iowa* steerin' and, let's see, I believe it was the *Minnesota*—that's when they were sternwheel boats. We left St. Louis about a half an hour apart, each one had six barges. Pat Wilson, you've heard of him . . . Pat was on one of the boats; I forget who the other one was on there pilotin'.[8] We had Silvernagle and . . . I think it was Peoria Johnny Brown. . . . We started out from St. Louis. They were ahead of us, and we was tryin' to catch 'em, and they didn't want us to catch 'em, you know, and we was racin' down the river there. Man, they was steerin' bends that they'd been flankin' to go down there at St. Genevieve. The guys'd [probably referring to the Corps of Engineers] built a dike plumb across the darn channel. Old Pat goes right on through that million-dollar dike, pilin' goin' up on both sides.[9] We come right down behind him and went right through there, too. We took out a little more, see. . . . So we got down there to Backbone. . . . All you can do is flank around it there when the water's low, without hittin' the bank. But the water was pretty low. Damned if they didn't steer that thing, and I mean to tell you that it liked to scare the captain on the other boat to death, and when we come down there— J. B. Simmons was captain, you know—Jimmy was standin' out there [paces back and forth moaning]. He couldn't even holler, he was so mad.[10]

Old Silver come on down there, and I bet you we didn't miss that bank with that wheel that far [shows about six inches]. Just throwin' the water all over. Just drivin' her. We went on down there to 76; well, that's when you went between the towheads. . . . Well, we had fair water; they went on across that'a'way, and ole Silver was on watch, and when he got nervous he'd always—settin' on that high stool, you know—he'd always kind of slide over and put his foot down on the floor. He'd start that and that foot'd go down. Now, you couldn't tell he was nervous. He smoked that stogey just as unconcerned, but you watch that foot. When that foot startin' pattin', you knew somethin' was comin' up. The captain was sweatin' and lookin' at that foot, he says, "Oh, my God, oh, my God!" He had an idea what he was gonna do. Silver went down instead of goin' across here; he had picked out a

---

[8] This is the same Pat Wilson featured in "The Legendary" section of this chapter.

[9] At that time, they constructed wooden dikes.

[10] See Glossary for distinction between flanking and steering.

way down through there and he went on down through there and we got ahead of the others. And we beat 'em into Cairo.

Well, then Patton was down there; he was about to have a hemorrhage too. Them two boats, everybody knew they was racin', you know, and the chances they was takin'.

About a year later, two other line boats raced between St. Louis and Cairo Point. Captain Harry Nichols, piloting one of them, misjudged his clearance and consequently parted company with the boat's jackstaff and smokestacks. He won the race, but he lost his job. "Thereafter, they never let two boats start out down the river at the same time. They'd hold one at least six hours after the other one was gone."

In the late twenties, Tippitt worked briefly on the *Choctaw* and as relief pilot.

When not there I was on construction boats, as they were putting in lots of revetment and dikes between Cairo and St. Louis. I could make more money on trip and construction jobs than working regular, per example if I worked twenty days, I made equal of Barge Line pay. Then I would have time to party and dance in town. Most of the construction jobs were daylight only and that left the nights free for roaming around.[11]

In 1929 he went with the Corps of Engineers and in the next decades ran pilot or captain on all varieties of their boats—survey, channel, dredging, revetment, and inspection. Like most other pilots, Captain Tippitt weathered the Depression years much better than the majority of workers onshore. During his career, which spanned Prohibition, the Depression, and World War II, Tippitt witnessed bootlegging and high times, the resurgence of river traffic credited to the Federal Barge Line, and major changes in river improvements and equipment advances.

Prohibition didn't really "take hold" in the lower Mississippi. Boatmen knew both the location of stills and the quality of brew all along the river. And, of course, they also knew where other pursuits of pleasure were to be found.

Oh, there was plenty of stills, there was stills all up and down the river. Cairo was kind of a supply center for St. Louis and northern Illinois, and down on Island No. 1 a fellow by the name of Bryant had very fine stills. . . . They was running all through prohibition. He was never

[11] Letter to J. Curry, February 23, 1981.

caught, because he made quality whiskey. You couldn't get no whiskey from him that wasn't at least six months old. He had some run up there at the last that was three or four years old. It was premium liquor. . . . White lightning they called it, yes, but it wasn't lightning—it was real whiskey, it was corn whiskey.

Now when you got up there around . . . Island 10 . . . that was good territory all in there for stills. Well, then you come on down the river there. On all the little islands there was stills and on the river bank. . . . In fact, down there at Rabbit Island below Memphis down here, . . . we could come up behind the island out of the main channels and that was—City of Memphis had sold a fire engine, you know, one that had boilers on it, pumper—they sold a couple of them here, and there it was, sitting down there on the banks, all painted up, just pumping away . . . and there you could see the big barrels of mash out there and you see the big copper still and she's furnishing steam there for all that. Just working day and night, twenty-four hours a day. And that whiskey all came to Memphis.

Tippitt willingly takes his listener on a guided tour of stills, with attendent recommendations regarding quality. Down by Helena at St. Francis Towhead; or, out behind Flowerhead Bayou was a wonderful place, but the whiskey was not too good up there. Memphis whiskey was inferior, too—did not have time to age. But down at Big Island near Rosedale, they had "some of the finest stills in the country and the finest whiskey." Premium or raw, whiskey was certainly accessible.

Tippitt also knew all the places where "you could get anything you wanted . . . from a black eye and a busted head on up and down." Even a town the size of New Madrid had a couple of bawdy houses. So did Carruthersville. On the upper end of town, somebody built an 80-foot x 80-foot building up there on pilings, up about twelve feet above the ground. "What it was built for was a honky tonk. Every time a boat came by, why we'd . . . blow the whistle and the girls would come out, and they'd heist their dresses up and shake it up for us, you know, as we went by. We'd just have a picnic!"

One owner in particular, Tippitt remembers, was exceedingly accommodating to rivermen. Jack's place was in Ashport.

Well, Jack had a place down there about 60 x 120 feet, and it was about eighteen or twenty feet off the ground because then they had to be that high up to keep it dry. So you climb these long steps and you get up there, and Jack had a bar down one side and the tables over there for gambling on the other side, and in the middle there was a space for dancing, and upstairs was the rooms for the girls. And you could go into Jack's there and you could find anything you wanted there at the price you wanted to pay. His prices was reasonable. He never overcharged; I think a beer was twenty-five cents, home brew was twenty-five cents a bottle, and whiskey was twenty-five cents straight or fifty cents for a set-up and everything.

All through Prohibition we would go in there, and if there wasn't enough girls, he'd just call Ripley up there and then he'd call around on the telephone. We had plenty of girls down there before the night was over. And you wanted to get in a fight, there was somebody there to knock the hell out of you. If you didn't, he tried to maintain order there among the people.

The joke of it was, though, when they got ready to go down them steps, man, that looked like it was a mountain of stairway there, and Jack generally had a couple local boys out there, they grabbed you when you come out, and they'd ease you down the steps, see, because you're liable to fall down and break your neck or something. He didn't want that to happen because he didn't want to hurt his steamboat trade.

But Jack knew how to treat them, and if they was too full, he always had an old car down there, and they'd load you up in the car and haul you back up to the boat and dump you off and holler out there for them to come and get you. . . . He delivered you back. . . . Well, we'd break a gut trying to get down there for a night; if we knew we was going to get caught a night, we'd even run a little bit after dark.

Didn't matter what time you got in there. Life would be going on down at Jack's. If you went in there at two o'clock in the morning and tied up and blowed the whistle a couple of times, by the time you got down to Jack's the lights would be on. And if you wanted something, he'd get it for you.

The old "hot spots" are gone now, of course. Places are built near the highways nowadays. Besides, as Tippitt concedes, "I'm too old to run around them things now, you see. I done lost my up-de-dump-dump." Asked where rivermen go for their entertainment now, he admitted, "I don't know. They don't go no place, by God. Fine thing. You get on a boat now . . . and you go thirty days there. I mean it's just watching and watching. . . . No, it ain't no fun doing it at all any more. Just work."

In the latter part of 1930, "things got tight."

They was really tight. You know that was about time it was really getting down, see, and so American Barge Line, they cut down expenses. They made their own men get licenses. . . . Business was getting kind of sticky and I had been loafing about three months, and I had an opportunity then to come down to Memphis to work for the government. So I came down there. That was the biggest surprise of my lifetime. I didn't know that there was such steamboat jobs as that, so I liked it so well I just practically stayed with them from then on.

Even though some boats were laid up, Tippitt recalls that throughout the Depression "there was a pretty good demand for qualified men. If you was qualified, you had no trouble getting work." River pilots had been organized into an association ever since pre-Civil War days. [12] But in the 1930s, it took an altogether different form with the involvement of the CIO — a step thoroughly unpopular with Captain Tippitt. What had been more of a fraternal organization became strictly a labor union.

It [association] had about nine lives. It survived and then it would die down and then a new group would get in there and revive it up until the late '40s. They were just an association, that's all it was. We was all just good fellows, you know, belong to it. You couldn't get 'em to stick to it. They were too much of an individual. You couldn't get the pilots to stick together like they do now. . . . Not a labor union like you've got now.

When Roosevelt come in, he put through that railroad pension, railroad retirement, and then he turned right around and give the CIO a wide-open hand. Well, that's where we steamboat people fell out with him. See the CIO pulled a strike on the Barge Line and they went to it. In fact, they had the strike broke, and then Roosevelt says, give in to them, and they made them give in to him.

I was a union man, too. But I didn't believe in that CIO business. . . . We wanted a union wherein it had respect not only for our trade and our ability but we respected the money that they had invested in there and all. We tried to work out a mutual agreement with everybody, see. We said when times were tough, we didn't expect the company to lose no money. We wanted to see them make money. The more they could make, why the better it was for us. That daggone CIO when they took over, they didn't care whether you made anything or not. They just wanted it their

[12] See chapter 7, *Life*, for Mark Twain's account of the power and tactics of the first pilot's association.

way, and they had it. I'll tell you, them boats was something awful to ride there when the deckhands were telling you how to run the boat—tell you to fire the cook, and you had to fire the cook. Tell you to fire the mate, you had to fire the mate.

During World War II, Tippitt joined the Coast Guard as a St. Louis-to-New Orleans pilot, moving war materials (submarines, LST landing craft) to the Gulf. Technology developed for the war effort later became standard equipment on inland river boats.

World War II was responsible for a hell of a lot of changes on the river. In the first place, you had the development of radar. Now see we had radars on them LST's, but nobody knew how to run them. And where they had them run, they wouldn't be worth a damn to a pilot. They had them back in the chart room instead of right there in front of the pilots. Of course they do different [at sea] . . . than we do on the river. So you had the development of radar, you had the development of the sounding machine. . . . And probably the biggest development of all was the perfection of the diesel engine where they had reliability.

We had tried diesel electric, we tried steam electric, and of course diesel had been coming along since the early part of the thirties, but about 1,100 horsepower was the biggest diesel engine you could get. They had an awful lot of trouble with them engines back there. And you really might say the development of the diesel engine didn't really take the full effect until the wartime when they got to turning them out in mass production. They had to get them where they could run and reliability.

After his Coast Guard war duties, Tippitt returned to the Corps of Engineers and retired about 1965. He did some trip work for a year or so and then settled into "building models of trains and models of boats and doing research on this old steamboat history, which I enjoy doing. . . . So now when I feel like it, I work. I don't feel like it, I don't." Fortunately, Captain Tippitt has retired neither the stories of his long career nor the zest of the telling.

This one's the best of all—talkin' about the *Mississippi*. "Duke of Paduke"—he was one of the big, blowed-up sapsuckers—he worked for Nickel Box Company for twenty years. They used to always have somethin' about Duke in the *Waterways Journal*. So, he thought he was better than any of us. Johnny-come-lately, and he was one of them dude-y dressers, you know, during the Depression. . . . Nickel had sold the *Exporter*, and he was workin' for the government like I was. So, we got on the *Mississippi* to take her to St. Louis. We got to St. Louis and we were there three or four days. Comin' down the river—we left there at nine o'clock, I was on watch—Captain said, "Now, back her out easy, round her to easy, and don't upset the commissioners. Be careful when you go to round to."

So, that afternoon he was on watch down there at Chester—big, wide river—oh, we was just pattin' our foot, we was about ten minutes late. The captain told him, too, to be careful in landing, not to upset her. [Gets up and acts this whole thing out]. Well, she had quite a bit of ground in her lower deck, all through her cabins, see. And they had this big long table settin' out there in the forward cabin which the commissioners set around, four on each side. And the president at one end and the secretary at the other. They was all glass in front there, just like she is now. They was holding a meeting before they got to Chester.

Old Duke come down there and he stepped on the whistle and he threw her hard down. Boy, she come around like a button on it, right out of the store. I mean, she laid over; I mean she really laid over. When she laid, old [captain] was standin' out on the head of the boat—that's when we had that bridge out there—and he went a jumpin' up and down, cussin'. You couldn't hear 'im 'cause Duke had his foot on that whistle, blowin' hell out of her. The daggoned table took way over; it went through the port bulkhead. . . . Old Duke come on around, throwed her back down, straightened her up, you know, to go into landin' and back went the commissioners and out went the door. And all the windows on the starboard side.

Table and all, he took 'em out. That great big old chair, lot of chairs, saved anybody from gettin' hurt. . . . I never will forget that. [Laughing uncontrollably.] Old Duke rang the stoppin' bell, set her full head astern, flipped the rudders around, pulled her in right quick, and made an eggshell landing. Hollered, "Drop the stage, Captain."

Captain was shakin' all over. Old Duke said, "Drop the stage, Captain, she's right on the minute." He said, "My God, so are we!" Boy, I mean to tell you, the special clerk they had on there said, "General wants to see ya. Right now." He was shakin' so hard, he could hardly get off of the steps. I don't know what the general said, but all the deckhands, everybody was up there cleanin' up the mess, and they wouldn't let people on till they got it all kind of straightened out. Old Duke, you know, he was pokin' around like a big pigeon. Captain comes up and says, "Captain Duke, you go to your room and stay there till we send for you." That old Duke swelled up, "What in the hell's the matter?" Said, "Didn't I tell you to take it easy when you turned this boat around? You just knocked both bulkheads out of the cabin. Damned near killed the committee and you almost got me fired! You go to your cabin and stay in it till I tell you you can come out."

'Course, direct order, nothin' he could do. Oh, he strutted out of that pilothouse cussin'.

Well, we laid there about an hour and we headed down for Cape (Girardeau). He called me, "Can you go up and take the wheel?" I said it was Duke's watch. He says, "You go up and take the wheel." I could see he was mad, and I didn't argue. And I went on up. He said, "Back this boat damned, damned easy. Don't rock or roll anything." And I backed her out on a slow bell, round her up, and got her to comin' ahead for a slow bell. Set out for Cape, only about an hour and a half's run; she was runnin' pretty good. We got out of Cape, and he said, "Now, Bill, our necks are both hangin' up like a goose right now. Back her out. Don't you even let a swell rock this boat." Well, I come around Cape on a slow bell. Soon as I got around to Cape Rock, I stopped her and let her float all the way down to the city front, backed her on a dead slow bell around and eased her into the landing.

I was 'sposed to go home that night from the Cape, see. He told me, he said, "You can't go no place. You got to take her out to Cairo. That man can't touch her." We got to Cairo. We'd both been down on the fleet layin' around . . . and we walked up the hill—Duke was madder than a wet hen—we got to the top of the hill and here comes Nappam runnin' up the hill. Old Captain Nappam. He was the man in charge of the first field area. He was our boss. He said, "Boys, I have to lay ya off. That's orders from Vicksburg."

I said, "Well, what in the hell we done?" "Oh," he says, "You know what happened t' Chester." He come over to me and he says [whispers], "Bill, you come back to work in about three days." And old Duke, they never did let him go back.

Clearly, careening through the bulkhead in his highbacked chair didn't appeal to the general's sense of safety or decorum.

Captain Tippitt's opinions regarding today's rules and regulations are couched in the same spicy lingo that peppers his stories: "poppycock," or "crazy," or "outrageous." Hardly reticent in dealing with what he perceives to be wrong-headed Coast Guard officials enforcing "blasted" rules, Tippitt seems to take delight in the contrariness allowed an old-timer. Told he must return to school to get a communication license, he informed the port captain, "That's a lot of poppycock. I talked over one of these things when you'as in diapers!" He adds, "Boy, they don't like dealin' with us old-timers. They ruined it. They ruined the profession. Coast Guard's ruined the profession."

Certainly not alone in these judgments, Tippitt is nevertheless no doom-sayer. When the man who met Horace Bixby speaks of his beloved profession, it is with the same pride and ebullience that characterized Bixby's cub, Samuel Clemens. He did indeed become a steamboat man and he was forty years a pilot on the Mississippi River.

Captain Ernest E. Wagner

*What's the use of being a
steamboat captain if you can't tell
people to go to hell?*

Remark attributed to
Captain Tom Leathers,
owner-captain of nineteenth-
century *Natchez* boats

*He would holler and scream
and jump up and down
and all that, but if he did get
unhappy, he'd cool off very
quickly.*

Captain Jim Blum, referring
to Captain Ernest Wagner

THE BIG CAPTAIN

It is rare nowadays to find men whose entire boating careers were served on excursion, passenger steamboats. [13] The old-time roof captains on tramping steamers have been replaced by the master-pilots on diesel towboats. But Captain Ernest E. Wagner—the Big Captain—with his sturdy stature (approximately 6'4", 250 lbs.) and booming voice was reminiscent of the image of famous nineteenth-century steamboat captains whose position and demeanor commanded nearly universal respect. In fact, when he appeared on the television show "To Tell The Truth" some years ago, panelists immediately guessed that Wagner was the authentic steamboat master. He worked on the *Island Maid, Island Queen, Avalon, Delta Queen,* and the new *Mississippi Queen*—all steamboats, all passenger boats. His river career started behind the Creamy Whip stand and ended as commodore of the Delta Queen Steamboat Company.

Captain Fred Way, Jr., said of him: "He was one of the few river mortals who was on top of every situation he confronted, and had uncanny instinct about when to shout and when to cajole, adept at both, and always fair. Fair and kindly. For under the skin he was a pushover for deserving old river guys who always found transportation, bed and board on Ernie's boat and to hell with what management had to say" (S&D *Reflector,* December 1979). He might also have added that Captain Wagner's sense of humor led him to play pranks—occasionally elaborate practical jokes—on other crew members.

---

[13] Captain Verne Strekfus and other Strekfus family members have spent their careers in the excursion, passenger trade, mostly on steam, but also on "dieselized" boats, like the *Admiral* in St. Louis and the *President* in New Orleans. Current roof masters—like captains "Doc" Hawley, Gabriel Chengery, and Jim Blum—on the daylight excursion steamer *Natchez* and on the only overnight steamers left in the country were brought along by Captain Wagner.

181

Even as dignified master of the *Delta Queen*, a post he held for sixteen years, the mischievous side of Wagner's personality found a forum. Mates or deck crewmen prudently practiced discretion until they had assessed his true mood. "He had a very good sense of humor, he really did. There's only one problem, though; you didn't play too many tricks on *him*. He played 'em on you. But you could never quite tell; he always acted like he was mad. . . . You took him at face value until he laughed. If he didn't laugh first, you didn't laugh. No, no, no, no" (Captain Jim Blum).

When he died in October 1979, testimonials to the Big Captain reflected the respect and affection the river fraternity felt for him. A riverfront park was dedicated to him and a monument erected in New Richmond, Ohio, where he lived for many years. At the time of his funeral services, "salutes were blown as the *Mississippi Queen* neared New Orleans; as the *Delta Queen* neared St. Paul; by the *Natchez* at New Orleans and by the *Belle of Louisville*.[14] And the citizens of New Richmond, Ohio, no doubt still hear many a whistle blown as passing boatmen pause to remember Cap'n Ernie.

In November 1978, Captain Wagner recalled his career on the river.

Beginnings: Island Queen

Born and reared in eastern Tennessee, Ernie Wagner took his first steamboat ride in 1927 aboard the *Island Queen*, operated by Coney Island in Cincinnati.

I got to talking to some of the boys behind the stand, how you went about gettin' a job on a boat like that, and they said, "Well, you have to see the quartermaster of the *Maid*. They're the ones that does all the hirin'." Well, I saw the quartermaster, talked to him, and he said, "Well, uh, I need a boy behind the Creamy Whip stand over there." . . . I said, "Well, I'll be glad to take the job." He said, "Well, the job pays $9.15 a week, room and board." Well, Monday morning, I come over and went to work behind that Creamy Whip stand . . . for three days.

I found out that the deckhands got a little more money. They made $14 a week and room and board. And I thought I would rather be a deckhand than I would a cabin boy. . . . I went ahead and finished out the season of 19 and 27 as a deckhand on the *Island Queen*. . . . After Coney Island closed, they took off on what was known as a tramp trip. They would leave Cincinnati

[14] Sons and Daughters of Pioneer Rivermen *Reflector*, December 1979. The *Belle* is the former *Avalon*.

and play the different towns up and down the river, maybe as far as Pittsburgh up the river, and sometimes they'd go as far as New Orleans down the river. But most of the times they only went as far as Memphis, Tennessee, down the river. Anyway, this particular year, the boat went up river as far as East Liverpool . . . and turned around and came back. But the deckhands on that trampin' trip, the river was down, had to make locks. The deckhands had to get up and make locks regardless of what time it was at night. And they had to get up at eight the next morning and get their breakfast and go on their regular job all day long just the same—paintin', scrubbin', whatever it might be. Well, about four or five days before we got to Cincinnati, I went to Captain Joe Heath and told him, I said, "Captain Joe, I'm gonna get off when we get to Cincinnati." I said, "I just ain't gettin' enough sleep." He kinda laughed. He said, "Well, you ole country boys, when you live up there," he says, "I know you're used to more sleep than you get on here." He said, "You'll get used to it." And I said, "Mebbe I will and mebbe I won't," but I said, "I'm going to give you a notice. I'm going to get off at Cincinnati when it gets back." And he said, "All right."

So when we got back to Cincinnati, I left, quit, and went home, back to Tennessee for awhile. But, in the spring of 1928, I was back up in Cincinnati and went back down to the *Island Queen* to see about a job. Sure enough, Captain Joe, he was still the mate. So, he gave me a job.

Wagner worked the 1928 season, was promoted to night watchman on the *Island Queen* and *Island Maid*, and made $17.75 a week. He worked on and off in '28 and '29, took a job in the Frigidaire plant in Dayton, worked as a truck driver, and generally alternated working on the boats and taking other jobs for a few years at the end of the twenties and beginning of the thirties. In 1935 he "went mate" on the *Island Queen*, where his penchant for pranks flourished.

We had a dance floor officer. He was a little related to the people that owned Coney Island Company. His name was Andy. . . . And everybody teased Andy all the time. Andy would sit around in a chair and go to sleep. Somebody'd come along and they'd get a pair of scissors and cut his necktie off. When he woke up, he'd just have a stub hanging there. Well, he'd get mad and throw his hat in the river. . . . So one day Captain Hall took me, he thought we oughta quit bothering him so much. So we all get together and said, "Well, we'd quit teasing Andy." So, four or five days, nobody done anything to him, didn't kid him, or nothing. So one day he come and he said, "Hey, Wagner," he said, "for God's sake, somebody do something.

I'm going crazy." . . . He thought everybody was mad at him, I guess. I guess this was in . . . 1937. It was right after the year of the flood.

We was down at Cairo, Illinois, in the fall of the year. And we laid there all night. . . . Some of the band boys set on top of the wheelhouse and was fishing. And one of them caught a big, long, ole big, big long eel. Well, the next morning when I got up, I come out past there, and I asked, "Been doing any good?" and a couple of 'em said, "Yeah, we got a couple of catfish." And one guy said, "Looky here what I got." He pulled that big ole eel up out of the water. I said, "How about giving it to me?" He said, "All right. You can have it." So I went back and looked where Andy was sleeping. Usually he always slept in the nude. And he usually left his winder down, down with screens over it. Anyway, I went back there and looked, and there laid Andy a-snorin'. So I went back and got that eel from that boy and I throwed that eel in there and I took off down the stairway. I went all the way to the main deck from the Texas deck. . . . I went down the port side, and the deckhands was gettin' ready to go to work that morning so I had some new brooms down there. So I picked up these brooms and carried them back up the starboard side of the stairway.

When I came back up, Andy was standing in the door with an ole 38 in his hand, wavering, cussing, raising hell! He said, "Wagner, did you see anybody go down that stairway?" I said, "No, I didn't, Andy." He was gonna kill the SB that throwed that thing in there on him. I said, "What's the matter?" He said, "Somebody throwed a snake on me." I said, "Oh, Andy, they didn't do that!" He said, "Come here and look." Well, I went back there and poor old Andy had tore the door off the hinge and broke his mirror in his room. Well, I picked the eel up and took it out. I said, "Andy, that's just an eel. I'll throw it in the river and get rid of it." He said, "I'll kill the so-and-so that throwed that in there!" I said, "Well if I find out who done it, Andy, I'll let you know." He said, "I'll sure appreciate it, Wagner, if you did."

Anyway, I got the carpenter to come up and fix his door back and I had to buy him a new mirror to put on his bulkhead. . . . And I never did tell him that I done it. He finally forgot about it, but I believe if I'd 'a told him I done it, within two or three weeks after I did it, he might'a shot me. So I kept it to myself.

After a disagreement with Captain Hall, Wagner left the boat in 1939 and took a job at Andrews Steel Mill, where he worked until 1942 when he was drafted into the service. Discharged in 1945, he went back to the steel mill, but was soon laid off. He returned to the *Island Queen* in the spring of 1946. The details of one of the river's worst explosions, which happened soon thereafter, remained vivid in Wagner's memory.

In the fall of 1947, after Coney Island closed, the *Island Queen* proceeded upriver and was going on into Pittsburgh on the tramp trip. We docked at the foot of Wood Street there on the Monongahela River. They had to get a little barge and put in between us and the dock for us to land agin. . . . And that third day, at about 1:15 in the afternoon, didn't have no trip out in the afternoon or anything. Freddie Dycko was doing a little welding on a stanchion out on a bow of the boat where they had a fence kept the passengers from getting out there on the bow. One of those stanchions had come loose. It had been riveted and Freddie proceeded to weld it. Well, I was sitting out on the bow of the boat when he started to weld and I said, "Hell, I wasn't going to sit there and git no flashes. Git my eyes burnt mebbe." So I proceeded to go upstairs and go to bed.

Well, I hadn't much more than got my clothes off, laid down, was fixing my pillow, it exploded. Well, I thought that an airplane had hit us because there had been a little seaplane. It was flying under one bridge and over the other down the Monongahela River. But, anyway, I proceeded to see what happened when I opened the front door of Texas [deck]. The flames was already so bad you couldn't go out the front door of Texas. So, Captain Jim Butler . . . came out, and I said to him, I said, "Captain, you'd better take a life jacket," and I throwed him a life jacket. He went back and jumped overboard on the afterend. I started to jump and I thought of my billford laying on my dresser. I run back and got my billfold, stuck it in my pocket, and started to go back through the back end, but I couldn't get out because there was too much fire. Joe Bond, one of the concessionaires, run the candy stand, he was there, kinda trapped, too. He didn't know what to do, and I told him, "Well, c'mon, Joe, we'll get through one of the musician's rooms." So I kicked the door down and kicked the winder out and that's the way we got off into the water because I knew it was only about six feet from the winder of the musician's room to the edge of the boat. And that's the way we got overboard.

Well, I got in the river. It was awful hot behind me cuz you could really feel that heat. And I swum ashore. *Charles T. Campbell* came along and lowered their lifeboats. When they come by and wanted to pick me up, I said, "No, I'm all right. I'll make it to shore." I said, "Go get some of the others there." Well, Butler was still in the river. So they picked him up.

When I got to shore, I had kicked my pants off because I didn't have no belt in my pants and they got down around my ankles and I had to push them off because I couldn't kick my legs. My shoes, I had them on, but they wasn't tied so they come off very easy. So when I got to shore, I tried to get ahold of that esplanade. It was slick and slimy and I couldn't make it. Some policeman was trying to hunt something to help me get up and over that esplanade with. Some colored guy was standing there with a cane. He walked over and stuck that cane down to me and helped me get up out of the river there with that cane.

The policeman came over and said, "You'd better come on and get in the ambulance here." I said, "No, I'm not hurt." I said, "I'm all right." He said, "Well, look at your arm there." Well, when I looked at my arm, I knew I was burnt pretty bad. So I proceeded to get in the wagon . . . and they took off for Mercy Hospital.

Well, when we got to the hospital the only thing I had on was a pair of undershorts. . . . I went into the main entrance of the emergency room of the hospital; and then they wrapped me up, gave me a sheet to put around me, and then the first thing they give me, I remember, was a big drink of whiskey.

When I went in that Mercy Hospital in Pittsburgh, the only thing I had was a pair of undershorts, a cheap cameo ring, and a wristwatch. Everything else that I owned was on the *Island Queen*, and it went up in smoke. . . . I only had those three items. I didn't own a pair of shoes. I didn't own a pair of socks, or anything. And that's gettin' pretty low when you're about thirty-seven years old—and that's how old I was when I went in Mercy Hospital there in Pittsburgh—a pair of undershorts, a ring, and a wristwatch on. I stayed in Mercy Hospital thirty-six days.

When I came out of the hospital, I came back down to the foot of Wood Street where the *Island Queen* was still layin' there in the river. And it was hard to believe, that a big steel boat like it was coulda melted down like it did. . . . I don't think there coulda been a living insect on that boat in three minutes' time after it exploded, because it was just an inferno that quick. Because when it blowed, the fuel oil went up in the air and the wind was downriver about fifteen miles an hour, I think they figured that day, and it just kind of saturated the whole boat in burning fuel oil.

There were nineteen crew members killed. I don't remember just how many was injured, but the Coast Guard came down, and they cut out the deck where Freddie Dycko, the chief engineer, was welding, and they proved that he was welding right over an oil compartment. And he got his metal too hot and he burned into this oil compartment. If he hadn't burnt through the metal, it probably wouldn't have exploded, but the fuel tank was less than half full, which made it a lot worse because that give a lot more room for fumes to accumulate in there. But Freddie Dycko don't know what hit him. He was on the outside of the rail. They found him in the river, but every bone in his body, I guess, was broken. Freddie Dycko was a mighty good engineer, but he had one bad mistake that he made, a real bad mistake.

After I looked at the *Island Queen* layin' there as I came out of the hospital, there at the foot of Wood Street, I came back to Cincinnati and I didn't do anything until the next spring. The Coney Island Company kept me on the payroll, they paid all my expenses in the hospital. . . . Insurance company made everything good that I lost. I never got gypped for anything.

Wagner worked in the park at Coney Island during most of 1948 and then ran a tourist court for his brother for about six or seven months. This marked the end of his association with Coney Island and its boats and the beginning of his long association with the excursion steamer *Avalon*.

Avalon Years

Wagner "kinda got homesick for the river," and Ernie Meyer, who had bought the *Avalon* in 1949, wanted Wagner to captain his new boat. At the time Wagner had only his mate's license, so he found a retired Coast Guard man who "schooled" him on what he "was supposed to know about going up and gettin' my master's papers," and in "19 and 50" mate Wagner became Captain Wagner.

It was on the *Avalon* that young Clarke "Doc" Hawley was taken under Captain Wagner's wing and eventually brought along to be a master himself. Wagner spoke fondly and proudly of Hawley's beginnings on the boat and his subsequent accomplishments. "Well, we came on back down the Cumberland River and up the Ohio, and we went up the Kanawha River to Charleston, West Virginia. And we were gonna stay in Charleston, I think, eight days. And that's where I met Captain "Doc" Hawley. At that time he was just a kid, fifteen years old, going to high school."

But young Hawley played organ in the theater, and Captain Wagner needed a calliope player. Hawley auditioned for the captain and was offered the job. After the young Hawley's parents were assured that Captain Wagner would look after him as if he were his own son, the deal was struck, and Doc even made the Pittsburgh paper as a local boy leaving to go away on a steamboat.

Sure enough, Doc met me in Pittsburgh, and he finished out the season as calliope player. He'd help out behind the popcorn, hot dog stand; he'd do anything that needed to be done. He didn't stand back and wait for somebody to tell him to do something. . . . Finally they kinda called Doc the Popcorn Boy and me the Hot Dog Man. They got real busy behind the hot dog stand, I'd get behind there and help them out, too. I never will forget. Doc was standing there, heard this man say, "Hey, Captain, I'll give you five dollars for a good hot hot dog." Because they'd been kinda putting them out so fast that they had a couple of roller grills that wasn't getting good and hot. So I let one roll good until it got real good and hot. I put it on the bun for him, the napkin, handed it to him. He give me the five dollars. I said, "Well, where's the quarter for the hot dog?" And he reached in his pocket and got the quarter and I give him the hot dog. And I done it just because Captain Doc Hawley was standing there watching me. And Doc couldn't get over that. The guy give me a five-dollar tip for that hot hot dog, then me asking for a quarter for the hot dog.

Anyway, while we were in Pittsburgh, we had a colored organization, church people, had the boat chartered. And there was one in charge of the boat ride. They didn't sell as many tickets as they thought they was gonna sell so they was almost down to where they thought they were going to lose money on the trip. But they finally got up to where they was making a few dollars and there were ten or twelve, looked like hoodlums, out there on the dock. They didn't belong to this organization, but anyway they come up and wanted to get aboard, and she wanted to let them aboard. I told her, I said, "Well, I think you're doing wrong, but if you want to let them aboard, go ahead." And she talked to them. She said, "Aw, I think they'll be all right." So she went ahead and let them aboard. Well, sure enough, just before we got back into the landing, they did, they started some trouble on the boat, and we got back in, got landed, got them off, and after everybody got off the boat, they went over there, and we could see them ganging up over there under the bridge, picking up broken bottles and pieces of brickbat and whatnot. So I took off to my room. I had an old shotgun up in my room. I took the slug out of it. It held five shells. Them old shells was real old. Anyway, I got that gun. I run outside and went out on the bridge. And them guys started back in on the gangplank. When they did, I cut one crack loose of that old shotgun and them pellets hit that steel deck and you should have seen them hoodlums take off! At the time, my first mate was Will Redd. He had a pistol in his pocket and he'd always pull his pistol out. But he told me later. He said, "Boy," he said, "I never heard any sweeter music in my life than when you cracked that shotgun," he said, "I knew you was riding shotgun." Well, like I said, them old shells I had, the fire flew out of the end of that gun all the way to the stage almost. But we never had anymore trouble while we was there in Pittsburgh.

Well, we went ahead, and Doc Hawley stayed with me as calliope player, popcorn boy, whatever not, every summer. He went to college. When he got out of college, he'd come aboard and work with me until he had to go back to school. But the day before he was twenty-one years old, we was in Burlington, Iowa. I told Doc, I said, "Doc, I'm going to send you back to Cincinnati to the Coast Guard office to get your mate's license. I'll pay your way to and from the boat if you pass the examination. If you don't pass the examination, I ain't going to pay you nothin'." Of course, I was only kidding him and I paid him anyway, but I didn't think he'd have any trouble. But the day he was twenty-one years old, he was setting there on the Coast Guard office, waiting for them to open, to go in and take his examination for his mate's papers. Well, he got his mate's papers, came back to the boat . . . and he took over as mate. And he run mate with me for two years. Then he had time in to go get his master's papers. He went up and got his master's papers. So he was a full-fledged captain.

This was a mutual admiration society between Captain Wagner and the young Hawley. In 1977 when Captain Hawley was asked just what it was that made Captain Wagner such a well-respected master, he was quick to answer.

He's a practical boatman. The old term, "once a mate, always a mate"— Captain Wagner is a mate captain. He's a working roof captain that doesn't mind getting his hands dirty, and everybody knows it. He'll get in there and splice line and do whatever he has to do. He's not a figurehead, prima donna-type captain, and everybody that works for him know that he knows what he's doing. And that's, I think, that's the basic reason for his great success. He's been everywhere on boats and done everything.

After Captain Wagner's death, Captain Doc Hawley recalled his eighteen seasons of association and friendship with the Big Captain. He remembered an incident that Captain Wagner had overlooked. Cap had always insisted that the boat's calliope be played as much as possible. "Once, while on our annual three-week stay at Pittsburgh, Cap decided to serenade the prisoners of the

Western Pennsylvania State Penitentiary with 'If I had the wings of an angel [over the prison walls I'd fly]. This impromptu concert caused considerable commotion among the inmates, and we were met at the foot of Wood Street by the warden, who strongly requested 'no repeats.' Cap responded by sending each prisoner a picture postcard of the boat, and free tickets for the warden and staff."[15]

After more than a decade on the *Avalon*, Captain Wagner went aboard the steamer *Delta Queen* as master on January 2, 1962.

The Delta Queen Years

A seasoned master by 1962, Captain Wagner continued to garner respect from members of the river fraternity and to play his pranks and bluff his subordinates.

First year, like I said, I was on the *Delta Queen* in 1962. January 2nd. It was a little something different for me, because I'd never worked on a boat like that before, but I got along pretty good.

I guess the first incident that happened on the *Delta Queen* when I'as on there, was — I guess it was 1964. We's comin' up the river on the lower Mississippi River, below Carruthersville, Missouri. The pilot on watch that morning was Captain Tommy Dunn, from Hendersonville, Tennessee. Captain Tommy dropped — had a stroke at the wheel — or while he was on watch. This happened about 11:00 in the morning. I got the boat to Carruthersville and got him off the boat; got him to the hospital about 12:30, 1:00, and he lived until 11:00 that night. But, that morning, around 8:00, I was in the pilothouse, and Tommy said, "Captain would you hold 'er a little bit; let me go get a bite of breakfast?" I said, "Yeah, I sure will." But he didn't like to eat breakfast at 5:30 or 6:00 in the morning. So, I let him go down to eat breakfast. He come back up and stuck his head in the pilothouse door and said, "Are you in a hurry to go down?" I said, "No, I want to go down to the lower deck, directly, when you get through." He said, "Well, let me go shave and I'll be done then till evening; I won't eat no lunch." So, he went and shaved and came back and took over.

I went downstairs and went all the way to the lower deck — the boys was painting the bow of the boat — and went back upstairs, and I started to go into my room, and I happened to look over to the pilothouse door and there was water runnin' out from under the door. I walked over and opened the door and there laid Captain Tommy Dunn, on the floor. Well, I beat it up to the pilothouse, right quick, and the boat was already off of its course — it was over behind the red buoy — 'course the river was up a little high and they'as water behind the red buoys — but I stopped the boat. Dr. Eckhard [boat's doctor] done all he could for Tommy — we got him on the stretcher and got him down on the lower deck, on the bow, and had the ambulance to meet us at Carruthersville. We got him off and got him to the hospital and I called his wife. But I had left a watchman there with him and one of the people out of the purser's office until she got there. That was kind of a serious situation, to have a pilot like that, have a stroke on watch, and nobody else in the pilothouse.

Another little incident that happened on the *Delta Queen* the first year I went aboard — Mrs. Greene had hired a young boy from Pittsburgh, Tennessee, I guess it was, as a clerk. His name was John Lewis. I was over in the wharf-boat office, and Mrs. Greene said, "Captain, did you meet the new clerk?" I said, "No." She said, "Well, he's over there unpackin' his clothes — gettin' ready to make our first trip." She told me who he was — so, I knew where his room was, so I went by. I had on an old pair of coveralls and an old, brown sloppy hat on. John was, what you say, a character — he was quite a character. But, anyway, I went by his room, and I stopped and stuck my head in the door, and he said, "Hello, hi, how are you?" I said, "Oh, I'm fine." He said, "Well, you lookin' for a job?" I said, "Yes, sir, I sure am." He said, "Well, you'll have to go back on the wharf boat over there and talk to Mrs. Greene, or Mr. Calwell. . . . So, I went on about my business, and a couple of hours later I run into John and I said, "Young man, come here," I said, "I want to thank you," I said, "I went over there and talked to Mrs. Greene," I said, "she give me the job as captain on here." Well, he looked at me — he was a pretty shrewd guy — but, he didn't know what to say. But he knew that I'd kindy pulled his leg, then I shook hands with him and told him who I was.

The seventeen years that I've captained the *Delta Queen*, we never had too many accidents. Nothing real serious; we did scrape the bridge at Madison, Indiana, one night, in the fog and high water. Nobody got hurt; we went on into Louisville and laid at Jeff Boat, I think two days. Let Jeff Boat straighten up the nosing and what-not, the bulkhead. And another time . . . we'as a gettin' out of a lock — Cannelton lock — foggy; there was a little sandbar there below the lock wall; got stuck on the bar and foolin' around there, tryin' to get off, and backed into the bank and tore the paddle wheel up pretty bad. One of the towboats that was waiting to get into the lock—he tied his tow off and come and got us, because he knew if he didn't, he'd never get into the locks—took us back down to the city front of Tell City. We laid there about three days, and repaired the paddlewheel up, and was back in operation again. That's the only two serious accidents that I remember havin' in the seventeen years that I was on board the *Delta Queen*. Nobody got hurt in either accident, and the Greene Line, I guess, really had a good record—eighty-some years and never had a casualty—nobody got killed or anything.

Another incident that happened on board the *Delta Queen* I thought was pretty exciting, was we backed away from Memphis, Tennessee,—Captain Gabe Chengery . . . was mate, at that time. We turned around and headed down river. Oh, the boat had just a little list, on the port side, so Captain Gabe had one of the deckhands [Vic Strattmueller] to back the Volkswagen over on the starboard side. [16] Well, something happened, his foot slipped, or something, and he backed right on through the gate and went in the river. And Captain Gabe called the pilothouse . . . and he said, "Captain, Vic just went overboard with the Volkswagen." . . . The port window was down and Vic was kinda small, but the Volkswagen bounced back up, and Vic Strattmueller, the deckhand, he crawled out that winder and crawled up on top of the Volkswagen, and I was on the radio, tryin' to get ahold of Waterways Marine, to let them send one of those speedboats out there, like quick, and get him. There was a towboat coming up river; he was just about at the bridge, and he radioed and said, "*Delta Queen*, don't worry about your man," said, "we've got a motorboat in the river, takin' a pilot ashore." Said, "We'll go get him." So this motorboat off of this towboat went and picked Vic up and brought him back to the boat, and Frankie and Johnny's motor store, right below the bridge, had two little tugs. They sent one of their tugs out. They got ahold of the Volkswagen and almost towed it ashore before it sank. But it finally sank, and a little later on, they had to get a little derrick boat, and they went in there and they picked it up and pulled it out on the bank, but we never did have it back on board the boat no more.

Captain Gabe Chengery, now master of the *Mississippi Queen*, well remembers the incident with the Volkswagen and the qualities of fairness, firmness, and humor that characterized his mentor.

[16] A Volkswagen "bug" was carried on the bow and used for running errands when the boat was landed.

No matter what caliber job a crew member had, even if he was just a pot washer, to treat that person like a man and not look down on him because of the menial work that the guy's doing aboard the boat . . . that's one of the key things I got from him. At times he was very very strict with me. At times I guess he needed to be; I needed a good kick in the backside from time to time. But always in some way he would show his love and affection for me. For instance, as I was in the deck crew, running mate, I used to make my mistakes like any young mate would do in learning the proper way of doing things. We were locking through Emsworth Lock going into Pittsburgh on the *Delta Queen*, and I was the mate. And the mate on the lock wall, the lock man, throws a small heaving line down to catch the big rope to pull up to tie the boat to the wall. I put two ropes on that one hook instead of one, and it was too much weight, and the lock man dropped his line into the river and lost his real fancy hook and his rope. Captain Wagner got real mad. He says, "Well, why don't you just go pack your bags and get off the boat in Pittsburgh when we get in." And that really got me kinda upset. Later on he cracks and he says, "Well, Gabriel, I'll at least ride you home in the car."

Captain Chengery particularly remembers Wagner's adeptness at playing practical jokes. The musician Vic Tooker had bought Captain Wagner a gift, a move that made Chengery play the role of scapegoat.

This gift . . . was a little statue of a monkey . . . stood about a foot and a half high, maybe a foot high. Big fat monkey, behind a pilot's wheel, with a big cigar in his mouth and big feet. . . . So Vic puts it in the captain's room, and it's sittin' on the desk. And I'm not insinuatin' that Captain Wagner ever looked like a monkey, but there was a certain comparison there with the cigar and the big feet and the husky thing and the pilot's wheel and the captain's hat there. Captain Wagner tried to have some fun with me. He knew that Vic Tooker got it for him. He gets ahold of me, says, "Come up in my room, Gabriel, and knock on the door!" I go inside of the room and he says, "Look at that!" points to the monkey on his desk there. . . . "Did you put that in there?" I go, "No, Cap, I don't know where it came from."

And I'm lookin' at it; I'm ready to bust out laughin'. And one thing, when you'd get chewed out by Captain Wagner, you don't smile or twitch a muscle because he interprets as you laughin' at him, then that just gets him even more steamed up. . . . And I almost lost it when his next question was, "Do you think that looks like me, do ya?" I said, "No, sir, Cap, sure doesn't, doesn't look like you at all." If this thing woulda been on film it woulda been hilarious. . . . "Find out who put that in here then if you didn't do it." I says, "OK, I'll ask around."

Detective Gabriel found out that his friend Vic was the gift giver but declined to offer the information to Captain Wagner, who, of course, already knew.

So, I would never tell a lie; I was always a basic honest kid. And that same evening, we're in the officer's mess havin' dinner there. Vic's on one end of the table; Captain Wagner's eating on the other end. . . . He's sittin' there chompin' his lips and smokin' his cigar. He says, "Gabriel, did you ever find out who put that monkey in my room?" . . . What am I gonna say, I don't wanna lie. "Well, Cap, I'm not quite sure." . . . And Captain Wagner just did that to see if I'd lie, and he caught me.

In keeping with the kind of sense of humor that prompted Captain Wagner to declare June 17 "Monkey Day" in honor of his statue and celebrate the holiday for a couple of years thereafter, Wagner's last full season on the *Delta Queen* yielded perhaps his most intricate prank of all. He delighted in retelling it:

I guess the latest incident that happened aboard the *Delta Queen* — monkey-business-wise — was with Captain Howard Tate. Captain Howard Tate just passed away last year, but he was my lower-Mississippi pilot for several years. We'as comin' up the river, in 1976, 'bout eleven at night, and Tate bounced off of a reef down there someplace. He was in his marks — he was between the buoys, and the river was falling. But, I just went down to my room, and I went back into the pilothouse and I told the watchman, I said, "Well, I don't think you done any damage, but go down and check in the boiler room, 'cause that's about where she hit." The firemen and all them looked and no leaks, or nothing, and so I went on to bed.

Next morning, Tate was down gettin' his breakfast at 5:30, and a couple of the engineers was in there, and they asked him what happened. He said, "Well, he let Captain Wagner hold her while he went to the bathroom," said "he's the one that hit that reef!" So when I come down to breakfast, the engineers asked me about it. And, I said, "Well, that lyin' so-and-so!" Well, 'course, I knew he was only pullin' my leg when he told 'em that. But, anyway, when I got through eatin' breakfast, I went in the pilothouse and I let on like I was mad as a bear. He said, "Well, now, Ernie, you know that I was only kiddin.' " I said, "Yeah, I know that." And I said, "Now them guys all think that I'm the one that hit the reef down there, last night." "Oh," he said, "don't think as hard about that." I said, "Okay, I'll get even with you."

So this was on a Saturday night when it happened, and Sunday morning we were gonna stop in Helena, Arkansas. . . . I'll take the Volkswagen and run up and get some papers. Lexie Palmore was on board. But her and Tate didn't get along too well. I mean, Tate was just a little jealous of her, or something, I don't know. But, anyway, I took Lexie with me to get the papers. And, while I'as gone, I thought of what I was gonna do. When we come back to the boat—I had a little portable radio in the room. I got it—took it down to the purser's office, and I got the boy that run the gift shop (who had a lingo that nobody would recognize, I was sure). So we got in the purser's office and we fixed us up a little script—what to do, and what to say, on the radio. So I told 'im, "Now give me five minutes, and I'll go to the pilothouse, and I'll sneak the radio up there on channel six, so that it doesn't go all over the country."

So I went up to the pilothouse and put the radio on channel six; Tate didn't see me. Sure enough, the boy come in on channel six, and he said, "This is radio station so-and-so—so-and-so, in Helena, Arkansas." I answered back, "This is the *Delta Queen*, let's go to six." I "reched" up like I'd punched channel six, and he come back and he said, "Who's this speakin'?" I said, "This is Captain Wagner." He said, "I hear you had a little accident last night, down the river—you hit a sandbar, or something, and knocked a lot of people out of bed? Did anybody get hurt?" I said, "No, nobody got hurt," and he said, "Was you on watch?" I said, "No, Captain Howard Tate was on watch." Well, I thought Howard would die! He turned around and he said, "God damn," he said, "I been out here fifty-five years—I hit one little sandbar" and, he said, "everybody in the country knows about it." I looked around to Lexie and I said, "Lexie, who'as you talkin' to when you's on the telephone, up there, at the newsstand?" And I thought he was gonna come out of his chair and go over and smack Lexie. But Lexie could'a killed me when I said that, I'm sure. But, anyway, the boy in the office said, "Well, I just heard it;" said, "we got news of it," and said, "I just thought I'd call you and see if anybody got hurt." I said, "No, nobody got hurt—everything's lovely—everything's fine." He said, "Okay, talk to you later, *Delta Queen*," and we signed off. Tate turned around to Lexie and said, "Lexie, you talk too damn much!"

But anyway, I was gonna do it to him again at Memphis. I was gonna have it like it was comin' over the Memphis station, but that afternoon, about four, I got up and went down to get me a cup of coffee, and Howard was already down there drinkin' his coffee and he almost had tears in his eyes. I went over and I said, "What's the matter?" He said, "Ah," he said, "I think I'm gonna get off." Said, "You've got another pilot you can get in Memphis. Get one, I'm gonna get off." I said, "Well, what's the matter?" He said, "Well," he said, "of all these years I've been out here and I touch one little sandbar and it gets out on the radio, everybody in the country knows about it." Well, like I say, it looked like he was gonna cry—and I felt so sorry for him, well, I had to tell him what I had done, and I didn't have the heart to do it again in Memphis. But he looked at me and said, "Ernie, you big so-and-so, you mean to tell me that was all put up?" I said, "Yes, Howard, it was all put up. Just like you tried to pull my leg about me hittin' the reef."

Captain Ernest E. Wagner, "the mate's captain," with a booming voice, kind heart, and prankster's sense of humor, was one of the last in a limited-edition mold: roof master on steamboats plying the inland waterways of America.

1. The sternwheel steam packet *Henry Frank*, with its record freight of cotton bales, circa 1878–84. Courtesy of the University of Wisconsin–LaCrosse, Murphy Library.

2. The *J. W. Van Sant*, in the Upper Mississippi, circa 1898, towing a log raft equivalent in area of six football fields. The bow boat is the *Lydia Van Sant*. Courtesy of the University of Wisconsin–LaCrosse, Murphy Library.

3

4

3. The gravestone of Captain Isaiah Sellers in Bellefontaine Cemetery, St. Louis, Missouri. Captain Sellers, a pilot during Mark Twain's time, commissioned his tombstone and carried it to St. Louis on a boat he was piloting. It was obviously important to him to be remembered as a pilot, with his memorial stone facing out over the Mississippi River. Courtesy of the University of Wisconsin–LaCrosse, Murphy Library.

4. A. U.S. Army Corps of Engineers boat, the *General Allen,* 1929. This boat was used by the Corps for buoy and channel work in the upper Mississippi. The master in the pilothouse is Captain William Henning; the man between the stacks on the hurricane deck is Pilot Allen Fiedler. Courtesy of the University of Wisconsin–LaCrosse, Murphy Library.

5. The sternwheel packets *Betsy Ann* and *Chris Greene* race on the Ohio River near Cincinnati, 1928. The *Chris Greene* won the contest by two minutes in one of the most highly publicized races on the Ohio River. Courtesy of the University of Wisconsin–LaCrosse, Murphy Library.

6. The *Alexander Mackenzie,* 1947, towing what was at that time the largest tonnage to come up the Mississippi River. The fifteen-barge tow, including the boat, is 1,182 feet long by 105 feet wide. Courtesy of Captain Walter Karnath.

7

8

7. Pilothouse on the 3,200-horsepower diesel towboat *Ann King,* 1964, owned by Mid-America Transportation Company. Note the hydraulic steering levers, the searchlight controls just inside of each lever, radio equipment, and the radar scopes. The two vertical levers in the middle of the console are used to indicate direction (coming ahead, backing up) and replace the round dial indicator on the older boats. The pilot sits between the steering levers in a tall, high-backed chair. Photograph by Russell Ray Studios. Courtesy of the *Waterways Journal.*

8. The *Jason* at Pittsburgh, September 1974. Typical of the most sophisticated and powerful diesel towboats now in service on the inland waterways, the *Jason* is a triple-screw, 10,500-horsepower boat measuring 190 feet by 54 feet. She was built by Dravo at Neville Island, Pennsylvania, and is owned by Dravo-Mechling Corporation of Pittsburgh. Courtesy of the *Waterways Journal.*

9. The *Shirley Bowland* is one of the Crounse Corporation towboats that runs primarily on the Ohio from Paducah, Kentucky, to Maysville, on the Cumberland and Tennessee rivers, and occasionally down to Memphis on the lower Mississippi River. Courtesy of the Crounse Corporation, Paducah.

10. Even given the variety of cargoes regularly transported by barge line, this sight must have turned more than one head. A Crounse boat is towing a cargo of coal and a NASA missile, 1960. From cotton bales to aerospace equipment in less than a century! Courtesy of the *Waterways Journal*.

11. A towboat pushing a fifteen-barge tow through the railroad swing bridge at Newport, Minnesota. The pilot communicates by radio and whistle signals to the bridge operator who monitors both rail and river traffic. Because of his speed and tonnage, the pilot must know well in advance whether he will have to wait or whether he can line up to run the bridge span. Courtesy of the U.S. Army Corps of Engineers, St. Paul District.

12. A tow locking through Lock and Dam No. 5 at Minnesota City, Minnesota. The dam is in the foreground, the lock chamber is near the bank. Since the lock is not long enough to accommodate the entire tow at one time, the first string of barges is uncoupled, locked through the chamber, and secured, after which the second string plus the towboat enters the chamber, reaches the same water level, and is then reattached to the first string. Courtesy of the U.S. Army Corps of Engineers, St. Paul District.

13. A towboat leaves the lock chamber at Lock and Dam No. 3 near Red Wing, Minnesota, with barges carrying coal and, probably, grain. The building parallel to the towboat is the lockmaster's headquarters, and the platform near the lock wall to its right is a visitor's viewing area. Courtesy of the U.S. Army Corps of Engineers, St. Paul District.

12

13

14. After waiting in the lock chamber while their boat and tow slowly drop to the lower water level, the crew would enjoy this view of the chamber while leaving. On the upper Mississippi River, a fifteen-barge tow usually requires approximately one to one and a half hours to complete the locking process. This lock is on the Green River. Courtesy of the Crounse Corporation.

15. Each era has had its highly touted record tows. The *Miss Kae-D* claimed a world-record tow on May 6, 1981, when she pushed seventy-two barges past Memphis, Tennessee. Photograph by Don Lancaster. Courtesy of Flowers Transportation, Inc.

15

16. The *Delta Queen,* one of only two overnight passenger steamers still plying the inland waterways, tied up at a landing as visitors admire her. The stage, which serves as a walkway between land and the bow, can be moved to either side for a landing and is suspended directly over the bow during regular cruising. The antlers mounted atop the pilothouse proclaim a victory in one of her recent races, probably the Kentucky Derby Race against the *Belle of Louisville.* She can display the trophy until she loses the next race and then must pass the antlers to the victor. Courtesy of the *Waterways Journal.*

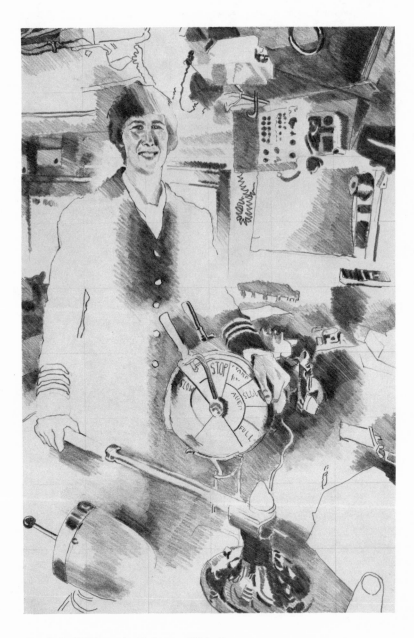

Captain Lexie Palmore in pilothouse of *Delta Queen*

The Youngsters

CAPTAIN LEXIE PALMORE

Captain Lexie Palmore is an atypical riverboat pilot because she is a woman, because she learned on steam in a diesel age, and because she is also an accomplished artist. Historically, piloting has been a man's profession; none of Mark Twain's "monarchs of the river" were female potentates. However, while Captain Palmore is one of very few present-day women pilots, she is by no means the first of her sex to frame her license with justifiable pride. Among her better-known predecessors were captains Mary M. Miller, Mary Hulett, Callie French, Blanche Douglass Leathers, Mary B. Greene, and Nettie Johnson—all of whom piloted steamboats, except Captain Miller, who was the first woman to receive master's license (1884).

There have been at least fifty-three women steamboat pilots and captains, the majority of whom were licensed between 1900 and 1930. Twenty of the women, engaged primarily in the ferryboat or harbor-tug trade, worked at stationary locations such as New York Harbor, the Great Lakes, or West Coast areas.[17] Some women captains seldom ran the boat or stood a watch at the wheel. Their titles were more honorary than pragmatic. Others served their apprenticeships (often with their husbands as tutors) and steered the boat regularly. Captain Hulett, for example, received her pilot's license in October, 1891, after serving several years of apprenticeship with her husband, Captain John Hulett. She subsequently worked on the Illinois River for over fifty years. A *Waterways Journal* article said of Captain Hulett: "Those who knew her declare that she is fully competent to do so and also look very knowing when

[17] I am indebted to Sandra Miller of Louisville, Kentucky, a descendent of Captain Mary Miller, for supplying me with information from her research on women pilots and captains. She reports that she has also located three women engineers, two mates, and one male impersonator (who apparently worked on the *Sprague*).

they assert that all on board from Captain down to roustabout had better look spry when she is at the wheel if they want to keep out of trouble. . . . He (Inspector Gordon) now has a wholesome respect for the ability and firmness of character of the first and only female pilot on the river."[18]

Captain Callie French, not Hulett, claimed to have been the first licensed woman pilot, receiving her second-class pilot's license in April 1889. She helped her husband, Captain A. B. French, and after his death in 1902, took over the running of French's showboats with the assistance of another woman pilot, Ida McNair (and her husband, John, as well).

When Blanche Douglass married Bowling Leathers in 1880, she moved aboard the *Natchez* to be with him. She eventually held both pilot's and master's licenses, but the actual amount of steering she did is uncertain. In newspaper interviews she regaled reporters with accounts of her apprenticeship, of the anxiety she felt when first standing her watches, of the range of her responsibilities. "I have done everything [on a steamboat] but marry people." Records confirm her licenses, which she renewed regularly, even in retirement, until her death in 1940. However, her brother Allan Douglass suggested that she was never "a bell-ringing, whistle-tootin', wheel-turnin' captain."[19] According to him, she generally took care of the cash and the bills but left most of the "captaining" to Bowling and the men.

Mary B. "Ma" Greene secured pilot's license in 1896 and captain's license in '97. Working alongside her husband, Captain Gordon C. Greene, she became well known along the Ohio River. "In 1897 she was taking the *Bedford* between Cincinnati and Louisville during low water, and the 'lady captain's boat' became extremely popular for its dependability and for its air of refinement. Captain Mary Greene's biggest moment perhaps came when she took the Greene Line's newest marvel, the side-wheeler *Greenland*, from Pittsburgh to the St. Louis World's Fair in 1904. The crowds went wild over her."[20] Most veteran pilots who knew Ma Greene say that in later years, at least, she rarely steered the boat but instead served as the ultimate hostess, treating passengers as if they were guests in her home. Even today aboard the *Delta Queen*, once a Greene Line Steamers boat, one hears tales of the "friendly ghost" of Ma Greene keeping an eye on her latter-day charges.

[18] *Waterways Journal*, October 31, 1891. The statement that she was the "first and only female pilot" is incorrect.

[19] Samuel, Huber, and Ogdon, *Tales of the Mississippi*, pp. 187–91.

[20] Ibid., p. 187.

Captain Nettie Johnson's grandson, Captain Fontain Johnson, proudly talks of a take-charge lady, "a Steamboat Annie from the word 'go'." She ran a packet from Memphis to St. Louis hauling bootleg whiskey. "And she'd get into Memphis with a load of whiskey whatever time in the morning, . . . unload it, and they'd pay all the deckhands off in cash—the roustabouts. . . . Then she opened the bar and then got all her money back. . . . And that way she had a crew goin' back because they was all broke." Captain Fontain heard another story from one of Captain Nettie's former pilots involving the "little, bitty" 116-foot-long *Nettie Johnson*. "She'd come into Memphis and landed, and here comes the *Kate Adams* or . . . one of those big packet boats . . . and she'd walked back there with a 45 and run 'em away. . . . Wouldn't let 'em land against her. . . . She was tough!" Captain Nettie Johnson was an active pilot and master who did the work because she wanted to and because she liked it.

Whether motivated by a desire to work with their husbands, by financial necessity, or by the challenge, women have followed the profession; and not without the customary difficulties encountered by women who seek acceptance and respect in hitherto male strongholds.[21] The first to hold master's license, Captain Mary Miller, initially served as clerk on her husband's boat, the steamer *Saline*. After Miller had placed his boat in the Red River trade, the owners of a competing boat complained to the Steamboat Inspectors that the *Saline* was not in compliance with the law because Captain George "Old Natural" Miller acted as both master and pilot of the vessel. Thereupon, Captain Miller offered his wife as an applicant for the master's license, a move which occasioned much consternation and buck-passing among various bureaucratic levels. She stood the examination, passed without difficulty, and made official application in November 1883. Mary Miller's first visit to the Steamboat Inspection office in New Orleans prompted the Inspector of Hulls to query, "But, madam, how can we 'captain' a lady?" The telegraph was kept busy between New Orleans and Washington, D.C., in an effort to answer this very question. One telegram from Washington asked, "Has Mrs. Miller a husband living?" Finally, the secretary of the treasury supplied a final answer, though one with which he obviously was uncomfortable. The secretary "objected to the issue of the license upon social grounds, as having a tendency to degrade the female accepting such license." However, apparently the solicitor

---

[21] A licensed wife-captain saved money. Another captain would not have to be hired each time the husband stayed ashore to attend business.

refused to accept those conclusions and advised "that Mrs. Miller be granted her license if fitted for performing the duties required in spite of her sex."[22] Her license was officially dated February 16, 1884.

Nearly a century later, Lexie Palmore joined the exclusive ranks of women pilots and captains. Born in 1947 in landlocked Tyler, Texas, Palmore remembers a lifelong fascination with boats of any kind. Whenever she saw a steamboat, an ocean-going vessel, or even a canoe, she wanted to be on it. She was first exposed to steamboats at the age of ten when she rode the *President* in New Orleans and stood awed by the power of the huge steam engines. That fascination with boats was reawakened in 1970 when she drove to Vicksburg, Mississippi, to see the steamer *Delta Queen*. At that time, the *Delta Queen*'s future was being threatened by the safety-at-sea law, and Lexie Palmore, a commercial artist working in Dallas, was determined to photograph the last overnight passenger steamer before its imminent demise. Fortunately, the steamer won reprieve, and Palmore signed up for a cruise in 1972. During that trip she decided that she must work on the boat: "It hit me like a sack of lead or something. You know, 'just what am I doing wasting my time at a drawing board in Dallas, Texas.'"

After fruitless attempts to finagle a job aboard the steamer, she went back to school and earned a master's degree in art. But working on the *Delta Queen* remained an unfulfilled dream. She had been a paying passenger; she had even been smuggled aboard by a friend on a dinner cruise; finally in December 1974, she landed her job. As stated before, the customary route to the wheelhouse begins with working as a deckhand, then as mate, perhaps as steersman, then finally as pilot. Palmore's was an alternate path: maid to steersman to pilot.

In the fall of 1979, after piloting regularly for one year, Captain Palmore discussed various aspects of her new river career. While Lexie the maid had admired the men who steered the steamer up and down the Ohio and Mississippi Rivers, it hadn't occurred to her to aspire to such a position.

I thought it would be a neat thing to do, but it never occurred to me that I could physically do it myself. You know, it just seemed like a far-off impossibility—I'd sooner try to be President of the United States. . . . I didn't even know what was required to become a pilot. I had no earthly idea what it took, or anything. But I said, you know, it would be a nice thing to do because then you would really be involved in the industry itself, actually

[22] Again, from Sandra Miller. Also see Samuel, Huber, and Ogden, *Tales of the Mississippi*, pp. 185–93.

working with the river and the boats. And it would be better than being a maid. It'd be more applying yourself to the actual events.

But I really thought it was an impossibility, so I never really gave it any serious thought until I was informed by several people on the boat that it was a serious possibility.

Encouraged by Captain Ernest Wagner, the boat's master, company officials, and some pilots—and sponsored by the Delta Queen Steamboat Company—Palmore enrolled at the river academy in Helena, Arkansas. Palmore realistically accounted for this unusual range of support:

Well, I think their [company] purpose was twofold. They must have thought I had some kind of possibility, or they wouldn't have approached me on it anyway. They're just not prone to do that kind of thing—the pilots aren't. No matter who I am. There had to be some possibility there. . . . [the company] had to put out money to send me to that river academy. So . . . it was a twofold thing. They thought, "Well, if she holds out and goes through all this and makes a pilot—good. If she doesn't—or however long she lasts—we're getting a lot of good publicity out of it anyway." I mean, they hit me with the publicity bit right off the bat. It's tapered off now. . . . They're not sicking 'em on me anymore.

QUESTION: Was there any negative attitude because you are a woman and this is considered a man's profession?

PALMORE: A little bit. There were some pilots that had to try to pick fault with everybody, and this was their good out. So, you know, with a woman—one in particular said I didn't have the constitution to pilot a boat, you know, that women don't have the constitution for things like that. . . . 'Course, stuff like that just made me more determined—all it did. It didn't discourage me at all. And then there were some that started helping me, and they got something in their craw, or somethin', you know, or decided they didn't really want to do that much for me. But the majority of them, 90 percent of them, were very helpful.

And they all just sit me down there and say, "Steer the boat." And the first things they told you—when you're just first learning to steer the boat, you don't know anything about where you are—they'd tell you to hold on something, maybe a daymark, or a water tower, or a tree, or something. And so you'd try to steer as straight as you could for that little item right there ahead of you. And then when you got to the point where you didn't need that anymore, they'd say, "Now, bring her around on this next dayboard right up there, or that point," or something like that. You know, you'd steer from one point to another. And then maybe the next time I went over that route, they'd say, "Now, what do you do here? What's the name of that light," or something like that—"What's the name of that point?"

And not tell me quite so much. Or they'd say, "Don't bring her around yet, just hold on that a little longer," or "You'd better bring her on around now." They'd see what I could remember from the last time and just tell me things when I needed to know, when I wasn't doing it right. And, of course, each time we went over it, they told me less and less about it—about a particular stretch, say—until finally they didn't have to hardly ever say anything.

And then they'd let me steer it, and under a little bit more difficult circumstances, like at night, or when it was raining, say, or on a stretch of the river that was maybe more difficult than when I'd started out. Until, as the time went by, I was steering just about everywhere. And the next thing after that, once you more or less got steering the boat up and down the river, you understand what's going on. And places you've been over several times, you know where the channel is and where to go. Then after that, you have your maneuvering and handling the boat. And when they feel like you're ready for that, then they might let you make a little landing at a bank somewhere where the bank slopes gradually down into the river, and it's mostly sand or something like that. You just drift the boat into a certain bank. See how well you can do on that. You can't hurt anything; it's a nice easy landing.

QUESTION: So when they let you go into the first lock, you know that you're doing pretty well?

PALMORE: Yeah. Oh, I thought I was gonna have a hissing fit if I didn't get to make a lock. You know, I waited so long for that. And what it was is the pilot and the captain were at odds, kinda not really comprehending that one was waiting for the other one to say something. The captain was waiting for the pilot to say I was ready, and the pilot was waiting for the captain to give the order to let me. So they were just kinda waiting for each one to say something for a long time. Meanwhile, I was sitting there watching one lock after another go by, and I was just about to scream! 'Cause I knew I was ready to try to learn this. And I had to try to learn it and do it.

I had made landings. Even made a few difficult ones, like in New Orleans, and that kind of stuff. The worst kind of landing is against a wharf. So I knew I could do that pretty well. . . . The thing about waiting so long to get to do that is you start building up this anxiety about it, and then when you finally get to do it, you're a nervous wreck. The first lock I made was McAlpin. I had to go land up against the wall to wait for another boat to get out of the lock and then go into the lock. Captain said, "Well, why don't you let her make the lock?" "Okay." Then after we got out of the lock and we get ready to leave the lock, "Let's let her take her out of the lock." "Okay." We go up the Portland Canal there and he says, "Well, she might as well make the landing."

Graduating from the academy after a two-year course, Palmore sat for her mate's license in August 1977, and in November she began drawing stretches of the river for her first-class pilot's license. In May 1978, after working as mate for several months, Palmore got her first chance to pilot on one of the first trips up to Cincinnati that season. Like all pilots, Captain Palmore remembers that first trip vividly.

I got on at Paducah. I'd just had Ohio River license, so that was my first shot at it. It was that horrendous University of Nebraska cruise that was supposed to go from New Orleans to Cincinnati and hardly made it. . . . See, they had an impossible schedule so they were way behind, and they had fog so they got even farther behind. They were so late getting to Paducah that instead of being there at noon, they were there about 2:00 a.m. the next morning. And I'd been going around holding my eyes open, you know, thinking, "What am I gonna do?" But I did get a few hours of sleep before I went on watch.

QUESTION: Do you remember the first watch you stood?

PALMORE: Oh, yeah! We were at Bay Creek on the Ohio and going up the river, and it was a little bit fuzzy. It was kind of foggy, and I couldn't really see too well, but it cleared up. The sun burned it off pretty quick. And I thought I was gonna be a nervous wreck, but I didn't think about it too much. And I just started steering like I had when I was steering for the pilots, you know. And just steering the boat up the river. Everything was very routine, didn't get hysterical, or anything. The next morning it was a reason to be hysterical because we lost one of our boilers, and we had a towboat helping us up the river. We're in a horrendous thunderstorm — two of 'em. One of 'em right in front of the boat.

Lightning strikes the boat. What next, you know. It was kind of like that. And I just weathered it all fine, didn't have any trouble at all. The river was kind of high, so I wasn't worried about running aground or anything.

And that same lightning bolt, we figured it struck the flagpole right outside the pilothouse, and there were three or four of us in the pilothouse. And that's where we figured it hit, and yet we didn't feel any sensation of electricity or anything. But then we found out that supposedly Vic Tooker got knocked off his feet down in the Texas Lounge—he was in the front of the Texas Lounge looking out the window, and all of a sudden he went back like on his rear end. And that's what they think it was.

But anyway, what couldn't happen! And then we got a bigger towboat to help us push up the river there right at Brandenburg, and something got hung in the rudders, and we were right above the bridge. And that was another cutie. . . . And then he got off of us, and we had to make the McAlpin on a slow bell, and that wasn't too cool. Here I am, this is my first week as a pilot! And we finally got our boilers back up above Louisville somewhere. It was fairly routine the rest of the way in, although we had to put half the passengers off at Markland Lock, and things like that. Otherwise it was a routine trip! Captain Wagner said it was one of the smoothest trips he'd ever been on! [Laughs.] But he's been known to fib. So, anyway, that was how my first watch as a pilot ended.

Captain Palmore works less than six months a year as a pilot, which gives her ample time to pursue her other career—art.[23] When asked why she had chosen to draw the river (obtain first-class pilot's license) when most pilots obtain operator's license, and to pilot on steam when most boats are diesel, she answered as both pilot and artist.[24]

It's just where I ended up. I like it, though. I wouldn't have gotten on there if I didn't like it in the first place. . . . It's built into me to like that kind of thing. Like I say, when I was on the *President* when I was ten years old, I was quite taken by the big machinery that drove the boat. I always had a little mechanical leaning. And I guess something like that to me is beautiful. It's like a sort of art form, you might say. You know, even like to watch the machinery moving on an old steam locomotive or anything like that. So I

[23] Her first pilot wage was seventy-two dollars a day. By the time of the interview, it was ninety-two dollars; *Delta Queen* salaries are considerably less than wages earned by towboat operators. In 1979, she received sixteen days off for every thirty worked; in 1980, it was twenty for thirty.

[24] Pilots on steam vessels over one hundred tons are still required to have first-class pilot's licenses. Pilots on diesel vessels can get an operator's license, which doesn't require drawing the river.

enjoy that kind of thing; the means of propulsion was interesting to me. And it's sort of a unique thing to experience. There must be something poetic about it because so many people enjoy it and like to see it and like to go down and see the engines work and everything moving up and down. You know, it's power on display. It's right there where you can see it. Not just a big lot of noise and you don't see anything happening.

Would Captain Palmore stay on the river if steamboats vanished altogether?

Oh, I think I made my mind up a long time ago on that. In fact, even if the *Delta Queen*, if they quit running overnight steamboats, you still got your excursion boats, like the *Natchez* and the *Belle of Louisville* and those. I think I'd still look towards the direction of the towboat because I'd miss the river just running up and down one little harbor. The river means more to me than steam propulsion, I guess you'd say. And I've gotten that. I've gotten enough of it now. . . . I know what steam power's like; I know what an old steamboat's like—one that carries passengers. I guess I'm as close to the packet boat days as a person can get in this century—at this time of the century. So I've fulfilled that dream. So I'd want to go on and stay on the river and see the river. I've got a license on it, I know it, I enjoy seeing the scenery. And I might work on, say, an excursion boat, some, just for the fun of it every once in a while. But I'd have to go the route of the towboat in order to see the river. And I think I would enjoy 'em. I've been on a few of 'em, and there would be a challenge there to know how to handle something like that.

I make a lot of friends just talking on the radios, say, to a lot of these towboat pilots and talking about everything—not just the river. And try to make friends with them. I think they kind of get the idea that I know what I'm doing and I enjoy what I do. A lot of them invite me to come ride on the towboat and all. I think they have some faith in me. Anyway, if I really did want to get into it some way, I wouldn't start on fifteen barges—anybody that would is kind of crazy, anyway.

Captain Palmore pursues two separate but interlocking careers. Her art work often portrays river subjects in the kind of detail a pilot's perspective can provide. She wants to portray various aspects of the American scene. "Because they're [artwork and piloting] so different, that's what makes it good, because I wear myself out on one, and I need the other one as a release and also a replenisher in order to go back to the other."

In her art she depicts past, present, universal, and unique features of everyday happenings "with the touch of America, with my own homeland sort of thrown in to show that I see that it's a little bit unique here." Both of her careers involved extensive apprenticeships, and both take her on journeys through a hall of mirrors reflecting tradition with one glance, the present with another.

It's [piloting] a very traditional thing. It's probably one of the few things that you can do that has a long history of tradition that's being perpetuated not by education institutions but simply word of mouth and the process of apprenticeship. And it has changed very little from, actually, its beginning of early steamboats over a hundred years ago. The boats have changed, the cargoes have changed, the operations have changed. But there's so much of it that hasn't because the river itself dictates how things are done, and those things really don't change that much because a river is a thing that takes centuries to change. So even though man has done a little bit to make things easier on the river, there's so much about it that's exactly the same as it was a hundred years ago.

You say maybe I'm dwelling on the past and painting steamboats and all, but it's really not that much of the past because I'm living it right now. It's part of the present for me. And the only reason I'm doing the old steamboats and stuff like that is because to my artistic eye, a modern towboat is not as beautiful as an old steamboat. If they were, I would do them. And I still may yet, you know, if I get on that subject. But I haven't cleared house as far as the old subject goes yet. So nothing's really hit me about a real modern towboat era as far as art work goes. I've done a few towboats for people, but they're more or less a display of power and strength more than beauty. And I have to come up with a way of picturing that.

[On a steamboat] you can see what's happening. In itself, it's a beautiful thing. And there's beautiful things going on inside of a diesel engine, too. Basically, the same thing's going on inside one that's going on with a steam engine, but you just can't see it. It's doing it too fast that you couldn't see it—you wouldn't enjoy it anyway. But a steam engine is a slow-moving thing. You can see how everything's working. There's something about the motion of it and all that's sort of rhythmical and fascinating, musical maybe even. And you can't see it with some of the modern things now; technology takes care of that. So everything happens and you never see a thing happen.

It just happens invisibly. Well, that's great, but you know every once in a while, we like to see things happen.

As yet, Captain Palmore has no tales of harrowing accidents, but she knows what she's up against as a pilot.

Piloting an airplane, or a boat, or a bus, or whatever—you usually have got somebody's life in your hands, and you've got some odds stacked against you, too. No matter how many modern conveniences you have or how much you know, when you're on something that's moving, you've got an odd against you there—a big odd. It's moving, and therefore it can move into something else. Ultimately, you try to occupy the same place that something else is some time—at some point in time—and so that's what you're always fighting, and it's a challenge to try to avoid this. You don't always win, but you can always hope that it'll never be something that can't be—as one pilot said—"repaired or replaced."

She relishes challenges, tackling the difficult and calling forth what is best within her. She hopes to continue both careers and preserve the cross fertilization they provide one another.

By 1980, after two full years of piloting, Palmore had accumulated approximately seventeen hundred miles of first-class pilot's license, including stretches from Cincinnati to Cairo on the Ohio, the Mississippi from New Orleans to Hannibal, Missouri, and a few miles on the Tennessee. She also carries master's papers. Like the lady captains before her, she is establishing her own niche, aware and respectful of tradition but determined to imbibe the challenge, adventure, people, and scenery the river offers its devotees.

Blatz "Butch" Harrington aboard *Shirley Bowland*, 1981

CAPTAIN H. B. "BUTCH" HARRINGTON, JR.

RIVER

River flow long—river run wide
I don't know why that I keep coming back
I hate her when I'm with her and I miss her when I'm gone
Oh, River—why can't you just leave me alone (Refrain)

I'm a riverboat man and I reckon I'm proud
A hard-working man—Lord there ain't no doubt
Back-breaking work just to earn my pay
And every minute I'm thinking, I'll leave her someday

(Refrain)

It's a love-hate situation oldtimers say,
Though a man leaves the river—well his memories never fade
They say he will pray for his happiness
But the river don't let go—there ain't no rest

(Refrain)

Oh river sing a song—I'm way away from home
I'd like to see my wife, I've been three weeks gone
Sing a song—make me laugh no time for tears
Maybe I'll leave this way of life—well maybe next year.

(Refrain)

Words and music by H. B. Harrington, Jr.
Sung by Splitwater Creek

Born in Paducah, Kentucky, in 1951, "Butch" Harrington[25] has been working on the river for four years—just a little less than the total river time of Samuel Clemens. His route to the river has been circuitous. He showed promise as a baseball player but quit school after one year of community college because he had "picked up on music" and wanted to sing locally. Instead of returning for his second year of college, he worked in the alloy plant at Calvert City—"the dirtiest one they have"—sweeping the floor around Furnace 16. The constant black dust didn't appeal to him, so at nineteen, when he was offered the chance, he joined a band, Our Brothers' Keepers, and traveled with them for three years.

> At times we thought we had a chance to do something; we released three singles, and one was with Columbia. That last one was with a company called Star King of Nashville, and it was gettin' a lot of air play in Paducah, which really doesn't mean anything, but it got air play in larger markets like Boston and Chicago. So we went back on the road thinking that we might have something here. And then the company went broke. And I met Alison [Bradford] at a place here in town and that pretty well ended that.

Just before his marriage to Alison, Harrington made one trip on an Alter boat, then returned home, worked in a music store for six months and in clothing stores for another two years. Then he became a carpenter's helper for awhile before finally turning back to the river in 1977. "The clothing business just about drove me completely out of my mind, and I knew that I just didn't have the hang of bein' a carpenter. I liked the hard work that goes along with it, but I just didn't care for it that much. So I went back."

Now, the songwriter feels he will never again be completely away from the river. Like so many of the old-timers he talks to, Harrington learned the river and learned to steer by working his regular twelve-hour day as a deckhand and then steering for six hours on his off-watch. And the lyrics to his song, "River," show that this young towboat operator is kin to those who have come before him. He is proud, hardworking, ambivalent. The mystery that is the river still "don't let go."

Regularly employed by Crounse Corporation of Paducah, Harrington talked of his river experience on May 17, 1981, two days after returning from his first

---

[25] Though he has his towboat operator's license and has steered his first trip as regular pilot, Captain Harrington pleads embarrassment at being called "captain" just yet. He feels he has not earned the title. So henceforth I'll alleviate the blushing by calling him "Harrington."

run as a trip pilot aboard the Malloy boat *Sipsey*.[26] Word is that deckhand Harrington is ready to be "set up" as a Crounse pilot and will be "turned loose" soon.

Starting on the River

Uncle Pud worked on the river back in the fifties, and I'm thinkin' that he may have worked for Mechling back then. . . . I have one other relative . . . still workin' on the river. Besides that, I don't know, I don't have any idea why I started workin' on the river. Unless at the time I was just lookin' to make more money. Because at first I was really intimidated about going out on the river. I didn't have any idea what it would be or what the people would be like. From the standpoint of being able to go up and down the river, I thought I'd like that. But thinkin' back, I have no idea what started me to work on the river.

I sort of play dumb, well I have played dumb in fact ever since I've been on the river, that I ever traveled with the band or that I was ever even a musician. That I even knew what a guitar looked like. I wasn't really paranoid about it; I was just sort of backward about it because I didn't know how they would take it. Because of the reputation people got from the sixties and so forth. I figured they'd look at me as if I was from outer space, but since this album came out, you know, a bunch of the guys around the river bought the album. You know, they're all lookin' at me sayin', "What in the world are you doin' out here?" They think that I should be back here playin' music and makin' a million dollars because they all think that automatically because you got an album out or a song, you're worth a million dollars. It's hard to explain to them that, you tell 'em, "Well, I like what I'm doin' here." They think you're crazy then too. Although they know what you're talkin' about, they'll look at you like you're crazy.

The river is in some ways a lot like any other thing, like the truckin' industry, for instance. I always wanted to be a trucker, but to be a trucker you always had to have two years' experience. So I asked these people, how do I go about getting two years' experience? They said, "Well, we don't know, but that's what we've got to have." Lot of times it was handed down in the family in order to do something like that. 'Course it's not that way

---

[26] At the time, Crounse boats were idle because of a coal miner's strike.

with the river, but it's gettin' worse all the time, as far as tryin' to get on with the river, than it used to be.

Used to be a green man could just pop right on a boat. I made one trip seven years ago, right before Alison and I got married, and I just got on a boat for Alter. And then about that time was when they was startin' that school down at Helena, and I think at the time it cost $150 to go to it. And it was more or less just a safety course and stuff like that. Back then, if you went to that school and stayed on the boat for thirty days, the company would reimburse you the money you paid out to go to that school. Now then, they'll only give you a third, or two-thirds, or something like that back; I think a third. So now, then, it costs a man to get out on the river now; he really needs to know if he wants to work out there 'cause a lot of companies are requiring that you go to this school before you can even get a job out here.

QUESTION: So you did go to Helena?

HARRINGTON: No, I never did. I was hired green with Alter that first trip, which was right before my wife and I married. And I was twenty-two years old then. . . . I told Alison—'course the way two young people are right before we were to get married and all this and couldn't hardly stand to be away from each other for two or three minutes—I said, "Well, they're going to call me right before Christmas, I know they're going to if they call me at all." And sure enough they called me December 19. Well I headed out along with a lot of tears and all this. It was terrible up on the upper end [Mississippi River] that year . . . it looked like Antarctica up there.

Well, I was so green I didn't even know the difference between a load and an empty. I can't remember exactly where we were; we weren't way up on the upper end. We were still on the lower end of the upper Mississippi River, but ice started to get in. You could see deer walkin' across the ice. And we had just a few barges. I was on the *Rene G.* . . . . That one trip I sort of got my feet wet, I guess, or wore out a pair of boots, or whatever. I liked it, but Alison she just, when I got back she wouldn't have anything to do with it. If nothing else, I wanted to make one more trip because I was gonna buy her a wedding set, you know, with that. But couldn't even work that out, but I did finally go back three years later, I guess it was.

In March of 1977, Harrington hired on as deckhand aboard the 1,800-horsepower *Frank Alter*, running the upper Mississippi, and later switched to the 5,600-horsepower *Bernard G.*

I worked for Alter for about a year and was on the *Bernard G.* about eight months, and then I started workin' for Crounse.

QUESTION: Well, now at this point had your wife accommodated to your going back on the river?

HARRINGTON: Yeah. At that time, it was fine with her. I mean, it wasn't fine, but I was bringin' in more money at the time than what we were used to. . . . Started at fifty dollars a day is what it was. That was straight time, that wasn't day for day. I mean I made fifty dollars a day when I was on the boat and I didn't make any money when I was off.

QUESTION: And how many days would you work usually before you took time off?

HARRINGTON: While I worked for Alter I don't remember ever working less than thirty-five days. Lot of times I'd work up to between thirty-five and forty; one time I worked forty-five and then another time . . . I remember working up to fifty-some-odd days one time because my younger brother said he was gonna get married. And he said, "I want you to be home for the wedding." I said, "Sure, work it out." I had to stay on the boat instead of gettin' off. Well, I stayed and I stayed and I got numb, I was stayin' on the boat so long. Finally got off, and when I got off, he said, "Well, I'm not gonna get married after all." I took him by the neck.

His move from Alter to Crounse was prompted by both practical reasons and his sense of pride.

One reason [for the change] is, of course, better pay. Goin' from fifty dollars a day to eighty dollars a day, plus day for day. So I was gettin' forty dollars a day when I was on and forty dollars when I was off. And they worked twenty-one and twenty-one; they'd swap whole crews out. And of course Crounse is right here at home. And Crounse's been in business for almost thirty years. It's just, you could almost say it's political, you know, in order to get a job at Crounse. It's that hard, no matter if you've got a thousand years experience, you don't go in there and just get a job. My uncle, he was the personnel manager down there and they used to have breakfast and so on, that's how I got an interview. Because I had called Crounse's office back in August of the previous year, and I wanted to know if I could get an application. And I was politely told that they don't even give applications out.

QUESTION: This seems very strange given there's a real shortage of pilots. So they're banking on their reputation to bring them the best people.

HARRINGTON: Right. A Crounse anybody has probably one of the best reputations on the river. A Crounse pilot, even though he's—all they have is single-screw boats, the largest boat they have is 1,800 horsepower, but they're like gnats, they're all over the river—and a Crounse pilot probably has as good a reputation as anybody. . . . A lot of people laugh, you know. Lot of 'em are called cowboys because it is about like ridin' a wild horse sometimes if you got a lot of current in the Ohio River and you got 1,800 horses tryin' to stop—see if there's enough current, you'll have trouble stoppin' nine barges sometimes. Comin' down on these locks, it can get you up out of your chair sometimes.

In an age of corporate subsidiaries, Crounse Corporation "is still George Crounse's Company" and the atmosphere is one that clearly appeals to Harrington: "When you walk in the office, you're called by your first name by everybody. Everybody knows everybody; it's almost like a big family." Still, it is more difficult to realize one's pilot ambitions at Crounse because, unlike some other companies, they have no steersman program. "The very first thing when I came over, they told me, there's a way that everybody else does it on the river, and then there's the Crounse way." But, although there is no regular program for apprentice pilots, Harrington was allowed to steer the boat on his first trip out with Crounse. "If a man wants to learn the river, if he wants to become a pilot with Crounse, then he really has to want it pretty bad." And Harrington wants it pretty bad.

Learning the River

Like the pilots before him, Butch Harrington learned the river from a seasoned man. Two pilots served as his mentors.

Started out workin' with Dub Hamilton. . . . And I would guess that Dub is basically a Tennessee River man; he's run the Ohio a lot but . . . if he wanted to be put anywhere, he'd want to be put on the Tennessee River and no other place in the whole entire world. That's where he started workin' in and that's where he ended up now. But he's been on the river close to thirty years, I'd say. . . . But he has the most phenomenal memory on anybody I've ever seen because he could name all the lights all the way up and down the Tennessee River, all the way up and down the Ohio to a certain place where he used to always run. And he wouldn't only name the lights, he'd give you the mile and the tenths of the light.

You had to win Dub's trust before—he was never out to do you any wrong, but he wouldn't do you any favors either, until he knew whether or not you could be trusted. . . . And I worked under Dub for a year and a half and we got real close, closer than I ever thought I'd ever be to anybody. Not exactly father-son type thing, but we were really close. He helped me a whole lot; I always paid attention—some of the younger guys don't care to hear all this rigamaroll about what the river used to be or what the river used to look like. But we would be comin' down the Tennessee and Dub'd say, "Well, the channel used to run over here behind this island, now they've got the channel runnin' this other way." Or, "There used to be a sandbar built up right there." You know, I take all of this stuff in and I liked hearin' all that stuff, always have.

But I worked for Dub for a year and a half, worked under him, and he was probably as fair a man as I've ever worked for. 'Cause he would shoot straight with you, he would never come around a bend with you and along that way; he'd shoot straight whatever situation you were in. He was some gutty dude. . . . You know, in some cases, as men get older, they get a little bit more cautious than what they were when they were younger, say they lose a little bit of their nerve. But that wasn't so with Dub; I mean, the hotter it was, the more he liked it. He'd just get up out of the chair and you'd see this wild grin come across his face. I remember one time we were comin' out of Pickwick Lock—it gets extremely hot up there with that current—we come around what they call Big Bend right below the lock, and the buoys are pinched in right next to the shore; I mean we always come out with empties and you've got to keep your empties practically running over the buoys the whole time on these blacks [buoys, kept on right side of boat going downstream] runnin' out. And on the shore you've got rock all the way up and down the bank, and in the first place, when they made that channel there, they moved the channel—I suppose with dynamite or whatever—out of shelf rock, so you're runnin' in a channel just in between rock. And, Lord, it was runnin', I mean it was runnin'! He came out and we had, I guess we had nine empties. And you just go 'round that bend completely sideways, you just keep pointin' your buoys all the way around, and when he came out of the lock, he come down to Wolf Island—and it *is* a nice little bend there—and I remember Dub gettin' on the radio. He never was one to cut up or anything like that on the radio. On the work channels, you know, he just came on and gave his call letters and told anybody that was comin' up says, "*Patricia*'s downbound and she's a-slippin' and a-slidin', better get out of my way!" He was cacklin' like a rooster up there. He took her right around that island, and he never let up on it.

I've gone through two different learning processes 'cause I learned a lot of basics under Dub, but when the time came to make the things that I needed to such as bridges—Dub . . . didn't have the patience of a younger man. You could steer open river, parts where he could sit back on the couch and relax. But if we got to a tight spot, he'd usually have to take it 'cause he just didn't have the patience for a younger man to sit up there; it was just a lot easier for him to get up there and do it himself.

About six months after Dub Hamilton retired, Harrington transferred to the *Shirley Bowland* under Captain Tam Young.

He's a younger guy; I'd say Tam's in his real early forties. And right now I guess Tam's probably considered the best pilot that Crounse has. He was different than Dub in that he'd let a man sit down, and whatever came up, he only took the sticks from me once or twice. In other words, when I sit down, I might as well know that even though I've got a man sittin' behind me that I'm not gonna be gettin' up, that he's not gonna take 'em. If I get myself into a situation, I better figure on some way of gettin' it out 'cause I'm not gonna be able to stand up and say, "Well, you better take her 'cause I don't know what to do." 'Cause he'll have you sittin' right back down whether you like it or not. And at that point in time, that's the kind of trainin' I needed. I needed somebody that when I was gettin' ready to make a bridge, he would give me an idea; he would tell me how he made it. He'd say, you know, "when you get set up, I'm sure you'll probably have a different way of makin' it. But this is the way I make it and you can try it for now and see how it feels. It may variate sometime in the future." He always has the easy way of makin' it; he always has a way of keepin' a man out of a hard steer. That's just the main thing, keepin' it out of a hard steer as much as you can. And it's not easy to make pilot under Tam. I know, I've worked under him for a year. It's not like he just works a man down, but when you work for him, you know, you *work*. Because he keeps the boat up, he keeps it immaculate. I mean it is completely immaculate. You're constantly moppin' decks, and he keeps up a boat.

He's the captain. And he keeps the boat painted. You know a man has to work a whole lot; he takes a lot of pride in his boat because of the way Tam keeps one up. I'm sure this'll probably rub off on me in later years. It's funny—see now, when you steer under somebody, even though some of these older guys . . . sometimes they'll criticize certain things about the people that they learned the river under. And what's funny, they'll turn right around and be exactly like the person they were criticizin'. . . .

Tam, he really studies the river. A lot of the people I know who's out on the river will learn the river enough to get up and down it, and then after that then they don't go on any further with it, on their education of the river. They learn just enough at that point to where they really want to learn, to where their interest is still real keen and they're pickin' up on all this stuff—almost like a child, it's just constantly stored information—but once they get set up and once they get comfortable with their job, that's when their learnin' process stops, seems like. They don't try to pick up on anything. But Tam is one—I worked with another, too—constantly they're pickin' up information and constantly learning because, you know, there's going to be something different on the river every day; you learn something different every day. And the learnin' process never stops; that's what I like. Because I hope I'm never like what I'm sayin' these other guys are; I hope that I never want to stop learnin' what there is to learn out there. Because if you do, it just seems like that takes a whole lot out. That's all you're doin', just sittin' up there steerin'.

So, though he had tried several jobs before turning to the river and had nurtured no longtime ambitions to be a river pilot, Harrington quickly became so obsessed with the idea that he routinely worked eighteen-hour days.

After the very first trip. I knew that's what I'd end up doin'. And after a while it almost—well it did—became an obsession. That's all I thought about, that's all that was on my mind as far as the river was concerned. And I sort of tiptoed through . . . without wantin' to get on people's nerves, but wantin' to get up behind the sticks so bad it just hurt.

I've been with Crounse for three years this month. . . . And I've been steerin' for three years. . . . I've been able to make a serious effort since last year. You know, it would be comparable to a man with a bigger company bein' set up as a steersman for a year. That's about the way you would compare it 'cause I've been seein' every part of the river that I could and that's why I was workin' eighteen hours. I worked the after-watch so I could stay up with the captain, and I'd go up at six at night. Most times stay up . . . till I had to go back on watch at twelve midnight. . . . I took full advantage of it for a full year.

Reflections on his Profession

Such a schedule leaves little time for "recreational" activities other than eating and sleeping. But since he's not fond of watching TV on the boat, Harrington claims that he can make it fine if he has a radio for music. He tried taking his guitar with him but found that, generally, it didn't work out.

'Course on Crounse boats, they're not insulated like these bigger boats. I thought, too, when I first started workin', I thought, "Well, this will be the perfect thing." I just thought it'd be perfect, but it's not. It's just two different worlds interferin' with each other. When I'm out on the river, I'm out on the river. And music, as far as concentratin' on tryin' to write music, it has no place.

I wrote the river song while I was out on the boat; I didn't have my guitar and I wrote two songs while I was out there that time. And they both came rushin' at me . . . I've never had anything happen to me since like that time. What I'm used to doin' is—my father-in-law writes the lyrics and I been writin' the music, for a number of years. And the lyrics has not been easy to me. But these, they just fell all over me, and I was just writin' furiously, and I wrote both lyrics in three or four hours' time. As I was writin' the river lyrics, the melody was already runnin' through my head, and I was like a zombie for a number of days on the boat 'cause I was constantly hummin' this melody because I was afraid that I might forget it. And we were a pretty good way away from home, and I was just waitin' for us to get close enough to home so I could get off and run home and put it down on tape so I could at least have it there waitin' for me when I got home and could finish it, you know, refine it. Which I was able to do. I was pretty crazy there for awhile.

When he was ready, Harrington applied for and received his towboat operator's license. Shortly before his examination, he jawed with his Uncle Pud one day in a bar.

I was tellin' him about havin' to go get my license, what I was gonna have to go through, what I'd studied, you know, and I thought this would really impress him. Because I'm havin' to do a whole lot to get my license. And it didn't impress him very much because it turned out that what he had to do back in the fifties to get his mate's license was about twice as much as what I had to do to get my pilot's license. It really was, it was outrageous. It took him a number of days to get his mate's license back then, and they had to write all their questions and answers out in longhand.

Though he is not required to sit for first-class pilot's license, this neophyte operator plans to do so.

I'm gonna get just as much of it as I can. I told Alison, I'm just gonna be licensed to the teeth. But as far as first-class pilot license, I can't put it in words. . . . If a guy can go through twenty-five or thirty years just on an operator's license, I don't see anything wrong with that if that's what he wants to do. But without sounding super gung-ho, I just want to be as qualified as I can possibly be because I take that much pride in what I do and that amount of pride goes over into being licensed.

Unlike some of the younger men on the river, Harrington listens to and respects the experiences of old-timers. And he's developed a few opinions of his own as well.

And I agree with a lot of the old-timers in that the river was harder to work back in their day. There have been a lot of changes in the river just in ten years time, especially in twenty years time, a phenomenal amount of change out there. I was listenin' to one captain, he was tellin' me about talkin' to another captain, and they were talkin' about the computers that'll eventually be comin' into the river and the traffic control that will eventually be comin' into the river. [27] And this one guy said that before long, anybody can walk off the hill and run a towboat. And he said he didn't want to see it become that easy.

Right now it's a specialized job that takes a special person and special knowledge in order to work the river, in order to be a pilot. And it still runs fairly true right now; just not any Joe can come off the hill and go out there and do what we do. But they keep makin' it easier and easier all the time, and, like the captain said, in one instance they're takin' a lot of challenge out of the river and in another instance, they'll be negatin' a lot of jobs. The easier they make it to work on the river, the easier it'll be for anybody to come out and do the job. And that's not such a welcome possibility as far as I'm concerned either. I know back then they had to know the river a lot; they had to do without. It wasn't that many years ago that they didn't have radar

[27] To some extent, traffic control is here. See Chapter 2 on the VTS traffic-control system.

and neon lights and all this other stuff. They had to *know* where sandbars were, they had to *know* river stages and where they could run and where they couldn't run, which you still have to know now — not out of necessity but just simply out of makin' better time. You can run behind certain islands if you know certain stages of water, and that'll make better time. Because they don't have all the channels buoyed off, not all the time they don't — a lot of times you don't have any buoys at all. Like when we were comin' down this first trip, there were hardly any buoys on the upper end there because of the high water, and the high water fallin' now, and we were beatin' some buoy boats, in other words some Coast Guard boats. There weren't any buoys out; there was just enough water to cover the dikes, which is actually pretty touchy.

Although he prefers not to talk about the more unpleasant aspects of life on the river, Harrington did reluctantly acknowledge the drug-abuse problem now facing most companies.

The old guys that I work with are mostly, they're all characters, of course. And they used to do so many things, you know, and I envy the things that they used to do. They sound like they used to have so much fun, and everything. 'Course they've grown up on the river and they've gotten old on the river — and they take everything seriously now. And there just doesn't seem like, maybe when I get older I'll think back and remember things that — but now it just doesn't seem like they do things, everything is more serious now. There used to be on the boats — 'course I don't know so much about other companies — there used to be a lot of drinkin' and stuff on boats, which is just not even thought about now. I'm sure there are some people that bring a bottle out, but even then if they do, you don't know about it.

QUESTION: But what about drugs now?

HARRINGTON: Yeah, that's a different story. It's evidently getting worse all the time, and it's a real touchy topic. And I hate to even speak of it because, I mean as far as associations with the river, 'cause I hate for people to read about that. But it's definitely there. . . . I know that the two companies that I've worked for — Alter and Crounse — I know that they're makin' more of an effort to not only look into it but to try to stem a lot of it that's goin' on. People in these offices, they hear a lot more than what you'd ever think they would. I know that they do, because so many men that come in and say just a few things here and there. And these little things that kind of just run through the office, they all add up to a story before long. And so they know what's goin' on out there, and I know that they're makin' an effort to stop a lot of it. There's been cases I know that it's been stopped at Crounse. . . . And it wasn't bad when I first started workin' out there; I'm sayin' that's a short period of time ago. But I've seen it steadily get worse since I've been out there. And like I say, it's just a touchy subject to talk about.

Of course, the drug problem is general in the culture and not particularly connected to river life, and, as Harrington observed, it affects a wide age range from twenty-year-old deckhands to sixty-year-old engineers. Another unpleasant aspect that is traditionally tied to life on the river is the sacrifice of time with one's family, a sacrifice felt even more keenly by men with children at home. Though he has no children, Harrington sympathizes:

You know, with Crounse we run around close, we run the Tennessee, and they allow us to get off the boat for anywhere from three or four hours to maybe eight or nine hours, get off at a point and catch 'em back on up the river. . . .
    Even if it catches you on your watch, somebody will cover for you. And I've seen guys get off the boat and go by home for a few hours. They might have a two-year-old child, just old enough to talk. And they're always real close to their daddies it seems like 'cause they always have a terrible fit, you know. Even at that age evidently they get conditioned to know when their father's gettin' ready to leave back out again, and evidently they can really make it rough on a man because I've seen guys come back and you just can't even get close to 'em for a few hours until he gets over it because it just really does, it hurts 'em bad. They've got this little one that's got his arms outstretched, you know, beggin' for daddy not to go. I know it hurts. I've often wondered what I would do, you know, if we did have children, how I'd handle it, because it'd probably kill me, I guess, havin' to leave one.

But such problems, hazards, or sacrifices do not dampen Harrington's enthusiasm for his new career. Just returned from his first trip as regular pilot standing solo watches, he gave an account of that run that will undoubtedly be etched in his memory and repeated over the years just as their own first runs have been by the old-timers. In fact, in his case, the operation was probably more akin to the experience of those veterans than to contemporary pilots because his "little ole boat" was running without benefit of radar, sonar, or complete communication. Besides that, he had never been on the lower Mississippi and their run took them as far as two miles below the Huey P. Long

Bridge at New Orleans—an area known as the "combat zone" because of the number of river and ocean-going vessels always plying that stretch. Accustomed to working those eighteen-hour days on the Crounse boats, Harrington found himself unable to sleep during his off watch and "about to go crazy" because there was no music in the pilothouse.

And it was just six hours of watchin' the river, which wouldn't be so bad except that this old boat we were on, it worked a man to death because . . . there was about four or five inches of play in the rudders, the bushin's were wore out, and it looked like a snake goin' up the river, you were just from one side to the other.

The boat is owned by Malloy's, here in Paducah. It's called the *Sipsey*. It's a small boat, fact I, well, I'm not puttin' the old boat down because it'd done a lot of good work in the past, but it's rated at 1,050 horsepower, so it's a real small boat. But I wouldn't rate it much over 700 or 800 horsepower, if that much. We caught the boat at Cape Girardeau, went on up the river light boat and picked up a couple of lash barges from somebody comin' down from St. Louis. . . . Like I say, there were just scattered buoys here and there. I was actually scared to death of that river there.

I've never even been behind the sticks on the Mississippi River. . . . and they've got huge maps for both those rivers, compared to what I'm used to usin'. And you have your map and you have your light list, so I looked at the map and the best that we could do was just follow the sailin' line, best that we could see. And that's why it was so much trouble; we didn't even have a radar to even see an outline of the river. . . . It just wasn't workin', so they took the power unit off.

Besides that, we had a radio that was out. We only had one radio. And we were goin' down—it was right after we left Cairo—we were goin' down the river, so besides havin' the radar out, besides havin' the radio out, somebody killed a damn snake down on the deck. A snake was up in the boat. And I *do* not like snakes at all! And to even think the snake'd get on the boat was just not good at all! God! I didn't know what I'd gotten into. The captain, he was goin' crazy anyway, he said, "Butch, what have we done?"[28]

He said, "What have we gotten into?" I said, "I don't know. I swear I don't know." He was real good to work for because the very first day I took the sticks—he knew I was green, and I was afraid everybody else on the boat would know I was green; I didn't know if they knew or not, 'course I was

[28] The other pilot-captain was also a Crounse pilot doing trip work.

sorta sensitive about that. I wanted to walk on there and act like an old, seasoned pilot, see, just knew right what I was doin', but I was so self-conscious, I don't believe I said five words in between gettin' on the boat. . . . But, he said, "If you need me for anything at all, don't worry about gettin' me out of bed. It's no problem." He didn't really treat me like a green man, he more or less said it tactfully to where, you know, "Neither one of us know this river, so a lot of times two heads are better than one." But that's the last time he had to say that; he didn't ever say anything else about it. I got word from one of the crew—which helped me out a whole lot as far as my confidence—I got word from one of the crew members that he was talkin' about that if ever I needed a recommendation, he'd be more than glad to give me one. Evidently, he must have been impressed that I could handle the job, I guess.

Well, we had a cook, evidently it was his first time on the river; he was a twenty-year Navy man, skin diver, and he was a little man, real hyper, always buzzin' around. And he didn't go to sleep for almost two days. I know he stayed up for probably forty-two, forty-four hours of the first forty-eight. And he sat up in the pilothouse after about three or four days I'd been on the boat. And he said, "Well, Butch, I just haven't been able to sleep. But it looks like you're gonna handle it all right." I was kinda tore up 'cause he knew that I was green, I guess, and a lot of these guys were impressin' him that the Mississippi River was the ultimate for a man to get onto. And it's pretty wild for a man who doesn't know the river to git on it, let alone a green man that doesn't know the river to get on it. So he came up . . . and I felt really flattered because he said, "You're cool; nothin' seems to upset you." Said, "You're doin' just fine. I believe I can get some sleep now." [Laughs.]

Oh, when we got into Baton Rouge. Well, in the first place, I remember makin' Greenville Bridge, by that time we had . . . ten loads on this little boat. I was comin' down on my watch, it was about two or three in the morning. I heard a lot of activity [on the radio] around this bend they call Old Town Bend. And the *Dennis Hendricks* had busted its tow, he had twenty or twenty-five loads, I never did really know, I just know he had 'em all over the river. And he got down in that bend too far and he broke his tow up, so I set her to backin' right up above that bend there. This boat wouldn't stop these loads. The most it would do was stop 'em to current speed.

The current was probably runnin' I would think anywhere between four and six mile an hour. And besides that, these barges were all boxes that didn't have any rake ends on 'em, faced up the boxes, just pushed square in. When you back on it, just seems to naturally want to turn around. Just wanted to flip around me, so I got it in some kind of bad shape. I mean I was goin' down into the bend sideways, not really havin' control. I didn't really have control of the tow, the best I was gonna do if I'd a kept on that course was just to land against the hill. There was a boat down there helping the *Dennis Hendricks* put his tow back together, and I was afraid I was gonna get down on him. Everybody was on a different channel; there were some on 67, there was some on 14, Coast Guard was a-hollerin' back and forth, and there was everybody tryin' to get ahold of everybody, and nobody could seem to get ahold of anyone. And I finally got ahold of the *Dennis Hendricks.*

I told him what kind of a tow I had and what kind of situation I was in—I asked him if there was any kind of hole down there I could get through. He said, "Yeah, I think you can get through here." So I told him, "Well, I don't have much choice. I'm gonna have to come ahead on it or you all gonna be pickin' up my barges too." So he said, "Yeah, go ahead and give her a whirl there." So I came ahead on her, which is not sayin' a whole lot on that boat, but it was better than backin' up anyway. So I got on down through that bend and kind of weavin' back and forth; there was a boat in front of me with a unit tow, and I noticed he had his light about two or three miles down the river below this bend. He had his light on some barges; I could see that far. It looked like they were right against the bank, and I thought they were tied off. They were tyin' off barges all around there. Well he kept his light on these barges all the way down until he made—there was another bend—and he made that bend. So when I got halfway in between that bend and the hill where those barges were, I threw my light on 'em, and like I said, it looked like they were tied off. The closer I got, I noticed it, you know, besides me goin' down the river and me keepin' a line with what I was doin', I noticed that they were movin' about the same speed that I was. And they were just gettin' down the river. They were almost movin' as fast as I was! And so I was gettin' ready to make that bend, and just as I was gettin' ready to make it, these barges, they were in two groups. One was in a group of three, one in a group of two. It was like they had rudders. They turned, too. And I was tryin' to judge whether or not I was on a collision course with 'em, and I thought I wasn't but I decided it was gonna be plenty close. So I was right on the verge of hittin' the general alarm and gettin' everybody up in case something did happen because I was in a slide and they were turnin' with me.

They were almost stayin' up with me. I told the captain, I said, "If it hadn't been so serious at the time, I'm sure I'd been on the floor laughin'. This little old boat tryin' to outrun these empty barges runnin' down the river. That's really stupid." Didn't say a whole lot for what we were on. But I had a twenty-five-barge tow and a thirty-barge tow comin' up and I had an empty gasoline tow, gasoline barges comin' up. And they were askin' me, and I said, "Well, y'all got a place to hide, you better find it, 'cause they're comin' right down on you and they're comin' down in the channel. It's just almost like somebody's steerin' 'em, they were followin' the buoy line." And this gasoline tow, he's already gotten behind the point. He was well hid and he wasn't about to poke his head out until those barges got out of the way. But I don't even know what happened; I know these tows came on up and then I was relieved by the captain. So I told him, I said, "Well, you got five of 'em that are loose runnin' right down on your stern there." And I told him about tryin' to outrun 'em. He just shook his head, like that was just par for the course, I guess.

On the way down river, the *Sipsey* met the *Miss Kae-D* coming upriver with her record seventy-two-barge tow.

It seems like I was right above Vicksburg, best I can remember, a wide stretch of the river. Well, thankfully enough, there was extra water down there because I was watchin' him and wasn't payin' attention—I mean it just had my mind completely off center because I was lookin' . . . at these red buoys, the red buoy line, and I was still thinkin' about these seventy-two barges, I just couldn't believe it. I know I read about the old days of steamers, I'm tryin' to remember, I just got through readin' it in *Waterways* some records they had, but I thought this seventy-two deal must be a record. Gotta be, of some kind! I was runnin' on the wrong side of the red buoys just gettin' down the river; then all of a sudden I thought, "Those dudes are supposed to be over on my port side!" I ran her hard down and got over inside the buoy line; it's a good thing, I know I was runnin' over a bar. If we hadn't had some extra water, I guess I'd a had some loads on the ground. It unnerved me; I couldn't believe that anybody could be behind that.

It's unreal! Well, after awhile when you get down there, it all becomes commonplace to see twenty, twenty-five loads, that's not so much. It doesn't even impress you that much. What really does impress you is that river is so big down there, in some places it's just so big. And I told my wife, I said, "I felt like a mackeral in a sea of whales." Because you don't see anything down there hardly, I mean just people that all the time run that river down there, you don't see 'em on hardly anything less than 5,200-horsepower boats. And that's just the average-size boat. But you see a lot of triple screws down there, you see a lot of 6,300 horsepower, lot of 7,000, and a lot of 8,400, and then once in awhile you run into some of these 10,500s. They are just immense. It's unbelievable!

Well, we finally got radar in Memphis. . . . It was a big help because the searchlight we had was probably not much more than—we had one carbon light and one bulb light. I told one of the boys that the bulb light, you know, we may as well have a guy sittin' up there with a frog-giggin' light or something. And the carbon light wasn't but about twenty-five amps, so it was real small. . . .

We didn't have any sounders at all. We made that trip practically about the way the old guys used to have to do it. I can't say I particularly care for it either. [Laughs.] As far as modern technology, that radar is real nice.

After trying other trades, Harrington has settled on the river, he says, for basically two reasons: "economics and likin' the job." And, he admits, for that dash of romance.

There's a lot of things about the river that's hard to put down. With that song I just barely touched what I really say about the river without trying to sound like an amateur cornball tryin' to spout off stuff. 'Cause I know it wouldn't come out right if I tried to say exactly why I stay out on the river. But there's a lot of pride a man can take in what he does out there. He knows that he does something special, and he knows that he does something that nobody else will do.

I'm sure there's a romantic aspect to it goin' back to the steamers, 'cause I've always liked to read about stuff like that. But I'm sure that's part of it, because especially on summer nights, or full-moon nights, or lot of stars, or early in the spring just when everything is comin' out, or in the fall, you can see things on the river that people won't ever see in a lifetime. They just won't ever know it's there, just as far as lookin' around at what they would consider nothin' because you don't see anything but banks and trees and hills and houses and stuff like that. I've told Alison—she's only been out with me one time and she didn't really get an idea, but as soon as I get established in the pilothouse and on a boat that's comfortable enough where she can come on and stay with me for about a week—'cause I've never really been able to tell her in words what it's like out there, and I want her to get an idea of what it is like.

Like Captain Lexie Palmore, who pursues dual careers of piloting and art, Harrington will continue to write songs on his days off. Despite the ambivalence reflected in the lyrics of "River," Butch Harrington seems irrevocably drawn to the river and plans to maintain that connection regardless of what successes or failures his music career may hold.

I was talkin' to a boy over on the Mississippi . . . and he was talkin' about how it was just gettin' harder for him to go back on the river every time. And we got to talkin' about, there's nothing we'd rather do on the bank, and it kinda goes back to almost what I was sayin' in the song—when you're out there a lot of times, you say you'll never come back again, but after you're home two or three weeks, you're ready to hit it. Just back and forth all the time.

I started out, I wanted to become a pilot in the first place because I never was self-conscious about the fact that I didn't go all the way through school. But it did bother me because I didn't have anything to fall back on. The only thing that college ever represented to me was from the standpoint of security; you had a piece of parchment there or something, it may have been because of the way I was brought up or the time I was brought up in, but that piece of parchment always meant security. Whether or not you could make over one hundred dollars a week, you still had that degree, whether or not you were workin' in it or not. And that was always supposed to be a standpoint of security. There was never anything in school that really interested me, so the way I've looked at it is that I've put four years into the river, which is basically what I would put in school. And I've been paid to do this; I've been paid for this education, paid fairly well. And once I get in the pilothouse and established with experience, I can do anything I want to. . . . That means if I wanted to go back to music and pursue it, I think I'll have more security to fall back on than any amount of college education I could have gotten in anything that I can think of. And probably end up making more money at it than just about anything that college could've prepared me for.

At one time I was wonderin' whether I ever would find anything, until I started workin' on the river. If I ever did go back to Nashville and start peddlin', walkin' the streets and so on, if things got bad enough for Alison and I, I know that—the way the river stands now and I think it'll be for quite awhile—the only thing I'll have to do is make one phone call, and the very next day I'm sure I can be workin'.

A Crounse pilot is makin' $165 a day; we're up for a raise here next month, should put 'em up close to $175 a day.[29] There's pilots for some companies on the lower Mississippi River makin' $182 a day. Trip pilots down there are makin' $210 a day.

I told [Alison] even if we were worth just a bunch of money some day, . . . that I'd always keep my license up to date, and if things got just a little bit too rough, the pressures or whatever, I don't ever feel like that I'll be too far away from the river. If I get away from it, I don't believe I'll ever be too far away from it. I don't think that I'll ever be able to just stop it completely and say, "Well, that was just a phase of my life; that's what I did for a number of years there and now this is what I do now." I don't think there'll ever come a time till maybe if my eyes ever get bad, or something like that. A long time from now I hope.

Through his music, pilot Harrington may capture a little glory for the modern-day riverman whose world is generally inaccessible to the people "on the hill."

I think it probably flatters any riverman for anybody to take any interest in what he does. I don't know of anybody I've ever encountered who takes as much pride in what they do and probably get as little acknowledgment for what they do except for when they're out there among their own people. It's a different world. I've written a song about the truckers, how they sing songs for truckers, make a shrine out of railroad men, why doesn't anybody sing of the riverman. . . . Any of the songs that are written always go back to the steamboat days, which I don't begrudge, but there's a different river out there now.

---

[29] By $165 a day, Harrington means day-for-day. He is paid $82.50 a day while on the boat and $82.50 a day while he is off.

I'd rather pilot a steamboat than to eat.

Captain J. Emory Edgington, 1957

Well, a riverman is just like a coal man. A riverman starts as a riverman, he's goin' to finish up that way. A coal man starts in the coal digger, he's goin' to finish a coal digger. You can't break him. . . . You see some mighty exciting things when you're on the river.

Captain Gale Justice, 1979

The facet that is the most intriguing to me is the fact that you never know what is going to happen. It's a very unorderly existence, but certainly it isn't boring. It has some other drawbacks, but boring is what it is not.

Captain Donn Williams, 1979

Well, I suppose a great many of these men will never go down in history. They'll be anonymous at least. And their names will be forgotten. But in their day and age they were probably known from one end of the river to the other.

Horace Lyle (boat agent, clerk, Greene Line Steamers), 1957

CHAPTER SIX

Legacy

Captain Joseph "T. Joe" Decareaux on the *President*, 1977

A story is told of the "glory days" of steamboating when a "lanky country-man astride a mule hailed a steamboat tied up at a small landing. He insisted on seeing the captain, although every man on board tried to learn his business without disturbing that august personage. Finally, the irascible captain strode out on the deck and demanded what was wanted. . . . 'Just wanted to know, can my mule take a drink out of your river?'"[1]

Indeed, a steamboat captain in those early years was often the owner and pilot as well. Pride in his craft and his authority over its operation went unquestioned. Generally a one-man or a family venture, the "fleets" of these independent operators often included only a single boat. Some famous owner-captains like Captain T. P. Leathers, a red-headed, red-bearded, massive man nicknamed "Old Push," built a series of boats, each to replace the last one lost to service because of fire, or war, or "graveyarding." Captain Leathers commissioned the building of eight boats named *Natchez*, the first in 1848, the last in 1896. In *Look Down That Winding River*, Ben Lucien Burman passes on one of Captain Jake's pilothouse stories about some "mighty fine boats" and "mighty fine captains":

> "That Captain Leathers beat 'em all," put in Captain Jake. "One day he seen a young fellow that was a passenger whittling at the railing of his new boat. He doesn't say anything, just gets a big knife in the galley and begins slashing the fellow's fancy suit."
>
> "'Hey! What are you doing?' says the young fellow. 'You're cutting my coat!'"
>
> "Captain Leathers takes another good whack with the knife. 'Yes, sir! Damn it, sir! You're cutting my boat!'" [P. 65]

[1] Told by B. A. Botkin, *Mississippi River Folklore*. Original source cited as *Papers in Illinois History for the Year 1940*, pp. 18–19.

In addition to individual owner-captains like captains Leathers and Cannon in the lower Mississippi and captains Throckmorton, Davidson, and Reynolds in the upper Mississippi, joint-stock business associations were formed as early as 1810 when Robert Fulton, Dewitt Clinton, Nicholas Roosevelt, and others incorporated under the name of the Ohio Steamboat Navigation Company.[2] Later, because of ruthless competition among boats servicing the same routes, and because of the lack of regularity, reliability, and punctuality of transient steamboat operations, individual owners sometimes joined together in packet or line companies, retaining ownership and operation of their boats but cooperating in the determination of routes, schedules, and rates.[3] Before 1870 the corporation played a relatively minor role in the business of steamboating.[4] It was primarily in the towing industry after 1880 that large-scale corporate enterprise came to river transportation.

The decline in river traffic—attributed to competition from the railroads, undercutting techniques among boat owners, and eventually the advent of paved roads—reached its lowest point just before World War I. Old packets and old pilots were resurrected to contribute to the war effort. Formation of the Federal Barge Line in 1923 provided the boost of government ownership and backing that spurred revival of inland river transportation and served as the training ground for a new generation of pilots. When both World War I and the Barge Line created a new need for pilots, old packet men tried to adjust to handling tows but were often reluctant to train cubs who would eventually compete with them for their jobs. But by the 1930s river traffic had been steadily rebuilding and pilots found once again that they had prospects of steady work and good pay, particularly relative to the scarcity of land jobs.

[2] Louis Hunter, *Steamboats on the Western Rivers*, p. 309. For an extensive discussion of the organization of steamboat transportation, see chapter 7, pp. 307–56.

[3] Transient steamboats followed no particular schedule and roved from trade to trade, announcing readiness for business by putting up the boat's "shingle" and distributing handbills. A boat would not leave until a satisfactory cargo was on board, making departure and arrival times uncertain. Remaining a mainstay of western river transportation, these transients were not outstripped by the growing packets and lines until after the Civil War. The packet was a vessel that made regular trips at prescribed, stated intervals. A line consisted of two or more steamboats offering packet service in a particular trade route. Again, see Hunter, *Steamboats*, chapter 7.

[4] In fact, in assessing records from 1830–1906, historian Louis Hunter found that throughout the steamboat era, approximately two-thirds of all steamboats were owned by four men or less, nearly one-fourth owned by single proprietors. By 1906, nearly half the steamboats were owned by individual proprietors but the aggregate accounted for only one-fifth of the tonnage. Corporations, on the other hand, owned fewer than three-eighths of the steamboats but accounted for three-fourths of the total tonnage. See Hunter, *Steamboats*, pp. 331–2.

Many pilots, in fact, proudly point to their good fortune in never having been out of work during the Depression.[5]

Private companies followed the government's lead and began investing again in barges, boats, and crews to ply the once-sputtering river trade. Just as they had been in World War I, during World War II pilots were generally deferred from active military service in order to perform vital homefront work in transporting coal, oil, landing craft, and submarines to key destinations. With the post-World War II boom in commerce and the adaptability of war-generated technology for use on domestic carriers, pilots were once more in great demand.[6] Now, many towing companies are but small subsidiaries of giant, diversified corporations. There is a critical shortage of qualified, experienced pilots and increasing concern among the "old heads" that standards have been relaxed and licenses degraded in order to keep up with the numerous boats regularly being added to company fleets.

One might expect that this change of organization from individual owner-captain-pilot to joint-stock associations to government sponsorship to corporate subsidiary would substantially change the role of captains and pilots who command and steer the vessels.[7] It is unlikely, for example, that a country rube would assume the river itself must belong to the master-pilot of a diesel towboat. If Mark Twain's unfettered, independent "monarch of the river" ever did exist, have his traits been obliterated by the workings of corporate reliance on "team efforts," efficiency goals, and prescribed authority hierarchies? Have "controlled" rivers and sophisticated equipment made mere technicians of these august personages? Have revised licensing procedures and abundant Coast Guard regulations whitewashed the prestige and hogtied the independence of contemporary pilots?

When pilots assess their own profession, they articulate both the significant changes from the old traditions and the endurance of qualities, skills, and pride

[5] This may have been more true, however, of pilots employed by the Corps of Engineers or Federal Barge Line, both government-run operations. Some pilots working for private outfits may have faced harsher prospects.

[6] Especially important technological advances for the river were radar, depth-sounding, and radio communications.

[7] At least one owner-captain-pilot venture still survives. Captain Dennis Trone supervised the building of the *Julia Belle Swain* while he was still associated with a Dubuque boatyard. Subsequently, he bought the gingerbread-laden steamer used in the 1980 PBS production of *Life on the Mississippi*. He is owner-captain-pilot of the Peoria, Illinois–based excursion sternwheeler that still makes occasional tramping trips to such traditional events as the Kentucky Derby-week steamboat races on the Ohio River.

linked with the occupation of piloting since the early nineteenth century. Of course, when Mark Twain evaluated the profession, he eulogized the dignity, independence, skill, and power of the steamboat pilot whose "pride in his occupation surpassed the pride of kings." Mark Twain's contemporary, George Merrick, positively glorified the ennobling devotion and the "artist incarnate" in the pilot.

> The man who has once mastered the art of steering a steamboat on Western waters, never loses his love for it. . . . For forty years, since leaving the river for other pursuits often harassing and full of care, I have dreamed, time and again, of holding a wheel on one of the old-time boats on which I served as a boy. In my sleep I have felt again the satisfaction in work well done, the mortification of failure, and have felt again the cares and responsibilities that weighed so heavily when beset with difficulties and dangers. It is all as real as though I again stood at the wheel, doing real work, and achieving real victories over besetting difficulties and dangers. Mere work, as a means of earning a living, would not take such hold upon one's nature. It is the soul of the artist incarnate in the pilot. [*Old Times*, pp. 104–5]

In Captain Donald T. Wright's introduction to Ben Lucien Burman's *Big River to Cross*, written in "the bustling, hustling America of 1940," Wright claimed "the river was and is one of the fundamentals in making and keeping the United States the home of the individualist." Burman himself observed the 1930s riverman and, like Merrick before him, rhapsodized about the pilot as changeless artist, adapting to modern conveniences but preserving the core of tradition.

> There has been no change; no pilot has thought of changing. For the towboat pilot, like his brother the packet pilot, is an artist, a poet, not a mere driver of an automobile who can learn the trick in several weeks of practice. . . . Hour after hour he stands at the wheel, drinking his black coffee as in the olden days, joking, arguing, seemingly unconscious of his task, yet in reality always alert, and watching each line and shadow in the yellow stream that winds in ever changing pattern before him. [Pp. 145–46]

One need not travel far before encountering a pilot who would heartily scoff at being characterized as a poet or an artist. Yet, forty years after Burman's observations, and over seventy years after Merrick's, pilots still "put their spirits to the task" and wrestle the ambivalence of their love-hate relationship with the river and their craft. For the most part, they retain that quality of individualism that Burman admired while at the same time affirming their positions in a specialized group. The same advice given to a young Fred Way, steamboat clerk, in the 1920s would probably hold true today. In order to persuade the lockmaster to release water so that the *Crowder* could move on, Way told a lie. Upon learning what Way had done, the captain sternly cautioned him: "I've hoofed it up to that telephone for two days . . . and told them the truth every time. I told the truth because, as you'll come to learn, all we fellows who make a living down on the river here are sort of a fraternity, and we can lie to outsiders all we want to, but we don't lie when it comes to earnest business between ourselves" (*Pilotin'*, p. 183).

In pursuing that earnest business, pilots have, of course, been interested in the availability of berths, the wages drawn, and the respect rendered them as professionals. These concerns have sometimes prompted them to form associations with varying degrees of influential clout. The individualistic, independent pilots who people Mark Twain's memory once formed an organization "for the protection of their guild." Too many pilots had been made and the "growing swarm of new pilots presently began to undermine the wages in order to get berths."[8] Twain describes the formation of The Pilots' Benevolent Association which, after a somewhat shaky beginning when they were the "laughing stock of the whole river," became "perhaps the compactest, the completest, and the strongest commercial organization ever formed among men."[9] Initially enlisting only the incompetent, unemployed, and fledgling pilots eager to receive pension benefits of twenty-five dollars a month after surrendering only a twelve-dollar initiation fee, the association remained the butt of jokes as wages gradually increased again to the two hundred fifty dollar rate set by the association guidelines without directly benefitting a single member of that body. However, when business trebled and upper-river boats entered the New Orleans trade, pilots were suddenly in great demand and the supply was scarce. Former scoffers now turned to the association for pilots, but the association pilots then refused to partner with nonassociation men. They

[8] The wages for some time had been $250 a month, but had fallen to $100 with the surplus of pilots. See Mark Twain, *Life*, chapter 15.

[9] Louis Hunter takes exception with Mark Twain's account. "Mark Twain's further account of how this organization grew powerful, forced all pilots to become members, raised wages to an unprecedented level, and ruled the whole river with an iron hand is too like the lyric dream of a labor organizer to be altogether true. A more reliable if less colorful picture can be pieced together from other sources." See *Steamboats on the Western Rivers*, p. 471. For a comprehensive account of steamboat labor, see chapter 11.

created another advantage by passing along river information exclusively to other members.

> At every good-sized town from one end of the river to the other, there was a "wharf-boat" to land at, instead of a wharf or a pier. . . . Upon each of these wharf-boats the association's officers placed a strong box, fastened with a peculiar lock which was used in no other service but one — the United States mail service. It was the letter-bag lock, a sacred governmental thing. . . . Every association man carried a key which would open these boxes. That key, or rather a peculiar way of holding it in the hand when its owner was asked for river information by a stranger . . . was the association man's sign and diploma of membership; and if the stranger did not respond by producing a similar key, and holding it in a certain manner duly prescribed, his question was politely ignored. [*Life*, Chap. 15]

In those boxes pilots deposited association blanks that they had duly filled in with information of crossings, soundings, marks, and comments concerning the stretch they had just steered. By reading these fresh reports, pilots could become thoroughly posted. Nonassociation pilots, having to rely on much less recent information, began to have many more accidents that did the association pilots. Finally, even the hold-out captains were forced to discharge outsiders and employ association pilots because of the demands of insurance underwriters who had also noticed the greater safety secured by the report system. Eventually, all recalcitrants were brought into the fold, wages were boosted to five hundred dollars a month, and the association seemed invulnerable. But, as Mark Twain lamented, the new railroad and the Civil War combined to "annihilate" the steamboat industry for several years. After the war, steamers commonly towed a dozen cargoes "down to New Orleans at the tail of a vulgar little tugboat; and behold, in the twinkling of an eye, as it were, the association and the noble science of piloting were things of the dead and pathetic past!"

Mark Twain's admiration of the Pilots' Benevolent Association's tactics and resultant power is unequivocal. Subsequent attempts to organize have, until the mid-twentieth century, resulted primarily in associations that did not consider themselves to be bargaining agents but rather subscribed to the "strength in numbers" philosophy of a professional group addressing professional issues. Among the more visible of these groups was the Master, Mates, and Pilots Association, reorganized about 1939. But the labor union did come to the river as it had come to industry and mining. Many present-day pilots

were deckhands when the CIO attempted to organize on the boats. Both pro-
and antiunion men remember the various responses to these efforts. Captain
Lester "Whitey" Schickling remembers his first post-union check because he
was "rolled" by another deckhand on payday.

Well, actually, the union came on the river in 1939—that's when they
were getting $47.50 a month. In fact, they pulled a strike in order to get the
union in there. And the union came along, they organized a strike, and then
they signed up. Then in '41 they went from $96 to $115. . . . This was the
Master, Mates, and Pilots, and the NMU [National Maritime Union] came
in. Now the Teamsters, they didn't start union locals until, I believe it was
about 1962. I think maybe they might have fooled theirself into thinking
they could [provide more benefits than Master, Mates, and Pilots], but they
really couldn't. They just came in, and like I said before, they didn't try to
organize any new companies. All they did was raid the companies the
Master, Mates, and Pilots had, and for awhile, they had orders to lay off the
NMU. . . . That's the deck crew, and apparently they had a falling out and
they started raiding them then too. But I don't know one new company that
the Teamsters organized.

A prounion man since the 1930s, Captain Arthur McArthur catalogued
conditions on deck that had precipitated the advent of labor unions.

He [captain] always called me Mr. Mate, or Mr. Man, you know. I worked
with him for a long time; he was a good captain on the boat. 'Course when
the unions started organizin' and gettin' organized around here, he was one
of the first captains to kinda go ahead and change over right quick, you
know, to see the changes comin' and go to it. We didn't have all that kind of
union trouble with him. Puttin' clean linens on the beds, sheets instead of
usin' mattress covers and all that, and havin' blankets laundered instead of
when you turned your blanket in and it was never warshed and then it was
reissued to somebody else. That's the way they were, you know.

   That's what the conditions were. That's what brought the labor unions in
for some of the conditions years ago. . . . another thing they wanted to
change was, whenever they changed the captain on the boat, the captain
used to bring his own mate with him and then he brought his cook with
him. And the cook brought his second cook. So, when they walked aboard
the boat, and they changed the captain, well the cook usually wound up and
fired everybody in the cookhouse, and the mate he went around and fired

everybody on deck. Well, that was all uncalled for, and pretty good men was bein' eliminated. So, that was a lot of the cause, too.

Then they wanted fresh milk on the boat and different things like that they never did get. They wanted vacation time and sick-leave time and all kinda hours that they were workin'. Instead of six on and six off and then they called 'em out any time, they wanted—and if you were off of watch and we got into port and the mate didn't feel good and you asked permission to go to town, the mate used to say, "Well, you got all the time in the world to go but none to come back." It was according to how he felt, you know. And you could even be off watch. You didn't dare leave, 'cause you had so many people standin' on the wharf waitin' for jobs.

Another thing they had too; they had . . . what we called two pots. They had the officer's pot and the crew pot. The officers would set over there and they got iced tea and we would bring stores on in New Orleans. I was deckin' under the same conditions. We'd bring crates of oranges aboard the boat and the crew didn't see that. . . . So we'd bring hams aboard the boat; we didn't see ham on the table for breakfast, you know. They had ham, ham and eggs. . . . They cooked out of two pots.

Another thing, then they'd make coffee at say seven o'clock at night for the crew in those big urns and they didn't make any more coffee till four o'clock the next morning, or half past four when the cooks got up. That coffee run all night long. *But*, in the pilothouse, you could make coffee in the pilothouse up there for the pilots when they changed watches. He could have fresh coffee any time he'd want. All right, in the engine room, it was always fresh coffee for the engineers on watch and strikers, but the deck crew, they didn't get any of that. They were left out, see, they were just what you call the underdogs.

No advocate of unions, Captain William Tippitt points out what he considered to be the unreasonable excesses of labor organization.

Well, the conditions on the river today are 100 percent better. . . . They were different now from what we're talkin' about. We're talkin' about when the CIO took over, that is, when the deckhands and the politicians took over the operation of the Barge Line. When the captain couldn't even go in and paint the—I wish I could call it what we called it—paint the toilets. No, the deckhands would vote the cooks off, vote the mates off, vote the captain off.

As in other unionizing efforts, there was some violence involved—both by organizers and by captains reluctant to give in to perceived coercion.

It was up around Caseyville. And we had a few instances there at Paducah where they tried to organize, and they boycotted a fella down there named Hugh Edwards, and he was an engineer, a good one. They never would work him, only just when they had to. They come to the point where they couldn't get an engineer, they'd give him a job. He was tryin' to organize a union. And they had—up there around Caseyville—they had a lot of shootin' up there, where they'd load the coal you know and bring it down to Paducah. But around Paducah we didn't have no trouble there. Just up there around Caseyville and the mines. . . . Some of the boats up there, they'd shoot at 'em. Yeah. Come in there to get that coal, they'd just shoot at 'em. [Captain Ben Gilbert]

Captain Loren "Shorty" Williams angrily recalls physical intimidation by union organizers.

It was coercing these guys to go into the union is what it was. . . . [They would beat up pilots] or anybody else they'd catch out. If there was enough of their damned cowards to corner one of 'em, they'd beat 'em up. . . . [To son] You know Cody Grant? Well, could of killed him. They drug him right out of bed—on the boat! And damned near killed him. He was in the hospital for months! . . . He wouldn't go in [join union], and I don't think he ever did neither.

You know, I'll fight for a man's right to join the union, if he wants to, but I'll also fight for his right *not* to join the union, if he wants to. . . . I can join the Knights of Columbus, or I can join the Masons, which I have, or I can be a Moose or an Eagle, or whatever, if I want to. But by God when somebody says I *have* to, then I back up. That is not the American way. . . . I joined because I had to. I felt forced to. I felt like I had to buy a job from somebody that had no work for me to do. In other words, I had to join the union, but I wasn't workin' for them—the other company was payin' me. But it was very much against my principles.

Some captains retaliated with real or threatened violence of their own.

It was tough on the river. The deckhands, the union, the CIO, they were trying to organize the deckhands and the working on deck. And the Master, Mates, and Pilots were trying to organize the pilothouse. And they had some real tough times there. And one particular instance, there, we was in Cairo, Illinois, to Point Pleasant, West Virginia. We was towing chemicals. And we got to Cairo there. We knew there was somethin' brewin' there because on the radio, you know, you listened to the Cairo stations. . . . So, anyway, this one particular towboat had pushed their oil barge into Cairo. And the night before these people that were organizing had come aboard and beat up the crew. And so the captain said the next day they were comin' back and sign 'em up.

So the next day, they come back. But the first guy that stepped on the barge, the captain was there with a shotgun and shot him. Knocked him off the barge. So the rest of them didn't come on. . . . And so, then, of course, that stopped that right there. So then this towboat got under way then. [Captain Joe Toomey]

Captain Roy Boyd recalled Captain Russel Warner's response to intimidation tactics.

I don't know what it was, the union or what, they had dropped big rocks off of the bridge where they had to go through. Next trip up, he [Warner] had a machine gun settin' on the front, the upper deck—where it was handy. . . . As he approached that bridge, they never had to use this machine gun. They sent a man out there with it. Didn't drop any rocks. [Laughs.] And he'd a used it too!

Once the union had been established, new contracts sometimes violated traditional protocol on the boats. A pilot, of course, cannot leave the wheelhouse unattended during his watch. One captain-pilot took a memorable approach to one of these new situations, avoided unpleasant confrontation, and made a lasting impression.

An old captain with Federal Barge Lines—oh, many years ago when they was operating old black boats, you know—the union, see, CIO had just taken over all the boats. So, come on back to midnight there . . . and he [captain] asked him, "Could you bring me a cup of coffee?" Deckhand told him, he said, "Captain, under the new contract we don't carry coffee in the pilothouse anymore." He said, "Oh, how come?" He said, "Well, that's just the way; we ain't gonna do that kind of work. We're deckhands; we're not gonna be waiters." he said, "OK."

About ten minutes later, he blew the whistle. Told 'em he said, "Tell the mate to come up here." Mate came up. He said, "That tree right up there;

let's tie her off up there. Engineer wants to do a little workin' on her." He [mate] drug that cable up the hill about five hundred feet [laughs], got her all tied up. "All right, captain, she's tied." So, he went down and got him a cup of coffee, and pretty soon he come back up, blowed the whistle, and said, "OK, let her go!" [Laughs.] He went up the river, and about two hours later, he blew the whistle for the mate. "Hey, Mr. Mate," he said, "there a tree up there?" He said, "Yeah." "Well, let's tie up." He said, "Captain, you gonna get a cup of coffee?" He said, "Yes, sir." "Don't worry about it; we'll bring it!" [Laughs.] [Captain Fontain Johnson]

Today several unions, including National Marine Union, Seafarer's International, and Marine Officers' Association (Teamsters), represent deck and officer crews. Master, Mates, and Pilots was eventually absorbed by the Teamsters, but at least two relatively new associations have been started to serve the particular interests of river pilots — The American River Pilots Association and the Professional River Pilots Association. The latter describes itself as embracing both union and nonunion members "as we firmly believe that pilots are a breed among themselves and by choice we can help one another." It is strictly a professional association aiming to reclaim the "measureless pride" as professionals that members feel has slipped in recent years. To that end the association hopes to set standards in wages, regulations, and safety guidelines. With regard to wages, the professed short-term goal of the association is to reach $45,000 a year day-for-day (one day off for each day worked). According to several 1980 newsletters, masters' wages averaged $2,600 per month day-for-day, pilot's averaged $2,400 per month, day-for-day. For trip work they hope to establish rates of $200 to $250 per day, depending on the type of unit and the number of barges. It may be that, just as Mark Twain described with the Pilot's Benevolent Association, the insurance underwriters are influencing the quality of piloting and hence helping qualified pilots to earn the top dollar rates.

My son told me before he left — $250 a day! . . . That's with the big tows. If a tow is leavin' Cairo goin' to New Orleans — got probably thirty to forty barges — the insurance company comes on there, and insurance insures all that cargo. They inquire who's pilots on that boat. And if they find out these — jack-leg pilots, just out of that training school in Helena there — they say, "This boat does not leave this port until they get a qualified pilot." The company would like to hire one for $100 a day, see. Instead of payin' $250 a day. But the insurance companies are standing behind them. They said with thirty or forty barges loaded with all this grain, there's a lot of money connected with it, and we can't afford any accidents. [Captain Charles White, Sr.]

The quality of piloting is of considerable concern not only to insurance companies but to pilots as well — particularly veteran pilots who note a perceptible downgrading of the profession. Two subjects likely to initiate a prolonged discussion or harange from pilots are licensing procedures and Coast Guard performance. Traditionally, pilots on steamboats were required to hold first-class pilot's licenses, which they secured by drawing the stretch of river from memory. [10] Or, in some cases, an applicant gave a detailed, verbal account of how to run a stretch to an inspector who was qualified to judge him.

You see, back in the olden days, if you couldn't draw . . . I've had a lot of pilots tell me that they didn't draw a license. They just sat down with the inspector and told him the river and just told him how to run it and what was where and how to do it. And a lot of those old-timers got their licenses in those days without drawing a map. But they could sit down — you had inspectors who knew what they were doing. And then you had inspectors who knew the river. They were steamboat men. United States Steamboat Inspection Service had a local inspector — you had an engineer who was the boiler inspector, and you had a pilot who was the hull inspector. But they knew their particular territory. A man up in Nashville was a Cumberland River pilot. Here in Louisville we had Ed Maylor who had been pilot on the *City of Cincinnati*. Cincinnati you had Benny Patterson who had been a Greene Line captain. And you had people in a territory that knew that river. You weren't putting anything over on them. They knew whether you were right or wrong.

But in those days I was going to tell you — we were talking about what they were saying, and how they feel today versus the old — this is an entirely different ballgame. Piloting is a cinch today. On a boat like the *Delta Queen* or the *Belle* or anything else — a loose boat. The real problem today is these tremendous tows and negotiating these locks and being able to negotiate the locks in all stages of water, handling all of that tonnage and knowing what your boat can do. There's . . . very few places, very little territory where following the channel closely is very important. . . . I remember Captain Mauer who was telling me one time, you see these packet boat pilots, they

---

[10] See Captain Way's explanation of the procedure, Chapter 1.

had to know everything within a matter of inches. We had two big boats here [Louisville] . . . the *City of Louisville* and the *City of Cincinnati*. But they drew five feet of water. And when you got down below five feet of water they couldn't run—they had to get a boat with a lighter draft. And the old man, Captain Ed, had been running all these local packets and two or three inches—well, can you make this landing or can't you make this landing? And the real skill of piloting in those days was knowing where you could run the willows and particularly on the Mississippi River even more so than up here where—what chute you could go on through and where you could get on the other side of the river, you know. That was a question of intimate knowledge, of when you were working in a local business. Where you could get in and where you couldn't get in. [Captain C. W. Stoll]

It is that "question of intimate knowledge" that some pilots fear is missing from too many operators today. While anyone wishing to pilot a steamboat must still draw for a first-class license, diesel towboat pilots are exempt from this requirement and instead need to qualify for a towboat operator's license, which does not entail the command of specific knowledge over discrete stretches of river.[11] In fact, one obtains an operator's license for "the Western rivers" rather than for the Cairo to Louisville, St. Paul to St. Louis, Memphis to New Orleans, and so forth, prescriptions of the first-class license. For several years after diesel boats arrived on the river, diesel pilots were not required to have any license at all. While most veterans will concede that "a license does not a pilot make," they nevertheless feel pride in their first-class licenses and, occasionally, scorn the operator's license as a "poor relation." Some towboat operators also sit for first-class license because of salary incentives and professional pride.[12] For many, there is only one "real" license. Old-timer Captain Russell Warner makes the clear distinction.

I started workin' for wages about 19 and 08; I was a coal passer. So I worked there until 19 and 13, and then I got my first issue of license. Had it ever since. . . . I been everywheres there's water, you might say it that way, but my license—when the diesel age come in you didn't have to have a license, so we didn't bother about gettin' 'em extended back in those days. But my real license went from Chester, Illinois, to Vicksburg, White River, and the Arkansas River, and all those little rivers where we logged.

[11] Even in "drawing the river" the procedures have changed. Applicants are now given an outline of the river and only have to draw a percentage of the stretch over which they wish license.

[12] Here, again, differential insurance rates motivate companies to offer salary incentives.

Other pilots commented on the effect of new licensing procedures and guidelines.

The rule is you have to have a license. But these boats [diesel] didn't because of the way the law was written. It just kept 'em out. And that's always what I heard. And my brother-in-law was in that business of giving the license out and that's what he told me.

So all these diesel boats, they started using men that weren't licensed. So here's some guy, he could run, say from St. Louis to Cairo. Never been above Cairo in his life. "Go on up to St. Louis." Said, "I don't know the river." Said, "Take a map." They used to call it road-mapping. They run by a map. Now, see, they got the radios. . . . That only came in on the river during the war.

See, they would be good pilots, usually, in river where they could run. But then as this all proliferated, all of a sudden it just exploded, and they couldn't train enough men fast enough. And it just kept developing. The unions and some of the companies were being hurt by these cheap operators. 'Cause they'd pay less money. . . . They kept cutting on the Coast Guard and congressmen and senators about changing the law . . . making all these men get licensed. But then the diesel-engine people, they happened to have a man named Eastman on their side and Stennis from Mississippi. So he introduced a compromise.

Now all they had to do was get an operator's license for a small stretch of river—that entitles them to run on anything you want to, see? And that's what these guys are screaming about now. Because some of those men do run up there, and they never saw the river before. [Captain Francis "Dusty" Walters]

Well, actually, when that new law went into effect, I think back in '72, they gave them until September 1 of '73.[13] They could go up and do the same thing as I had to do—take a pollution test and there were twenty-five pilot-wheel questions. See I had a first-class license—1,180.4 miles—and so I went up to St. Louis and I got western rivers and inland the same day. Then I went back and got Great Lakes. [Captain Lester "Whitey" Schickling]

---

[13] This was referred to as "grandfather rights." Diesel pilots who had been running the river for some time were essentially given their operator's license after minimal or no examination.

Captains Fred Way, Jr., and Charles Fehlig remembered a time when short licenses were the rule.

He, Doggy Cross, was an excellent pilot, and I don't know of any instance that he was even in trouble, and he piloted up until, well, he was in his seventies when he quit. He died. He was on all of those little wooden boats where you could get in trouble in a hurry, but he never did. But he only went from Pittsburgh to Charleston, West Virginia, and then he finally got extension to Cincinnati in order to get on the *Senator Cordill* and the *Queen City*. That was like going to Europe for him, and he never felt comfortable about that there. He'd get down below the mouth of the Kanawha River, he was just jittery all the way to Cincinnati and back. He didn't feel like he'as at home. Like he was in a strange country. After a lifetime of doing the short trips. Many pilots in those days made a whole lifetime living with a license 180 miles long or 200. {Captain Way}

At that time I learned it, there was no maps and no chart books. Hell, now, a nigger named Moe could take a damn chart book and learn the river. . . . We had to learn it by bits and pieces.

At that time, I'll tell you, if the boat went from St. Louis to New Orleans, you changed pilots about four times. Short licenses. And then the river was changing so constantly. You couldn't keep up with the long stretches of the license then. And to be a posted pilot, why if you had 300 miles to operate in a river, that was a long stretch. {Captain Charles Fehlig}

Even some of the younger pilots required to earn only a towboat operator's license go ahead and draw for the first-class pilot's license. Captain Larry Ritchie has done so, both because it's a family tradition and because of professional pride.

They should change the law, you know, to where you would have to have certain amount of trips over one stretch of river before you could be able to operate on it. This license now, if a man hadn't ever seen the Ohio River, he could get on the boat and say, "I've got my operator's license. Let's go." And if you've got a map there, you might make it all right, and then you might not. It's undermining the first-class pilot's license is all it's doing. You can only run in your stretch of river, you know, with what you've got. And these operator's licenses, you can go anywhere.

"Old heads" speak with pride of their first-class, steamboat licenses and of their professional standing.

Well, on those steamboats, before you could stand a watch, you had to take your license and hang it on the wall to show that you were a licensed pilot and you're capable of standing a watch. . . . I had to have three letters. . . . Yeah. I had to have three letters from captains I'd worked under and one engineer I'd worked under. Letters of recommendation. Now a cook on a boat can write to his company and ask for the length of time he's worked on that boat or for that company. He can go to the Coast Guard and apply for a operator's license.

I always judged it—so did my father and grandfather—I guess they judged it more as a profession, like a doctor or a lawyer, because they couldn't work unless they had that license hangin' up there. And you had to work hard to get that license. . . . Now, it's—I believe right now to tell the truth, if you got six deckhands on the boat, pilot and six that's got pilot's license, and they're workin' as deckhands waitin' for that pilot up there to get fired, so they can jump up there and take his job. [Captain Charles White, Sr.]

For the last fifteen years of my boating, it has all been on steamboats—on the *St. Genevieve* and on here [*Delta Queen*]. I'm pretty happy about that because to me it's pretty proud to tell people you're a steamboat pilot or steamboat captain. . . . It's just something about it. The steamboats go back to many years ago, where these diesel boats, or turpentine burners, or whatever you want to call them, they come out recently, and then you have to have a certain amount of license to operate on a steamboat. In other words, during the war . . . the government considered pilots during the war as professional people, you know. And it's a profession. Just like doctors, and those kind of people. [Captain Arthur Zimmer]

On a trip between St. Paul and St. Louis in August 1979, Captain Gordon Nelson, master-pilot of the *Ann King* and twenty-year river veteran, decried the "state of the art" on the rivers today.

He said to me, "Well, piloting has changed," he said. "In other words," he says, "you don't have to know a Goddamn thing to be a pilot." You can take a guy off the bank and put him out there, and every time he comes to some sort of an obstruction, just hire a damn tug. The reason they want to do that . . . they don't want skilled people because they'd have to pay 'em the skilled. . . . They hire 'em over the damn telephone, sight unseen. . . . When I went to work for Mid-America, I went to St. Louis and . . . was interviewed, and they checked with my employer and people that knew me, what kind of work I'd done.

I didn't get a pilot's license till I was thirty years old. A license wasn't required. All they're interested in is if you can do the work or not. . . . They would rather you have a license, but if you didn't have it, they wouldn't send you home.

QUESTION: Why did you decide to get a license, then, if you didn't need one?

NELSON: Professional pride. I can't think of any other reason. . . . Up until, we'll say the last probably ten years, I would say 90 percent of the pilots really took pride in their work. They tried to give a man 110 percent for a day's pay and try to take care of his equipment and get as many miles per gallon as they could to do the man the very best job. I think that's getting to be a thing of the past. There's gotten to be an element on the river that, they're there to make their days, and they don't care if they make it holdin' up, waiting on a lock, or whatever. Down on that lower Mississippi, they'll sit right out in the middle and let her drag instead of trying to get out and hunt some slack water, make a little time. They'll sit out in the middle of the river and try to get up the river and read a magazine at the same time.

QUESTION: Do you think it would improve if operators of diesel tows had to get licenses?

NELSON: Well, you know, a license don't make a pilot. A license is just a piece of paper. I don't think that the license is gonna make a pilot. . . . The barge industry and towing industry has gotten on the wrong course here. . . . I'm not saying that the river's full of misfits, but it's getting to be that there are more than enough. I, personally, think that the people that are calling the shots, the industry executives, have just pretty much given up on the young people. . . . They feel that they're all the same. They all have the same outlook on things, which is entirely possible. I don't know what the answer is. I know what the matter is. I don't know what the answer is. I do know this, that there are still excellent pilots, very good pilots. And there are some of these younger pilots are good pilots. The potential is there for them to make very good pilots, but they're going to have to have the proper guidance and influences on 'em to shape 'em. Where you've got a boat with the captain on a boat, he's smoking and doing dope or whatever, and the crew is, too, and you have stabbings on the boats, and you know that indicates to me that there is something bad.

Captain Nelson sees a breakdown in both competence and pride.

That's [shortage of pilots] the reason things have gone to hell in a bread basket. Pilots out here that—we run into one on the *Mary L* here two or three trips ago. Got down to Lock 22. We'd been followin' him down the river. They'd been holding us up at every lock. Got down to Lock 22 and that tug wasn't available. The man didn't know how to go. He didn't know how to get in the lock. He'd been a pilot for two years. And he never had made the lock without a tug on the side pushing him in on the wall. He didn't know what the hell to do. He had no idea how to go about gettin' in that lock. And Ted Dean [Nelson's partner on *Ann King*] sat up there . . . a couple miles above the lock, and Ted told him just what to do and how to get in there. That's not an isolated case. A tug's sittin' up there at Lock 20. There will be one down here at 21. There'd be one down here at 22, laying right here. They burn fifty gallons of fuel a day. Run out there and get on the side of the guy and push him in on the wall. Charge $150, or $200, whatever they charge. The river's just full of people, guys that they can't get in the lock without a tug because they don't know how to go about doin' it.

And, . . . well you're running into second generation. These guys have been trained by guys that don't know theirself how to get in a lock. So you're looking at the second generation. I'm not saying that they're twenty years apart in age or anything. But they're a generation of pilots that the captain don't know how to get in a lock and the pilot don't know how to get in a lock either. They run down in these bridges and they try to shoehorn 'em in there. They just run down in there and then back up and let her crash.

Back in the late fifties and the 1960s, they were kicking these boats in the river down there at Greenville once a week. They'd throw one of these little boats in there. And they'd run around with one or two barges. You don't have to have too much on the ball to make it with one or two barges. You know they get in trouble, too. They take a guy that . . . you know, a license wasn't required. And they'd put 'em on these boats and call 'em pilots. Well, those people, they worked on those little boats for a year or two years. And then they graduated to bigger and better things, more tonnage. It used to be they'd run a lot of 1400, 1600, 1800 horsepower boats up this river. But now this boat's 3200. And it's out of its class anymore because 5000 horsepower boat is considered a, you know, a mid-size car.

Another source of debate among career pilots is the performance of the Coast Guard. The Corps of Engineers had traditionally been responsible for main-

taining the channels and marking the river. Now the Coast Guard is in charge
of marking the river and licensing the pilots. Most pilots take a dim view of the
Coast Guard's record to date.[14]

> The Corps of Engineers took care of all the sounding and changing the buoys
> and making the channel. Then afterwards the Coast Guard horned in there,
> and they started coming in with people that didn't know anything, you
> know.
>
> That's the Hooligan Navy, the Coast Guard. They didn't know enough
> in the first place. And the Corps of Engineers they took it to the Department
> of Commerce. Said that the Corps of Engineers should take care of it. So then
> after they took it away from the Corps, they had the Lighthouse Depart-
> ment. And they did good work because they had regular old-time captains
> and pilots on there, you know. And they had good personnel. But then after
> the Coast Guard took it over, you know what I mean, it meant you had to
> put a lieutenant at the helm, and a lieutenant at so-and-so, and they didn't
> know nothing. And of course now they're gettin' so where they maintain
> these big buoys and everything. [Captain Allen Fiedler]

> They try to do a job but their reputation — see, they only allow them to
> work in one spot so long. By the time they learn what they're doin', then
> they send them someplace else. . . . They try to do their best but . . . they
> ain't got the knowledge. . . . That's [deep sea] what they're trained for,
> and to come out here and try to set up buoy lines up through a channel —
> with a man who's been out there for six months and don't know a hill of

[14] Of course, this is a book about pilots and we hear only their side of the issues. I talked with
an official of the Second Coast Guard District in St. Louis to ascertain the Coast Guard's
perspective on the major pilot complaints. With regard to the complaint that people are on the
river too short a time to learn their job before being transferred elsewhere, he says the Coast Guard
has recognized this as a problem, is keeping people on station longer, and is rotating them back
into their area of most experience. On the issue of mounting paperwork to report normal
occurrences of western rivers piloting, the Coast Guard is conducting a review. (Reports must be
made of all marine casualties [deep-sea or inland waters] that involve $25,000 in damages, loss of
life, or incapacitating personal injury, and groundings.) They are reviewing the need for reporting
groundings on western rivers.

While acknowledging that buoys are not always accurately "on station," the official said they
are often hit or moved by towboat operators or shifted by changing channels (the latter is now a
problem primarily on the Missouri River). Buoy tenders have to maintain a regular schedule
because of budgetary constraints, though there are now a number of vessels with two alternating
crews that are continuously underway to provide aids to navigation.

beans about how a big tow operates, sometimes it gets pretty nerve-wracking trying to follow their buoy lines. Looks like they dropped them out a plane or something.

Like down at the Greenville Bridge, we asked them to put up a light down below the bridge, you know, so at nighttime there's nothing down below that you can steady up on and you're going through the bridge. It's a long ways down before you come to that American Bar Island, and we asked them to put a light down below the bridge where you kind of steady up on it. Well, they did—they put it over on the Mississippi side and you can't even see the darn thing from the bridge. Just little things like that that kind of irritate you about the Coast Guard. But they are getting better. They're finally learning what they're suppose to do out there—besides save lives and jerk licenses. [Captain Larry Ritchie]

Some pilots are vociferously antagonistic toward the Coast Guard because they feel the Coast Guard is incompetent at marking the river, intrusive in compounding paper-yielding regulations, and insensitive to suggestions and complaints of working pilots. In a rambling pilothouse monologue one night, Captain Charles Fehlig left no doubt regarding his position on the matter.

Here's the Coast Guard. They're having a big navigational meeting in Memphis, supposedly better relationships between the industry down here on the river and the Coast Guard. They were fully cognizant of the fact that relations are very bad. And they called in their tender skippers. And there's a four-striper from Washington there with various and sundry lesser officers all the way down. So they're trying to decide how to better this relationship and get better aids to navigation and so forth out here. They made the mistake, the Pilot's Association, made the mistake of electing me as spokesman.

And I said, "Well, number one, when the Coast Guard moved out here from the coast, it was certainly against all of our wishes and desires. The Corps of Engineers was doing a great job out here. And the Coast Guard had taken over the inspection offices. And I scarcely say that there is one licensed person that likes to go to the Coast Guard office for a renewal, or a license, or what have you, or to merely ask a question, because he couldn't get an answer—number one. And number two, there is some ensign up there or JG lieutenant that thinks he's a rear admiral, that he's gonna lord it over you. And number three, there isn't a damn one in the office who knows what the hell they're doin'. . . . Well, this four-striper said, "Well, Captain," he says, "we realize that we have a lot to learn out here." I said, "That's right, but you had about twenty-five years to do it in. By God, it's time that you learned."

I says, "We have realized that there would be a transition period, and we accepted that, but by damn, the transition period has been goin' fifteen years now." And I says, "Consequently, we turn around and you hold these meetings to try and have a better relationship, get better aids to navigation. And what do we do? We request certain things. We know what we want out here. But the Coast Guard pays absolutely no attention." I said, "Such as the green reflectors on these damn buoys, every pilot on the river despises 'em. And we all wrote letters in, and you always come up with some damn farfetched answer. The Coast Guard is gonna do what they want to, no matter what. So why hold these meetings?" And I says, "Number two," I says, "you flooded the damn communication system with your Coast Guard broadcasts. Some of 'em are great. But, for instance, that ferry they're putting in up here on the upper," I says. "They announce it fourteen times a damn day, forty-five days. And consequently nobody listens to your damn programs anymore . . . your announcements." And I says, "The total inefficiency now if we run aground, we have got to report to the Coast Guard . . . when we are grounded at such and such a location. Every fifteen minutes they're callin' us on the radio . . . wantin' to know how we're progressing. And it isn't enough that we say we will report to you when there is any change in our condition. That doesn't help a damn bit. So consequently you can't do a damn thing for asking the Coast Guard on the radio."

"Now," I said, "here is my jewel. Sometime back I was aground up there. Well, I wasn't aground. I couldn't get over a crossing . . . at mile such and such below Lock 25. And I reported to the Coast Guard. Well, number one, they've got to have the tonnage of your vessel. They've got to have the registration number, how many people is aboard, when this boat was built, what is your propulsion. Jesus Christ, we haven't got time for all that crap. How many people are aboard? What did you have for breakfast?" Then I says, "I explained to the man on the radio that we have less than nine feet of water in the Project Channel. We have eight and one-half feet of water. We sounded it out personally." "Well, just a minute," he said, "I want to . . . let you talk to the officer of the day." Well, he comes on. Then he wants a repeat of everything. Then he says, "Did I understand you to say that there is less than nine feet of water in the channel?" I said, "That's right." He said, "Is that horizontal or vertical?"

And you should have heard all . . . there must have been one hundred fifty river people at that meeting. This commander got pretty hot at me. He says, "Captain," he said, "I think you're stretching it." I said, "Not a damn bit. That's the actual words the officer of the day asked me. . . . 'Is that horizontal or vertical?'" And I said, "You wonder why we don't want to communicate with your people?" Bunch of damned nincompoops. Admiral Siler was there. . . . Then he brought up the question. "Well," he said, "what are the feelings of the people out here towards the Coast Guard about bettering relationships?" Well, that Jerry . . . what was his name? He said, "Admiral, the feeling of everybody out here is for the damn Coast Guard to go on the coast where they belong." And that's about the feeling of everybody out here.

Though most pilots seem to share at least a moderate disdain for the Coast Guard's performance in replacing the Corps and its career river people, not all veterans share Captain Nelson's generally negative evaluation of the younger towboat operators. Of course, it is difficult to compare differential skills through time, and some old-timers in any field will always claim that the men were better in "our time." Many things have changed—the boats, the sophisticated equipment, the "controlled" rivers. Maybe the quality of pilots has also changed; such an assessment must necessarily be based on subjective opinion. But then it is natural to make comparisons between then and now.

Oh, yeah, the pilots that they've got on some of these towboats now, they have . . . the amount of barges, they've got more power, and they got a lot better boats, too. But the pilots comin' up today, they're good in their own field like they are. When they work out here thirty days, they're ready to go home because some of 'em on these big tows are comin' down the river meetin' all this traffic every little bit. There's a certain amount of tension all the time, watchin', you know. An almost constant form of watchin' and they come down with these big tows, and they have bridges and everything else, and a lot of times, the old-time pilots years ago didn't have all the bridges that they have today. And that's a danger to 'em. . . . It's like Captain Pete Briscoe told me, "Some of 'em if they're lucky to live to be forty-five years old with all that steel out there in front of 'em, fifty years old, they're gonna be lucky." 'Cause they're under a greater strain than some of the old-timers were, because the old-timers would turn around, and if things didn't look right to 'em at night, they'd turn around and back the boat in. They tied up; they didn't pass a landin'. They just didn't pass a landin'; if it was four o'clock in the afternoon and there was a good landin' and they thought they had a bad piece of river down below, they stopped and tied up there.

So, mostly boats now, these companies pushin' these men and they keep her on the go and are tryin' to get that last mile. When they complete thirty days out there, they go home and they're wore out, you know. And then it takes 'em awhile, and then all they can look forward to is they're comin' back to work that other thirty days again, see. They probably get off thirty more days. So, they do work under a strain with all that kind of punishment. You take 'em handlin' down the river maybe 50-, 51,000 tons of cargo, and that's a lot of responsibility. They got their crews on the boat, their lives are in their hands, and 'course everybody else. And all these high explosives. Years ago you didn't have these high explosives movin' up and down this river that you've got today. So, you have to take all that and consider the pilots today as good as they were in the old days. I'd say, yeah, they're just as good.

QUESTION: Do they know the river as well?

MCARTHUR: I think they do; I think they know it as good or better. Probably better 'cause they're gettin' over it more often than the pilots back in those days did. And the river's bein' sounded out more today than what it was in the earlier days. The Engineers' constantly sounded on this river; the Coast Guard has sounding boats and gettin' marine information and all that, so I think the pilots have better postin' than the old-time pilots was.

Old-time pilots had to swap their own information a lot of times when they got together with one another and what the height of this bar was and the height of that bar, and they tried to pass on the right kind of information. Today, these pilots talk on ship-to-ship radio and they'll ask such and such, "Did you sound up over some place? How much water did you get?" And the man furnishes the information back to him. Says, "Well, I ran maybe some point and I got so much water through there." Years ago, pilots didn't have that kind of communication. Pilots today are better posted than the old-time pilots were. [Captain Arthur McArthur]

Still, Captain McArthur thinks the profession has slipped relative to other occupations.

I've seen it go down too; it's not what it used to be. Prestige and everything else, you know. Far as money-wise is concerned on these steamboats, and on the riverboats, too, they used to get in comparison to what everybody else got outside in industry. Now, you take truck drivers and teamsters union and plumbers and electricians and all those, and they don't have no where near the responsibility of these fellas that tow 50,000 tons of cargo and stuff down the river. Those fellas are not even makin' the money that these electricians are makin', or a plumber makes. So actually, the glory of it is not here any more. You know, back when the pilots was gettin' $315 a month, back in the '30s, that was a lot of money. It certainly was; it was a world of money. And most wages, if anybody else even in the towns and cities was gettin' $80 or $90 a month, they were doin' good. They thought they were up in high cotton, but pilots was gettin' $315.

Others throw their lot with the superior abilities of the old-timers:

What I mean, you have such nicer boats, nicer equipment to work with, and the river has improved, which has been done by the Corps of Engineers. 'Course, now you have low water and you have the ice, we had an ice condition last year which lot of 'em was never accustomed to. They're just a different class of people than what—what I mean, not different class, just like times are changin' and they have radar and radios and sounding devices and all that. We didn't have that.

QUESTION: Do you think the older guys had to know the river a lot better?
SKIDMORE: They had to, yeah, because the river conditions was not like they are today. And they had to know the river a whole lot better than they do now. They didn't have the buoys. [Captain John Skidmore]

Of course, years ago you had to be a pilot. You don't have to be a pilot today no more. I mean, hell, I mean all you got is a wide river, you know what I mean. And you got it well marked. And of course you've got a hazard there at the locks and dams, maybe up high water, but outside of that, you don't have to be a pilot. You had to years ago. . . . One of the main differences is, of course, the narrow channel we had for one thing. And another main difference is that we didn't have the water. Of course, they didn't load the barges down like they do years ago, you know. And whatcha call it, now you've got to run with a searchlight, where years ago you didn't have to have a searchlight if you knew the river, you know what I mean. [Captain Allen Fiedler]

One second-generation pilot, Captain Donn Williams, and one fourth-generation pilot, Captain E. A. "Li'l Wamp" Poe, discussed their perceptions of both the changes and the traditional remnants of their profession.

I believe that lots of the stories, and lots of the conditions that existed years ago don't any more. Lots of stories were related to incidences that occurred on the bank, as they were tying up, as they were uptown, waiting for barges, or whatever, fuel and so on. But that part of the traditional river currents that was true of Mark Twain's days, and up until much more recently than that, aren't true any more. Because the traditional part of our business is going away . . . because of the change of the river attitude per se. Used to be very traditional, we did things this way, we've done it for a hundred years, and it's gonna be that way for another hundred. That picture's all changing 'cause there are fewer boatmen, traditional boatmen involved in the towing business now than used to be, on a percentage basis, and more business men. So, everything is run in a more businesslike way, than in a traditional way.

So, if there's anything that can speed up any operation, make it more efficient, and thus more profitable, that is certainly done. So, some of the traditional things—little episodes on the bank, lay-by time, fog, etc.,—some of it is the elimination of traditional attitudes, ideas, some of 'em are the result of this business attitude bein' added—takes away lots of the opportunity.

The operation of the vessels is done in a more businesslike way than it used to be. The pilots are, I think, still traditionally oriented and still enjoy all the same things that the old pilots did, but the opportunities to exploit the possibilities isn't there, like it used to be.

It surely is a different ballgame now. In a thirty-day hitch—more times than not, the vessel never stops, except for locks, to change tows, whatever. Even in the fog—unless it's real bad, they don't tie up any more. Conditions, even as few as twenty-five years ago, they would have dictated tyin' up—stoppin' the tow—don't do the same thing any more. They just keep on truckin'.

It depends on what part of the river you're in, and so on. But, used to be—in fact, I know one fella who—I accused him of sending the mate out to the head of the tow to blow on the flags so it'd be windy enough to tie up.

That happened frequently—it seems, around Muscatine or Davenport—good places to tie up, and it wasn't very far to walk up to town. There's a lot more wind in areas like that—according to the logs, certainly.

I know that that has happened and, certainly, some boats have more engine trouble close to town than farther away, but most of those are not the real money-making companies like Valley. . . . These are smaller outfits, and they have pilots that aren't as concerned with the maintenance of a good record—rather they're sometimes concerned with maintenance of a good record on the bank! And, they do whatever allows them to maintain that record. So that part of the business is changing and, it seems to me, quite rapidly.

The traditional things everybody still—they call on the radio and use the old whistle signals from the steamboat days,—you're still required to blow the whistle, but sometimes it doesn't get done because your communication is so much better than it was in the old days, it doesn't matter whether it's done, or not. And, sometimes it isn't. The Coast Guard, in the last few years, has finally recognized that the radio communication is an acceptable method of choosing passing signals. But, they still use the same terms. I'll see you on one whistle—see you on two—you've heard that—forever.

That's one of the pilot's traditional things that will continue, I'm sure, forever. It's still port and starboard and forward and stern, and all that sort of thing. That'll never change, I'm sure. But, the things that are changing is the attitude of the office.

Used to be that there were boat people in the office and boat people on the boat. Now—there's boat people on the boats and business people in the office. [Captain Donn Williams]

Captain E. A. "Li'l Wamp" Poe and his father, Captain E. L. "Wamp" Poe talked about many of the changes they had witnessed in their careers. Captain E. A. now works in the office of Nilo Barge Line and knows firsthand the clash between corporate assumptions and the characteristic independence of pilots. Captain E. L., who says, with a twinkle, that he "wouldn't speak to the common person" when he first earned his license, began his career when 60 percent of the boats on the river were still packets and most all of them were made of wood.

LI'L WAMP: It's amazing how it's changed, I'd say, in the last five years. . . . Well, maybe ten years. . . . We don't have today, to me, you don't have river people as much as you have people workin' on the river. Now I know that sounds a little bit. . . . But you know, like myself. Now Nilo, we have some older pilots. You know, I'm sayin' like from fifty on. And these fellas are interested in the river. And the boats. Not necessarily Nilo

Barge Line, but the river. What's good for the river is good for them. Some of these younger people, it's just a job you know. They could care less. . . . And you don't have the number of young people that want to become pilots. . . . They're content to remain on deck. They're content to live for today. And then, you know, you have naturally x-amount saying, "I want to be a pilot." When you set 'em down and say, "Ok, but you're gonna have to learn this, this, this, this, this, this, this." "I didn't know all that. I'm not gonna. . . . " And they're not interested in the history of the river, you know.

QUESTION: You think the ones who become pilots now are as good as the ones who used to become pilots?

LI'L WAMP: No. Well, now, I'm not talkin' about ability, but in a great instance, no, I don't think they have the ability . . . because we use horsepower for ability. We're doin' it today. We're usin' horsepower for ability.

There's something that's different, too. You know, Dad, when he got his license he was literally proud of it. Still proud of it. . . . We've got people today that, you know, it's no big, hairy deal. . . . You know, I think when Dad was workin' and myself. . . . And I'm gonna say 50 percent of the people out there are still thisaway . . . that they want the boat to move, and they want this, and they want that. But you do have a great amount of people today that really aren't that interested in it. They're just there bidin' their time. They're interested in days off. They're interested in the money. But they don't really care that much about the river as such . . . to get up and really fight and argue to keep this, this and this and this. Now one thing I think that brought this about. . . . Up until . . . by the time Nilo Barge Line was formed. . . . say in the mid-sixties or early sixties, all your towing companies were private-owned, family . . . not all of 'em, but 90 percent of 'em was owned by the Hoaglands, the Igerts, and the Mechlings . . . these type of people. And it was a way of life, you know. I'm sure that somewhere old A. L. Mechling wanted his boys to run the barge line.

WAMP: They did. They did.

LI'L WAMP: Yeah. Anything that was good for the river would be good for A. L. Mechling and his family. Now I work for Olin Chemical. And Olin Chemical, we are strictly a cheap way to move something. And when push comes to shove . . . Olin Chemical could care less if the Mississippi River dried up and blowed away.

If it's cheaper by the railroad or truck or airplane or billy goat, then they'll be in the billy-goat business. And you've lost that. You can't sit down today, outside of the Igerts and some of the Greenville companies, that's the end of the family companies. Mechling is Union-Mechling, which is a huge corporation. Valley Line is Chrome-Alloy. Federal Barge Line is Houston Gas. Nilo is Olin. Mid-America is Peabody. And that's gone.

WAMP: Well, but you take . . . back when I started, like then, like he said, they owned the boats, and they were practical men. Now you take the Leyhes. Why, they were first-class pilots, engineers, deckhands. They lived that life. But you take his [son's] bosses, . . . they couldn't take a yawl down the river, let alone a tow.

LI'L WAMP: Yeah, but I mean people like myself and Jerry Tinkey . . . and these type of people, we are what's left. [15] Now, in a lot of these companies they never bring another man in off the river. Now like myself. I am sure that Nilo Barge Line will never bring another riverman into that office. They have too much trouble with us, you know.

They firmly believe you can run that tow boat like you do a chemical plant. And it cannot be done. It just cannot be done.

They have so much trouble. They have trouble . . . with my feeling that, you know, I might say that Nilo will do this or donate to this . . . because it's good for the river, see. And I've had 'em tell me . . . the higher ups, the vice-presidents and the corporate level . . . "You don't work for us. You work for the dern river." Which is true. You know Olin is like all corporations today. The public image is . . . And I might say somethin' as Olin, see, that . . . Oh, my God, they'd just be agin. You know, "Oh, don't do that, man. What are you talkin' about?" You know, for example, like to me the Coast Guard are totally incompetent. And this would scare them to death.

I think where corporations have trouble is . . . they want to think like a computer. You know, they want everything to be this, this, this, this and . . . fit in a nice, little notch . . . that's true. Now the next thing they have trouble with, and I think we have trouble with, with corporations . . . and that is the independence of people on the river . . . the pilots. You know they can't understand that I've got a Captain Herb Wilson that's been with Nilo Barge Line seventeen years—and Dad's a classic example of it, he's got no pension. And Herb Wilson, if you tell him to do

---

[15] Jerry Tinkey works in the office of Mid-America Towing, but, like Poe, had been a river pilot first.

this, this, this, and this, and he don't want to, he'll leave Nilo Barge Line in a minute. He has got certain principles that he's the captain on that boat. . . . In fact we just had a problem with him. We had some high corporate people on his boat, and they told him that they wanted this, this, and this done, and he informed them that they'd be gettin' off the boat at Memphis. And they said, "Do you know I'm so high in the company? And we'll have your job." and he said, "I hope you do. I've been wantin' to get off anyhow." And he told 'im, "Well, we're gonna call Captain Poe." He said, "I hope you do. I'll give you his number. But I'll be captain on this boat till I get off." . . . They have trouble with this. They really do. . . . It's the same thing as a lawyer being disbarred, if he'd lose his license. And then I still think that a lot of companies or a lot of people still have enough pride that they want their boat to look good and perform good or it will reflect their personality.

It [quality of independence] still exists today. In fact, I think it exists today, oddly enough, [in] some of these young people . . . that I would basically say aren't this good a pilots and all that, . . . they do have this independence. In fact, that's probably what saved us, to a certain degree, right now.

WAMP: I've had some pretty good jobs. Like I say, though, it's easy for a boatman to fool the higher-ups. Well, they don't know anything about it anyhow.

LI'L WAMP: Well, you know this basically is true . . . that for some reason people . . . you don't have to know that much about the river, and people think you know a lot about it. You know, that you've learned some great mystery. This is true, really. And 90 percent of it's just common sense . . . that . . . if these people would stop and think, you know, they would know a lot of it. That, plus it works just the opposite, too, I've said about corporate people. For some reason a man can get on an airplane and make a trip, but he doesn't think he's an aerodynamic engineer, you know. It don't enter his mind. But you can put one of these corporate people on a boat and haul him from St. Louis to New Orleans, and he firmly believes he knows all there is to know about that boat. Now I don't know why that is. . . . A good pilot makes it look so easy.

And a good pilot is often reluctant to retire. Few seem to leave the river only once. Some pilots "retire" three or four times before they actually give it up. Many retire from their steady jobs and then do trip work to keep themselves posted, to talk with old friends over the radio, to see the new boats and changes in the channels. Captain Arthur McArthur retired from the Army Corps of Engineers and stayed away for five years before returning in 1976 to do trip work on the *Mississippi Queen*.

> 'Course I used to say a long time ago like a lot of people, "Well, some day I'm gonna retire from this ole river and I'm gonna git me a couple o' oars on my back and I'm gonna start walkin' out through the countryside and when somebody asks me what those two oars are, that's where I'm gonna stop and settle." But that doesn't hold true. Like Mr. Guy Hurley said . . . "Once you ever get a drink of this old Mississippi River mud in your system, you just always come back to it." So I guess he was right.

For four decades Captain Carroll "Rip" Ware piloted oil tows for Pure Oil Company (later named Union 76), from which he receives a pension. Standing at the levers in the pilothouse of the *Delta Queen*, Captain Ware exhorts all within hearing distance to put their hands over their hearts whenever a Union 76 boat passes, "cuz I get a check from them people every month." In 1976 Captain Ware contemplated retiring from the steamer, saying that he just wished he could open up his head and let every bridge, every sandbar, every light roll out of it and give them to "some young fella comin' up." Then he could stop thinking about it and start collecting his rocking-chair money. Even when he was home, he saw that old river in his head. After the 1976 season, he did retire, briefly. But in August 1977 he was back, obviously overjoyed to be welcomed by the crew and by his radio river friends. Sitting on the farm in Pulaski, Mississippi, gave way once again to alerting passengers via intercom to the "confusion of the Ohio and Mississippi Rivers" at Cairo Point. "That settin' around will kill you. I'd get out there in that 96° heat . . . and I'd say, 'Well, I better quit this or I'll sure enough be dead.' . . . Like I told my preacher, 'I might not be here some Sundays; I won't be out there money-wise, I'll just be out there to be happy.' "

The river water is "in their blood" and transfusions rarely effect a "cure" for the independence and pride they take in being rivermen. So even as employees of giant conglomerates, pilots have generally refused to kowtow to corporate "higher-ups." They relish their special knowledge that still eludes the computer programmers. They continue to use the river as a school of natural and human variety.

Of his apprenticeship on the river, Mark Twain said:

I am to this day profiting somewhat by that experience; for in that brief, sharp schooling, I got personally acquainted with about all the different types of human nature that are to be found in fiction, biography, or history. The fact is daily borne in upon me that the average shore-employment requires as much as forty years to equip a man with this sort of an education. . . . When I find a well-drawn character in fiction or biography I generally take a warm personal interest in him, for the reason that I have known him before—met him on the river. [*Life*, Chapter 18]

Captain E. A. "Li'l Wamp" Poe likewise has met them on the river:

I'll tell you somethin' I think. . . . If a man works on the river . . . you do an awful lot of travelling, and it's amazing how different this country really is. There's people here in Cape Girardeau that, you know, they've been on a vacation to California or they've been to New Orleans, but they don't know the Cajun people. They don't know the . . . as we call 'em . . . hunkies, the colored people that stole from us, in Pittsburgh, the Smoke-Eaters. They don't really know these people and how different they live; where I do for the simple reason I have worked with 'em. You know I worked for years on a boat, run to St. Paul all summer, or run the Intercoastal Canal, and it's an education in itself. It's amazing to me how much you really learn about the country and the people . . . how different they are.

WAMP: Well, you work with all nationalities out there.

LI'L WAMP: Now like we've got right now a Cajun captain. This man can read you the weather forecast, and you'll die laughin'. Now he doesn't intend to be funny, but he is funny. You know, he's a pure Cajun. Couldn't even speak English till he was six, seven years old . . . and still really can't. He thinks he can, you know, and he can get by. But now, you know, I've known him and the kind of people they are and where they really are. And, like I say, the Scandinavian people that settled in the north, they are entirely different. Their food's different. Their music's different.

But I think that's somethin' that river people, you know, it's amazing. And you know what is odd about it? Now like Olin, we've got people that have plants all over the United States. And you've got people that have worked in Little Rock or Lake Charles. And for some reason these people transfer around to plants and plants, and they don't really get to know the people. They're a lot like the Americans that live in a foreign country. . . . Well, they seek out the, what you'd have to say is the mainstream of America rather than really gettin' involved, you know. I talk to people about tobacco. . . . I've worked on boats with guys that come off of tobacco, where their dad had a patch of tobacco . . . and cotton and, you know, the whole bit.

The echoes persist. And the tradition, if less immediately lived, is still actively remembered. The vestige of Mark Twain's American hero is now linked with twentieth-century corporate industry, but by most accounts he retains that cussed independence so admired by the river pilot's most famous chronicler and so troublesome to the corporate hierarchy. As Captain Francis Walters puts it, "The pilot has to be independent. Has to have a hard mind." Piloting requires some of the same skills it always has—memory, nerve, judgment—and some of the same sacrifices. Early pilots mastered both changeable rivers and the volatile technology of the steam machine. Modern pilots enjoy a more controlled river and sophisticated technologies, but even a controlled river offers surprise, and nature's storms are not harnessed. Sonar depth sounding has taken the place of the lead line, but each is a "technology" that had to be properly used and interpreted to ensure safe passage over uncertain waters.

Though the similarities of professional experience can lead one to suggest a composite portrait of pilots and to underscore both the continuity with past river tradition and the changes fostered by a new age, the individual defies generalization.

Yeah, well, people often asked what sort of persons are on the river. And of course it's like going in to an airplane or goin' on a railroad train, any public conveyance where anybody's allowed—the river people are the same way; they're just all stripes, from the sublime to the ridiculous. I've known some of them . . . could quote Robert Burns by the yard and then the next one was dumb as an ox, would reach in the plate to get his mashed potatoes with his hands. But still he was one of the best pilots on the river. So, oh boy, you've got the whole gamut. [Captain Fred Way, Jr.]

Even those pilots who, like Mark Twain in 1882, bemoan the demise of the old traditional ways do their part to keep them alive. They name lights after old-time, "lightning" packet men; they tell stories of their mentors; they salute the dead. Each generation has done likewise, and each generation in time becomes the "old heads." Because pilots are generally on the move, they are often denied the opportunity to pay their respects to a dead rivermate by attending the funeral. But, like Captain Ray Prichard who forty years after the death of his teacher was still blowing a whistle salute when he passed Captain Wethern's gravesite, they pay their respects by carrying them along by memory's tales. Salutes were blown in various parts of the Ohio and Mississippi rivers at the time of Captain Ernest Wagner's funeral. Salutes are blown on the *Delta Queen* each time they pass the grave of Doggy Cross, who died in 1938. And then someone tells the circumstances of his gravemarker. And someone tells a tale of Doggy's exploits. On the day Captain Prichard died, pilots aboard the *Ann King* told stories about Captain Ray and confirmed his tale of the big white ducks being locked upriver by the Tennessee lockmaster's little black dog.

And so the connections continue. The tombstone of Captain Isaiah Sellers, who was still an active pilot when Sam Clemens was cubbing, stands in Bellefontaine Cemetery in St. Louis, a pilot at the wheel of a steamboat. "Legend has it that Sellers had this tombstone of his made to order in some river city, Memphis, maybe, and had it brought to St. Louis on a packet he was piloting."[16] Captain Lester "Whitey" Schickling has had his tombstone in place at the cemetery in Prescott, Wisconsin, since about 1950. On one side is etched the likeness of the first boat he ever piloted. The other side is reserved for the last boat.

Even though "the undertaker hit him in the face with a spade seventy-five years ago or whatever," Captain Henry Nye's ghost is still called upon by Captain Gordon Nelson, a man who claims the traditions are fading.

Henry Nye was a famous old-time steamboat pilot. In fact, there's a Henry Nye Lake down there. And anytime we'd get in a little bind and get out of it . . . we'd say, "Well, old Henry Nye gave her a push."

I've been known to chuck a little salt over my shoulder. I don't think it does anything, but I don't think it does any harm, either, wards off the evil spirits. I do know one thing. I'm sure of one thing. A guy sometimes can get in a helluva pickle. I don't think you get out of all those scrapes alone. I think we've got some help, whether it's Henry Nye or Ray Prichard or Blackie Chriss or whoever it is that gives a little push.

The whistle salute echoes from the bluff over yonder and the tales carry on down the river.

[16] S & D *Reflector*, June 1980, p. 3.

APPENDIX

The following is a list of the pilots and captains interviewed, the date and place of the interview, and other pertinent data.

Boyd, Roy W. (1893–). Interviewed in his home at Rock Island, Illinois, on May 17, 1979. Started cubbing in 1921 after working for some time as a ship's carpenter. Retired about 1974.

Blum, James (1945–). Interviewed aboard *Delta Queen* in St. Paul, Minnesota, on October 10, 1980. Master of *Delta Queen*. Started on river in 1968.

Centanni, Samuel (1915–). Interviewed in New Orleans, Louisiana, on October 23, 1977. Started on river in 1931. At time of interview was pilot on steamer *Natchez*.

Chengery, Gabriel (1948–). Interviewed aboard *Mississippi Queen* in Vicksburg, Mississippi, on September 9, 1980. Started on *Delta Queen* in 1967. Is currently master of steamer *Mississippi Queen*.

Davisson, Joseph "Ted" (1951–). Interviewed aboard *Mississippi Queen* while cruising in lower Mississippi, August 10, 1977. Started on river in 1972. Has since started piloting ships from mouth of the Mississippi to Baton Rouge.

Dean, Theodore (1932–). Interviewed aboard Mv. *Ann King* on trip from St. Paul to St. Louis, August 25–27, 1979. Started on river in 1949, primary experience on diesel towboats with Mechling and Mid-America Transportation Companies.

Decareaux, Joseph (1905–81). Interviewed aboard *President*, August 14–15, 1977. Started on river in 1926, piloted for Standard Oil of Louisiana (later Exxon) for thirty-six years; pilot on *President* beginning 1962. Nickname, "T. Joe," is for "Tiny Joe," acquired when he was a 125-pound deckhand.

Fehlig, Charles (1919–). Interviewed aboard *Delta Queen*, October 2–6, 1977. Started working summers during the mid-'30s; 1940 started on *Admiral*. His regular job is as long-haul towboat pilot for Valley Line. He works as trip pilot on the *Delta Queen*.

Fiedler, Allen (1908–). Interviewed at his home in Fountain City, Wisconsin, October 17, 1978. Started on river in 1924; retired in 1968 from the Army Corps of Engineers with forty-two years' service.

Gilbert, Ben (1904–   ). Interviewed in his hometown, Huntington, West Virginia, February 27, 1979. Started on river in 1919; piloted steam and diesel towboats; retired in 1970 from Mid-West Towing Company.

Harrington, H. B., Jr. (1951–   ). Interviewed by telephone from his home in Paducah, Kentucky, May 17, 1981. Started in 1977 as deckhand with Alter, then Crounse Corporation.

Hawley, Clarke "Doc" (1935–   ). Interviewed aboard steamer *Natchez* in New Orleans harbor, August 15, 1977. Started in 1950; all of experience is on steam excursion vessels. Currently is master of the *Natchez*.

Hedrick, Truman (1901–82). Interviewed in his home in Moline, Illinois, May 17, 1979. Started river work in 1912 washing dishes on a contractor boat. Some work with Army Corps of Engineers; with Moline Consumer for forty-three years.

Johnson, Fontain (1917–   ). Interviewed aboard the *Delta Queen*, September 19–20, 1977. From a steamboat family, he was born on a boat in the middle of the Mississippi River at Commerce, Mississippi. Started working on river circa 1936. Worked for several companies including Federal Barge Line, Valley Line, Delta Queen Steamboat Company.

Justice, Gale (1877–1980). Interviewed in his home in Akron, Ohio, March 1, 1979. Started on river in 1890, piloted gasboats, steam packets, steam and diesel towboats. "Retired" in 1950, last trip circa late 1950s.

Karnath, Walter (1908–   ). Interviewed at his home in Winona, Minnesota, December 30, 1976. Started in 1922, retired in 1976. Steam and diesel towboats, trip pilot aboard *Delta Queen* at the time of his retirement.

Louden, Harry (1906–   ). Interviewed aboard the *Delta Queen*, September 18–20, 1977. Started in 1927 on *Sciota*. Retired from Corps of Engineers after thirty-eight years' service. Trip pilot on *Delta Queen*.

McArthur, Arthur (1918–   ). Interviewed aboard *Mississippi Queen*, August 13 and October 20–22, 1977; November 7, 1978, with William Tippitt in Hernando, Mississippi. Started on river in 1934. Currently is trip pilot on *Mississippi Queen* and alternate master on *Delta Queen*. Previously worked for Corps of Engineers and Federal Barge Lines.

McCann, Robert (1908–82). Interviewed aboard the *Delta Queen*, September 17–18, 1977, while kibbitzing in pilothouse. Was clerk on the *Betsy Ann* and Greene Line Steamers boats. Started on river in 1927; retired circa 1971. Only nonpilot-captain represented in these sources.

Nelson, Gordon (1937–   ). Interviewed aboard Mv. *Ann King* on trip from St. Paul to St. Louis, August 25–27, 1979. Started on river at age sixteen during summers, full time after graduation from high school circa 1955. Experience with diesel towboats, Ingram Barge, and Mid-America Transportation Company.

Palmore, Lexie (1947–   ). Interviewed in St. Paul, Minnesota, October 12, 1979. Started as maid on *Delta Queen* in 1974. Now pilots both *Delta Queen* and *Mississippi Queen*.

Poe, E. A. "Li'l Wamp" (circa 1932–). Interviewed in his father's home in Cape Girardeau, Missouri, August 30, 1980. Started in 1949, diesel towboats, Mechling-Olin, and Nilo Barge Lines.

Poe, E. L. "Wamp" (circa 1895–). Interviewed in his home in Cape Girardeau, Missouri, August 30, 1980. Started in 1910, many companies, steam packets, steam and diesel towboats. Has both engineer's and pilot's licenses. Retired from Mechling on December 31, 1966; tripped until about 1972.

Prichard, Ray (1906–79). Interviewed aboard *Delta Queen*, July 28–August 7, and August 29, 1977. Started in 1926. Was trip pilot aboard the *Delta Queen* at the time of his death.

Reed, Jesse (1902–). Interviewed in his home in Memphis, Tennessee, October 19, 1977. Started in 1921. Retired 1962, Army Corps of Engineers.

Richtman, Robert (1908–78). Interviewed in his home in Fountain City, Wisconsin, October 16, 1978. Started circa 1924. Retired circa 1966.

Ritchie, Larry (1945–). Interviewed in Paducah, Kentucky, August 31, 1979. Started on river in 1964.

Ritchie, Martha (1957–). Interviewed in Paducah, Kentucky, August 31, 1979, with her brother, Larry. Started on river in 1976. Since interview, she has married and is now Martha Ritchie Dennison.

Russell, Oren (1904–). Interviewed aboard *Delta Queen*, August 9 and 17, 1977, August 20–21, 1977. Started on river in 1928. Army Corps of Engineers, Mississippi Valley Barge Line. Still pilot for Delta Queen Steamboat Company.

Schickling, Lester "Whitey" (1923–). Interviewed in his home in Prescott, Wisconsin, May 8, 1979. Started in 1941. One of five brothers who were pilots. Federal Barge Line and Twin City Barge Line.

Skidmore, John (1918–). Interviewed in Vicksburg, Mississippi, October 20, 1977. Started circa 1925. Federal Barge Line, Corps of Engineers. Retired in 1966. Currently Port Director for Warren County (Mississippi) Port Commission.

Smith, Brady (1893–). Interviewed while he was visiting aboard the *Delta Queen* when it stopped in Marietta, Ohio, September 18, 1977. Started circa 1909. Steam packets, ferryboats, diesel towboats. Retired circa 1967.

Stoll, C. W. (1916–). Interviewed at his home in Louisville, Kentucky, December 19, 1978. A "gentleman pilot" for whom his pilot license and occasional piloting is fulfillment of a "Walter Mitty dream." Before retirement, his "regular" occupation was as a businessman. Pilots steam excursion boats, like *Belle of Louisville*.

Strekfus, Verne (1895–). Interviewed aboard the *President* in New Orleans, August 14, 1977. Also interviewed Captain J. Curran Strekfus, Verne's nephew. Verne started circa 1913. Strekfus steam excursion boats. Was aboard *J.S.* when it burned in 1910.

Tippitt, William (1900–). Interviewed at his home in Hernando, Mississippi, October 19, 1977 (with Ed Winford); November 7, 1978 (with Arthur McArthur); November 8, 1978. In addition, he made available to me copies of tapes he made for the Mississippi Valley Collection at Memphis State University in 1972. Eleanor McKay, curator of MVC, kindly provided clearer copies for my use.

Started circa 1915 (summers), full-time circa 1922. Retired from Army Corps of Engineers in 1966. Steam and diesel towboats, dredges, inspection vessels, showboat.

Toomey, Joe (1911–   ). Interviewed at his home in Brownsville, Minnesota, October 31, 1978. Started in 1926; retired 1973. Federal Barge Lines, Mississippi Valley.

Underwood, Harris (1897–1982). Interviewed at his home in Chattanooga, Tennessee, November 11, 1978. Started 1910. Has both engineer's and pilot's licenses. Steam packets, steam excursion, steam and diesel towboats. Retired from Corps of Engineers in 1956, worked on *Delta Queen* and *Belle of Louisville* 1962–1972. Semi-retired since 1972.

Wagner, Ernest (1910–79). Interview tapes made by Wagner from a set of prepared questions, November 1, 1978. Started in 1927. Entire career on steam excursion boats. Relief master on *Delta Queen* and *Mississippi Queen* at time of his death.

Walters, Francis "Dusty" (1912–81). Interviewed at his residence in St. Louis, Missouri, August 29, 1979. Started in 1930; retired circa 1974. Lighthouse boats, barge line, steam excursion (*Capitol*, *St. Paul*), diesel towboats.

Ware, Carroll "Rip" (1911–   ). Interviewed aboard the *Delta Queen*, August 22–September 2, 1977. Started in 1930. Retired from Pure Oil (renamed Union 76) after "thirty-one years and two months." Trip pilot aboard *Delta Queen*. Steam and diesel towboats, steam excursion.

Warner, Russell (1893–   ). Interviewed aboard the *Delta Queen* while it stopped in his home town of Memphis, Tennessee, August 22, 1977. Started in 1908. Steam and diesel, mostly towboats.

Way, Frederick, Jr. (1901–   ). Interviewed at his home in Sewickley, Pennsylvania, February 28, 1979. Started in 1919. Owned and operated the steam packet *Betsy Ann*. Author of *Pilotin' Comes Natural*, *The Log of the Betsy Ann*, *Saga of the Delta Queen*, *The Allegheny* (Rivers of America Series), compiler of the *Inland River Record*, and editor of the *S & D Reflector*.

White, Charles, Sr. (1904–79). Interviewed at his home in Paducah, Kentucky, August 30, 1979. Started in 1921. Retired in 1973.

Williams, Donn (circa 1937–   ). Interviewed at Williams Marine Service in Davenport, Iowa, May 16, 1979. Started 1963. Diesel towboats and harbor boats.

Williams, Loren "Shorty" (1909–1982). Interviewed with son, Donn, at Williams Marine Service, May 16, 1979. Started in 1926. Federal Barge Line, Corps of Engineers, own harbor boat service. Steam and diesel, mostly towboats.

Winford, Edward C. (1909–   ). Interviewed aboard *Mississippi Queen*, August 10, 1977; October 19, 1977 (with William Tippitt in Hernando, Mississippi). Started in 1928. Corps of Engineers. Retired from Engineers in 1964. Worked for private companies (oil tows) for ten years. Retired again. Is now a regular trip pilot on the *Mississippi Queen*.

Zimmer, Arthur (1904–81). Interviewed aboard the *Delta Queen*, August 2, 1977. Worked for St. Louis Police Department as motorcycle policeman before starting on river in 1942. Trip pilot for many companies. Ingram Barge Company. Corps of Engineers. Steam dredges, steam excursion boats, diesel towboats. Working as trip pilot for *Delta Queen* before his death.

GLOSSARY

black boats. Also called "city boats" because they were named after various American cities. Called "black" because they were painted a dark green that looked black to pilots.

bow. The front of the boat.

bulkhead. Any wall or partition.

buoys. Anchored float used to mark the river channel or indicate obstructions. Red buoys are on the left side going downstream (left descending bank); black buoys are on the right, going downstream (right descending bank). Pilots refer to them simply as the "reds" and the "blacks."

capstan. Metal spool on boat deck placed upright, which is revolved either manually or mechanically and used for winding a cable or raising a weight.

cavel. Cleat secured to deck of boat or barge, which is used for securing mooring lines.

chute. Narrow channel often restricted by a dike; also the channel behind an island.

day-marks. Aids to navigation located on the bank, usually in crossings. Used to be large, wooden X painted white and nailed to a tree. Now it may be a freestanding triangular- or diamond-shaped sign, visible to the naked eye during the daylight hours and reflective of boat's searchlight at night.

dikes and wing dams. Structures, usually of rock or wood, built from the bank into the river, that served to funnel the water during drought times and thus foster self-scouring of the channel and provide an adequate amount of water in the channel. Since the construction of locks and dams, the wing dams are mostly submerged and can be hazards.

double-ender. A person who holds both pilot's and engineer's license.

double-tripping. Practice of tying off some of the barges, taking part of the tow through a lock or bridge or difficult spot, tying that part off, and then returning to retrieve the remaining barges, eventually reuniting all barges in the tow.

eddy. A current at variance with the main current in the river, especially one having a swirling or rotary motion. A small whirlpool.

flank, steer. Term used as in "to flank a bend" or "to steer that bridge." To steer, the pilot keeps the boat coming ahead, going faster than the current, and negotiates the point, bend, or bridge. To flank, he puts the boat "to backing," gets lined up, then allows the current to help him through the spot. The boat is going slower than the current and uses the pressure of the current against the hull to hold position in the channel. See pp. 69–70.

forecastle. The forward end of the main deck.

government lights. Beacons maintained by the federal government to aid pilots at night. Lights are named and numbered. Old-time lights were kerosene lamps maintained by lightkeepers who regularly received supplies from a government boat called a lighthouse tender. Most lights are now electric powered.

jackstaff. Flagpole. Pilots use the jackstaffs to help line up their shore marks.

lead line. See sounding.

levee. Sloping or graded embankment generally constructed to prevent overflow during high water or flood stage; also used to mean a landing place for vessels.

lock. Chamber built at one side of a river dam for the purpose of raising and lowering vessels wishing to pass the dam.

mud clerk. Second clerk, whose duties included going out in all weather on unpaved levees to receive or deliver freight. In rainy weather the levees were muddy, so this name became descriptive of both the work and condition of the second clerk. Steamboat term.

port. Looking forward, port is the left-hand side of a boat. Starboard is the right-hand side.

revetment. A facing of rock or masonry to protect an embankment. To prevent erosion, enhance flood control efforts, and assist channel maintenance, the Corps of Engineers has over the years tried to stabilize the banks using various kinds of materials (willows, rocks, concrete mattresses). Broken stones used for revetment are called riprap.

riprap. See revetment.

roustabout. Steamboat term. Man employed in the deck department who worked for the mate, generally carrying freight, cleaning up, and the like. Most roustabouts were black men.

sounding. Process of determining the water's depth. Old methods used either the lead line (pronounced "led") or a pole. A lead line was a sash cord about thirty feet long, weighted with lead (approximately eight pounds), and marked into specific units of measure (fathoms and fractions thereof) by pieces of leather. One fathom (six feet) is called "mark one," two fathoms is "mark twain," and so on. Above "mark four" is "no bottom." The person who takes the soundings and calls (sings) them to the pilot is called a leadsman.

The pole was twelve to eighteen feet long and marked off in one-foot sections, alternately red and white. On modern towboats, sounding is done automatically by fathometers attached to the lead barges. The pilot reads the sonar depth finder's digital readout in the pilothouse.

sounding pole. See sounding.

stacks. Smokestacks on a vessel.

stage. Sometimes called gangplank, this forty- to sixty-foot-long boardwalk swings out ahead of steamboats and is lowered at landings with the heel on the forecastle and the other end on the bank. Crew and passengers use the stage to get on and off the boat.

starboard. Looking forward, starboard is the right-hand side of the boat. Port is the left-hand side.

steer. See flank, steer.

steersman. Also called cub pilot. Person apprenticed to learn piloting.

stern. The back of the boat.

timberhead. Top end of a timber, rising above the deck, for line or wire to fasten to. On modern towboats, these are cast-steel posts.

tow. One or more barges being transported by a self-propelled vessel. Hitching the barges together to ready them for moving is known as "making up tow."

towhead. A new or small island.

towboat. River vessels designed to push barges. Though the word *tow* seems to indicate pulling, in fact, towboats are push boats. The bow is square so that barges may be readily attached for transport.

towknees. Steel plates attached to the head of a towboat that serve as buffer between barges and boat. Small boats will have two, larger boats may have four. Place to attach barges.

trip pilot. A pilot who is not working regularly for the company. He hires out for certain trips and is paid by the day for those particular trips. Pilots often refer to this activity as "tripping."

wharf. Space (often paved) maintained for boats to tie up, usually supplied with ringbolts.

wharfboat. Usually privately owned and operated, a "floating warehouse" to which a boat can be moored for transfer of freight or passengers. In steamboat days, nearly every town of any size had a wharfboat.

whistle signals. One whistle indicates port; two indicates starboard. Example: If boats are approaching one another from opposite directions and the agreed signal is "catch you on the one whistle," boats will pass port-to-port. If boats are running in the same direction, the indicated whistle is that of the passing boat; i.e., one whistle means they would pass on the port side of the overtaking boat, starboard side of the boat being overtaken.

wing dams. See dikes.

yawl. A rowboat or skiff that belongs to a large boat.

SELECTED BIBLIOGRAPHY

Bissell, Richard. *High Water*. Boston: Little, Brown and Company, 1954.

———. *My Life on the Mississippi: Or Why I am Not Mark Twain*. Boston: Little, Brown and Company, 1973.

———. *A Stretch on the River*. Boston: Little, Brown, 1950.

Blair, Walter A. *A Raft Pilot's Log*. Cleveland: Arthur H. Clark Company, 1930.

Botkin. B. A., ed. *A Treasury of Mississippi River Folklore*. New York: Bonanza Books, 1978.

Burman, Ben Lucien. *Big River to Cross*. New York: John Day Company, 1940.

———. *Blow for a Landing*. Boston: Houghton Mifflin Company, 1938.

———. *Look Down That Winding River*. New York: Taplinger Publishing Company, 1973.

———. *Mississippi*. New York: Cosmopolitan Book Corporation, 1929.

Cable, George Washington. *Gideon's Band*. New York: Charles Scribner's Sons, 1914.

Drago, Harry Sinclair. *The Steamboaters*. New York: Bramhall House, 1967.

Ewing, Raymond P. *Mark Twain's Steamboat Years: The Years of Command*. Hannibal, Missouri, 1981.

Fugina, Frank. *Lore and Lure of the Upper Mississippi River*. Winona, Minnesota: By the author, 1945.

Gould, E. W. *Fifty Years on the Mississippi or Gould's History of River Navigation*. Columbus, Ohio: Long's College Book Company, 1951 (originally published 1889).

Hanson, Joseph Mills. *The Conquest of the Missouri: Life and Exploits of Captain Grant Marsh*. New York: Murray Hill Books, Inc., 1909.

Hartsough, Mildred L. *From Canoe to Steel Barge*. Minneapolis: University of Minnesota Press, 1934.

Havighurst, Walter. *Voices on the River*. New York: Macmillan Company, 1964.

Heckman, William L. *Steamboating: Sixty-Five Years on Missouri Rivers*. Kansas City: Burton Publishing Company, 1950.

Hereford, Robert A. *Old Man River: The Memories of Captain Louis Rosche, Pioneer Steamboatman*. Caxton Printers, Ltd., 1942.

277

Hunter, Louis. *Steamboats on the Western Rivers*. New York: Octagon Books, 1969.

Knoephle, John. Collection of taped interviews, 1957–58. Inland Rivers Library of the Public Library of Cincinnati and Hamilton County, Cincinnati, Ohio.

Lee, James, ed. *Tales the Boatmen Told*. Exton, Pennsylvania: Canal Press Inc., 1977. (Stories of boatmen who worked the Morris Canal in New Jersey.)

McDermott, John Francis, ed. *Before Mark Twain: A Sampler of Old, Old Times on the Mississippi*. Carbondale and Edwardsville: Southern Illinois University Press, 1968.

McNeely, S. Blake. *Papa, the River and Me: True Experiences Along the Mississippi*. Privately printed, 1975.

Merrick, George Byron. *Old Times on the Upper Mississippi: The Recollections of a Steamboat Pilot from 1854 to 1863*. Cleveland: Arthur H. Clark Company, 1909.

———. *Steamboats and Steamboatmen of the Upper Mississippi*. 4 vols. Clippings from the Burlington, Iowa, *Saturday Evening Post*, September 1913–December 1919.

Morris, Wright, ed. *The Mississippi River Reader*. Garden City: Doubleday (Anchor), 1962.

Petersen, William J. "Captains and Cargoes of Early Upper Mississippi Steamboats." *Wisconsin Magazine of History* 13, no. 3 (March 1930): 224–40.

———. *Steamboating on the Upper Mississippi*. Iowa City: State Historical Society, 1968.

———. *Towboating on the Mississippi*. New York: A. S. Barnes and Company, 1979.

Quick, Herbert, and Quick, Edward. *Mississippi Steamboatin'*. New York: Henry Holt and Company, 1926.

Raban, Jonathan. *Old Glory: An American Voyage*. New York: Simon and Schuster, 1981.

Rosskam, Edwin and Rosskam, Louise. *Towboat River*. New York: Duell, Sloan and Pearce, 1948.

S & D *Reflector*. Quarterly publication of the Sons and Daughters of Pioneer Rivermen. Marietta, Ohio.

Samuel, Ray; Huber, Leonard V.; Ogden, Warren C. *Tales of the Mississippi*. New York: Hastings House, 1955.

Saxon, Lyle. *Father Mississippi*. New York: Century Company, 1927.

Seelye, John. *Prophetic Waters: The River in Early American Life and Literature*. New York: Oxford University Press, 1977.

Twain, Mark [Samuel Clemens]. *Life on the Mississippi*. New York: New American Library, 1961. (Originally published in 1883.)

U.S. Army Corps of Engineers. Collection of taped interviews with retired dredgeboat pilots, captains, and engineers. Historical division, Washington, D.C.

Watkins, T. H. *Mark Twain's Mississippi*. Palo Alto: American West Publishing Company, 1974.

Way, Frederick, Jr. *The Log of the Betsy Ann*. Cincinnati: Ohio River Magazines, 1933.

———. *Pilotin' Comes Natural*. New York: Farrar & Rinehart, Inc., 1943.

Wayman, Norbury. *Life on the River*. New York: Crown Publishers, Inc., 1971.

Western Folklore 37, no. 3 (July 1978). Special issue on occupational folklife. See particularly Jack Santino, "Characteristics of Occupational Narratives," pp. 199– 212.

INDEX